From Maui to Cook

From Maui to Cook

The Discovery and Settlement of the Pacific

DAVID LEWIS

Drawings by
WALTER STACKPOOL

Doubleday, Sydney

First published in 1977 by
DOUBLEDAY AUSTRALIA PTY LIMITED
14 Mars Road, Lane Cove, NSW 2066

National Library of Australia
Cataloguing-in-Publication data

Lewis, David Henry, 1917-
  From Maui to Cook.

  Bibliography.
  ISBN 0 86824 001 X
  ISBN 0 86824 002 8 Limited ed.

  1. Pacific area—History. I. Title

990

Printed in Australia by Macarthur Press (Books) Pty Ltd,
Parramatta, NSW. Australia

Acknowledgements

I am indebted first of all to my learned teachers, the star-path navigators of Oceania, for their patient instruction ashore and afloat. Among them I would specially mention Tevake of Nufilole; Rafe of Tikopia; the Honourable Ve'ehala and other *tou tai* of Tonga; Abera, Iotiebata, and Teeta of the Gilbert Islands; Hipour, Piailug, Repunglap, Nomonour, and Epimai of the Carolines.

My research work in the Pacific was supported at various times by the Departments of Pacific History and Anthropology at the Australian National University, by the East-West Center, Hawaii, and by the *National Geographic Magazine.* I would like to thank the members of all these organizations for their unselfish, helpful advice.

Contents

Preface

This book could be called *"pages from* the exploration story", because I have deliberately selected characters and episodes that seem to me the most significant and, perforce, left out many notable explorers altogether (more comprehensive works — e.g. J. C. Beaglehole's *The Exploration of the Pacific* — are listed in the bibliography).

The Maui of the title is a pan-Pacific demigod or diety. He fished the north island of New Zealand out of the sea — hence its name *Te Ika a Maui* — the Fish of Maui. Similarly, far away beyond the Equator, this same Maui fished up the Carolinian island of Faiis from the ocean depths. Even in South America one investigator, Thor Heyerdahl, believes he has found traces of the Maui legend. What more suitable figure, therefore, to symbolize the first comers to the South Sea Islands, for they metaphorically fished unknown islands out of the sea.

In dealing so cursorily with Cook, the greatest of the Western explorers, I must plead guilty to a deliberate lack of proportion. That he should be dismissed in a few pages has simply been due to the sheer impossibility of doing him justice in a work of this length. There are many excellent books on Cook, not the least his own journals as edited by J. C. Beaglehole. I have contented myself, therefore, with the barest outline of the career of the great navigator and concentrated on a selection of his predecessors, great men in themselves, who are all too readily forgotten.

I have endeavoured to describe the exploration of the Pacific lands by *people* — not just by Europeans. Thus, part one of the book delves far into prehistory, from the time when the Pacific Islanders' ancestors breached the eight-hundred-kilometre ocean barriers to colonize the Marianas and Fiji nearly 3,500 years ago, to the navigation and voyaging techniques that made their subsequent feats possible. Exploration by the peoples of the Pacific rim — Chinese, Indonesians, Peruvian Incas — also comes in here.

Part two deals with the European explorers, beginning with Magellan and Drake and the Spanish mariners. Then follows an account of the centuries-long struggle between England (and Holland) and Spain for the Pacific. This section ends with the scientific explorers up to Cook — Tasman, Wallis, and Bougainville — and the battle for Tahiti and how the Tahitians had the last laugh on their conquerors.

Part three brings the Pacific Islanders back into their central place. There is the story of how the Tongans, now more knowledgeable of European ways, took by guile the privateer *Port au Prince*; how the English lad Will Mariner became a Tongan warrior chief and the record he left of this proud people; the adventures of Cannibal Jack Diaper, the beachcomber who helped bridge the gap between two worlds. The book concludes with the renaissance of voyaging that is now taking place — the great sailing canoes that are again ploughing the vast Pacific wastes, including the eight-thousand-kilometre voyage without instruments in the twenty-metre double canoe *Hokule'a* from Hawaii to Tahiti in 1976, in which I was one of the navigators. This section takes us well beyond the days of Cook — in fact, right into the present. But the Pacific Islanders and their cultures are resilient living realities; firmly rooted in a great maritime past, they are moving confidently into an unknown future, and it is here, on the threshold of their most challenging adventure, that we leave them.

I make no apology for placing disproportionate weight on places that I have myself visited in small yachts or in ocean-going canoes under the tutelage of Polynesian master navigators. For it is as one makes dubious landfall, as much prey to storm as the ancient pioneers, that the epic deeds of the great explorers, Pacific Islanders and Westerners alike, come most vividly to life. Thus, when traversing Drake's Passage below the Horn, alone, frightened and frostbitten, the true heroism of the great Elizabethan became apparent to me as never before, and I felt better fitted to write about his exploits with understanding and a sense of proportion.

ONE
The Founding Fathers

OROU,
MAILU.
S.E.PAPUA

Man Comes to the South Seas

Y A QUIRK of geography the Panamanian isthmus of Darien
runs east and west between the Americas, instead of north
and south as we might expect. Thus it was that, when Vasco
Núñez de Balboa, with 67 surviving conquistadores out of 190 and
his terrible war dog Léonico, sighted the pacific in 1513, he
named it "South Sea"; the Caribbean he had left behind became
the North Sea. They are so labelled on charts down to Dampier's
day. I make no apology, then, for reviving this historic term for
the Pacific and for including among South Sea Islanders not only
the Polynesians, but also the inhabitants of New Guinea, of the
Spice Islands, and of New Holland itself.

THE FIRST SEA CROSSING

Balboa, of course, was far from being the first man to view the
Pacific from American shores. Amerindian pioneers had preceded
him by something like four hundred centuries. Yet Australoid
man had reached the island continent on the opposite side of the
ocean a good ten thousand years earlier still.

All the continents save Australia and Antarctica were
interconnected during the Pleistocene Ice Age, when Bering Strait
was for long a land bridge and not even man-made canals
separated North from South America or Euro-Asia from Africa.
But Australia-New Guinea (a single land mass until the recent
melting of the ice-caps a mere ten thousand years ago flooded the
intervening continental shelf) stood isolated. It has never been
joined to Asia; there has always been a strait between Bali and
Lombok. The north-west side of this strait is Asia, realm of
monkeys, tigers, and elephants; across the narrow waters dwell
the kangaroos and emus of Australia.

Human beings of a sort seem to have evolved some three

million years ago in Africa; and from there the clans of the hunter-gatherers spread over Asia and Europe. Mongoloid nomads had yet to develop a cold-weather technology effective enough to enable them to brave the icy barrens between Siberia and America when the Australoids accomplished a feat of epic proportions—man's earliest known successful sea crossing. By later standards it was modest enough; only sixty-five kilometres or so, twice the distance from England to France, separated Bali from Lombok, but the traverse was an epoch-making event in that it signalled that the maritime era had opened and man was no longer an exclusively land-bound creature.

This first settlement of New Guinea–Australia took place something like fifty thousand years ago, at a time when Neanderthal man, not *Homo sapiens,* dominated the European scene and would long continue to do so. Nowadays archaeological discoveries are blurring the once firmly drawn divisions between *Homo erectus,* Neanderthal man, and *Homo sapiens,* but the Australian ancestors, unlike contemporary Europeans, seem to have been modern men. Obviously, we can never hope to reconstruct so remote a happening as the first sea crossing in human history. Apart from anything else, traces of camp sites and shellfish middens along ancient coastlines have been drowned beneath the Arafura Sea ever since the Ice Age ended. But we do have a few indirect pointers, nevertheless.

As well as the Bali-Lombok strait there was probably at least one other water barrier, that between the Moluccas and Irian Jaya, north-west of the then non-existent Torres Strait. Just how wide it was depends upon at what date the crossing or crossings were made. Archaeological evidence at present favours somewhere about fifty thousand years ago. This was a time when the ice sheets were near their maximum and the shallow seas were narrowest. But should new facts come to light further backdating man's advent in Australia (which is possible enough, seeing that only ten years ago fifteen thousand years was considered a daringly excessive estimate), the last Ice Age would not have begun and the seas to be traversed would have been wider—perhaps almost as extensive as at present.

Let us be content, therefore, with the figure of sixty-five kilometres, a formidable enough barrier in all conscience. How might it have been breached? Could a terrified group have drifted across clinging to the branches of some vast storm-uprooted forest tree? Currents and tidal streams do not run across straits but through them. Thus the wind would have been the only motive power. Even driven before the strong north-west monsoon, a waterlogged jungle giant, wallowing awash, would move very slowly indeed at right-angles to the current—three-quarters of a kilometre a day, perhaps. At this rate the party, which would necessarily include women of child-bearing age, would need ninety days for the passage of twice the width of the English Channel. One may, I think, rule out the possibility of survival.

But a successful accidental drift in some sort of primitive craft is another story altogether. What sort of craft? Inflated skin floats have been used since time immemorial throughout Asia and its American cultural offshoot, but they have never been reported from Australia. Similarly, though dug-out canoes of Indonesian–New Guinean types did spread from the Torres Strait Islands into northern Queensland, the dug-out was never a *native* Australian artefact. Even with the use of fire, the construction of a hollowed-out log canoe of any but the very roughest type requires a heavy stone or shell woodworking axe or adze. Such tools have generally been regarded as products of the Neolithic or New Stone Age, which began ten thousand years ago, but here, as in so much else, Australia does not fit in and caution is necessary.

Though the Australian Aboriginal culture was essentially hunter-gatherer, Palaeolithic or Old Stone Age edge-ground stone axes, some grooved for hafting and suitable for heavy wood-working, were being made in Australia twenty thousand years ago. Interestingly enough, domestication of animals and cultivation of plants are also regarded as essential characteristics of the Neolithic, yet the Australians of 8000 B.C. had their tame hunting dogs (dingoes), identical with the Asian village "pi" dogs; and the recently nomadic Pintupi of central Australia used deliberately to transplant the drug plant *minkulpa (pitcherry)* to the neighbourhood of their camps. It is all too easy to underestimate this ancient, highly spiritual and artistic culture, which was too successful to bother to borrow tedious agricultural practices from the New Guineans or Indonesians who habitually visited their shores. Thus some simple form of dug-out *may* possibly have been constructed by Australoids even fifty thousand years ago, though it seems unlikely.

Two types of seagoing coastal craft were, however, in use in Australia at the time of first European contact; the bark canoe and the raft. Bark canoes of all degrees of complexity were made in different areas. For instance, Matthew Flinders saw one in the Gulf of Carpentaria that was more than four metres long. Made of two pieces of bark sewn together, caulked with gum and framed with poles and vines, it could carry six people. Almost identical bark canoes were used, incidentally, by the Tierra del Fuegan Indians in the stormy waters round Cape Horn.

Widespread and ancient as is the bark (or sewn-skin) canoe, and readily constructed with Old Stone Age technology, there is a simpler and even more universal type of seaworthy craft, which is easier to build—the raft. Rafts are versatile and sea-kindly, and their distribution has been limited only by the requirement that the waters they float upon must, for the sake of their crews, be reasonably warm. Seagoing rafts were formerly used extensively on the Australian coasts, especially in the Gulf of Carpentaria and the north-west of Western Australia. It is of interest that the ones used north of King Sound were virtually identical with those of the Solomon Islands, India, and South America, in that they were made of an odd number of logs, their front ends were tapered, and they were pegged rather than lashed together. Another type, seen by John Lort Stokes near Bathurst Island in 1839, was 5½ metres long and 1½ metres wide and was being paddled by a man who was striking the water with a spear alternately on each side. Often the rafts seen by the early European explorers and surveyors were capable of carrying three or four people with their fishing equipment and catch.

The ancient Australoid rafts were probably not much different from these. The next question is, what were they made of? Except for Tasmania, "modern" Australian rafts were constructed of mangrove logs. The Canberra prehistorian Rhys Jones has re-created and tested one of the Tasmanian variety, which were generally of bark and rushes, and he found it became waterlogged after thirteen kilometres. This is significant, because the limits of Tasmanian settlement were, in fact, islands thirteen kilometres off shore. These water craft clearly proved inadequate for maintaining contact with the Australian mainland when the waters released by the melting ice sheets ten thousand years ago formed Bass Strait and cut off Tasmania. Reeds, then, seem an unlikely material for our purpose. Mangrove logs would be suitable, but less probable than bamboo, because the proto-Australians were coming from Asia, where bamboo is universally the raft-building material. The bamboo raft is by far the most likely vehicle to have transported that very "first fleet" of Australian settlers.

But would a raft drifting before the wind fare any better than a semi-submerged tree? Anyone familiar with bamboo or ambatch-wood rafts knows that they blow downwind with almost the same disconcerting velocity as rubber boats. Thus if a family fish-spearing off Bali on a bamboo raft were driven out to sea by the monsoon, they would conservatively drift at a rate of eight to sixteen kilometres a day and could make the other side within a week. This is well within the survival time of innumerable documented Pacific drifts.

There would be several such episodes, no doubt, in the course of a few thousand years. Nor must we neglect the likelihood that keen-eyed hunter-fishermen had seen the land beyond the strait, for it is probable that, then as now, high mountains stood sentinel over the waterway. The crossing might well have been deliberate.

However it came about, the first mighty step in overseas discovery and colonization was taken by the Australoids at a time unimaginably remote from the present. Forty millennia had to pass before the Ice Age ended about ten thousand years ago and the Spice Islands became separated from New Guinea, and Torres Strait and the Arafura Sea (not to mention Bass Strait) flooded what had long been dry land. Henceforth, though sea-borne commerce was resumed in later ages, the history of New Guinea and Australia diverged. Horticulture came to New Guinea, though not to Australia, about five thousand years ago. After their great sea-borne leap forward the Australians, like so many other continental peoples, confined their seagoing activities to estuaries and coastlines.

For the next steps in the discovery of the Pacific lands we must look to other peoples, notably Papuans and Austronesian speakers. We must also move forward in time from fifty thousand years in the past to five thousand—to a totally new era of agricultural and trading life-styles and capable sailing vessels.

THE AUSTRONESIANS' MARITIME REVOLUTION

The farthest roving of all early seafarers were not, as we might suppose, the Vikings or the Portuguese or the English, but Malayo-Polynesian Austronesian speakers. Their settlements came to span two-thirds of the earth, from Madagascar hard by Africa to Easter Island on the far side of the Pacific, and this was millennia before the Europeans first put to sea. Indonesia-Malaysia was the Austronesians' heartland, and they peopled, or helped to people, the Philippines, Taiwan, Madagascar, most of Melanesia, and all of Micronesia and Polynesia. Wherever they went, the Austronesians left an indelible imprint in the shape of the unique vessels they developed and in which they travelled.

Their sailing-ships were either outrigger-stabilized or double-hulled craft. Some could be reversed and sailed end-for-end. So characteristic were they that it is hard to distinguish a Madagascan outrigger from a Tahitian, or a Madras double canoe from a Tuamotuan. The *provenance* of the outrigger coincides with the Austronesian world. It is not found outside.

How did the Austronesians come to introduce the outrigger? Their South-East Asian heartland was the place where dug-out canoes attained their highest and most elaborate development, but the stability of a dug-out is, of course, strictly circumscribed by the narrowness enforced by the proportions of the parent tree-trunk. As we shall see, the great Austronesian seagoing expansion falls within the era of sail. But once dug-outs left river mouths for the open sea under sail, a stabilizing device was necessary for any serious off-shore work; the Austronesians came up with their own ingenious solution.

The earliest evidence of sail so far is a clay model from Eridu in Iraq dated about 3500 B.C. and resembling the later Assyrian hide-covered *quffa*. The linguist Andrew Pawley dates the break-up of the parent Austonesian language—and hence the beginnings of dispersal—at 3000 B.C. or earlier. He has pointed out that terms for sail (very significantly), outrigger, outrigger boom, connecting booms on double canoes, steering oar, and canoe rollers (only needed for large vessels) are found in all the coastal regions the Austronesians occupy. Some individual words have been lost in some places and some "borrowed" by non-Austronesian neighbours. But most occur from Madagascar to the Philippines and Polynesia. All these words, he believes, come from the parent Austronesian tongue.

The date of around 3000 B.C. for Austronesian expansion is supported by the simultaneous appearance of new styles of pottery and tools in the South-East Asian archipelagos, which had been isolated from mainland Asia since the seas enlarged after the Ice Age. The linguistic evidence clearly shows the central role of sail and outrigger-type stabilizing devices in these sea-borne migrations—which only ended with the colonization of New Zealand and Hawaii four millennia later.

The dug-out–outrigger picture is logical enough so far as it goes, but prehistoric events are rarely as simple as our scanty knowledge implies. While dug-outs are ubiquitous throughout the Indian Ocean and the Pacific to this day, Austronesian ships, including the great double voyaging canoes of Polynesia, were more probably *planked* craft.* The planks were joined to one another and to V-shaped inserted ribs in the Indo-Pacific (but not Mediterranean) manner by *sewing* or lashing, not by nailing. Sewn-plank construction goes far back in time to a remote ancestry in the Mesolithic sewn-bark or sewn-hide canoes that may antedate any but the rudest dug-outs. It rather obviously owed its origin to the substitution of wood for hide or bark when planks could be adzed into shape with the heavy blades of the New Stone Age.

Once outriggers had been developed for sailing dug-outs, the advantages of what today are called multi-hulls—speed, lightness, shallow draft—would have become apparent and the devices would have been applied to the sewn-plank vessels of the same vast culture area. This is exactly what seems to have happened. In fact, our earliest representation of an outrigger is in an eighth century A.D. Javan carving showing, not dug-outs at all, but substantial sewn-plank merchantmen—most, but not all, with outriggers. The Roman traveller Strabo mentions an outrigger ship in the Red Sea in A.D. 23 that seems to have been from Indonesia. Sewn-plank vessels, some with outriggers, were still in general use as late as the turn of the century in East Africa, Ceylon, southern India, Indonesia, the Philippines, and, in the Pacific, in the Gilberts, Marshalls, Tuamotus, Samoa, and Fiji. They had probably changed but little since Strabo's time, or, for that matter, for several millennia before that.

When and where man first abandoned the illusory security of rock-girt tide-swept coasts to seek safety and an unimpeded pathway on the open sea, we do not know. Mesolithic skin boats would have been quite buoyant and seaworthy enough for the role—as able, in all probability, as the ten-metre hide-covered curragh in which Saint Brendan voyaged from Ireland to Iceland and beyond. The great gulfs of the Indian Ocean—the Bay of Bengal, the Arabian Sea, the Persian Gulf, and the Red Sea—would be likely locations for the first truly off-shore passages.

Deep-sea navigation must necessarily date from the same remote epoch. Remarkably uniform techniques using stars,

---

* Haddon and Hornell in their classic *Canoes of Oceania,* citing evidence that the vessels of the proto-Polynesians were planked, refer to the functionless frames of dug-outs from Hawaii, Niue, and the Southern Cooks as relics of one-time plank and frame construction and mention the surviving sewn-plank canoes of the Gilberts, Fiji, Tahiti, the Tuamotus, Samoa, and Tuvalu.

winds, waves, and birds have been recorded all the way from the Mediterranean to the Pacific. Once perfected, these pre-instrumental arts had little reason to alter over the millennia, except in response to local conditions, until the advent of the compass on Chinese and Indian ships between the ninth and tenth centuries A.D. heralded the close of the era.

THE LAPITA PEOPLE: ANCESTRAL POLYNESIANS

This has been a cursory sketch of the Austronesian background to man's exploration of the Pacific Islands, for it has skipped over the centuries like a stone flicked across a pond. But now the protagonists are on the margin of the island Pacific, perhaps we should pause a while and study them as they stand on the threshold of the island chain of Melanesia.

It will be fifteen hundred years till the birth of Christ; even the full flowering of ancient Greece is still a thousand years ahead. One section of the Austronesian sea traders, known as the Lapita people after their handsome incised pottery, have pushed on to unknown islands off New Guinea from coastal trading settlements in the Philippines and Moluccas.

The sea-roving traders are tall, thickset, and brown skinned. For the most part they they wear bark cloth breechclouts or mat *lava-lavas,* but even the trade wind strikes cold at sea on a spray- or thunderstorm-drenched skin, and ponchos of overlapping *ti* leaves are stored aboard ship for bad weather. These are for the common sailors. Chiefs and navigators are decked out in dog-skin or feathered cloaks.

Yam and taro are the main crops cultivated at the settlements. When venturing into the unknown, shoots and cuttings of the root crops are carried under the deck beams, together with a score of other useful plants—sugar-cane, paper mulberry, pandanus, breadfruit, and the ubiquitous coconut—all carefully packaged in damp earth and wrapped in *tapa* cloth and matting. The pig, the dog, and the Indonesian jungle fowl have been brought by ancestors from South-East Asia, and these too accompany the Lapita people afloat. But these rovers do not rely solely on the land for their sustenance. The harvest of the sea and the reef-girdled lagoons is no less important to them; fish traps, pronged spears, and trolling lures are their fishing implements.

The Lapita ships are lofty, with slim V-sectioned sewn-plank hulls, from which spring rows of arching outrigger booms. In size they fall within the range universally preferred throughout the ancient world for deep-sea transport—ten to twenty metres. This may seem small by our standards, conditioned by super-tankers, but Columbus's ships were little longer, if more capacious; the Australian Bill Nance's *Cardinal Vertue,* in which he rounded Cape Horn and the world, single-handed and unheralded, in 1964 was only 8½ metres overall. My own ten-metre Antarctic *Ice Bird* was not much longer.

Double hulls are preferred by the Lapita captains over outriggers where traditional trading networks are well established and heavy deck cargoes of pots, giant clam shells, and obsidian have to be carried on the platforms. The mat sails, set on one or two masts, are of the fore-and-aft variety. In technical terms, they may be (*a*) canted square sails, which owe their ultimate inspiration to the middle Nile, and persist today in Madura (Indonesia) and Ninigo (New Guinea); (*b*) Indonesian boomed lateens, which developed out of the first type; or (*c*) inverted triangular claw sails, which are to become the hallmark of Polynesia.

Cooking fires are glowing on nests of coral gravel contained in ceramic or wooden platforms lashed to the deck beams. But, apart from fresh caught fish, the rest of the food has been prepared ashore—dried or fermented root vegetables for the most part. Water is carried in hollow bamboos, gourds, and green coconuts.

These are splended ships with—by this advanced Lapita era of 1500 B.C.—two thousand years experience of sail power behind them, and their learned navigators are heir to an even older tradition of naked eye deep-sea navigation. It is worth remembering that the vessels have been constructed with never a tool of metal, but only with the rectangular obsidian and clam-shell adzes and the sharks'-tooth-tipped drills of the New Stone Age

Carbon dating of refuse from ancient middens and charcoal from long-dead cooking fires has shown that Lapita settlements sprang up with extraordinary rapidity right along the 3,500-kilometre arc of islands from New Ireland and New Britain off New Guinea, through the Solomons and Santa Cruz to the New Hebrides and New Caledonia. Something of the extent of the Lapita trade networks has been revealed by Professor Roger Green and Dr Wally Ambrose. They found by chemical analysis that the obsidian used to manufacture the flake knives from a 1000 B.C. site in the Reef Islands of the Santa Cruz group had actually been mined in New Britain and transported no less than two thousand kilometres. This is no mean journey; even though much of the way would be "island hopping", there is one 330-kilometre stretch of unbroken sea that must have been traversed.

The Polynesian Santa Cruz Reef Islanders have remained notable sea traders. Down to the 1960s their big *te puke* outrigger canoes, with claw-shaped pandanus mat sails and thatched shelters on deck, were following age-old trading patterns beyond sight of land, laden with shell, pottery, and feather money. Their last great navigator, the far-travelled Tevake, with whom I sailed in 1969, was far more restricted than his remote forebears, even though he voyaged to the distant New Hebrides.

Eastward of the Santa Cruz group and the New Hebrides, the vast emptiness of the Pacific begins in earnest. The next land, Fiji, lies across the Melanesian Trench, a 670-kilometre expanse of open water without intervening islands. Beyond this again are the major archipelagos of Western Polynesia, Tonga, and Samoa. To make matters more difficult for the voyager, the passage of the Melanesian Trench to Fiji has to be made in the teeth of the prevailing trade winds.

Now, to test the possibilities of colonists having accidentally drifted ashore on the Pacific Islands, a remarkable computer study was mounted by M. Levison, R.G. Ward, and J.W. Webb, and later published in their book *The Settlement of Polynesia: A Computer Simulation*. The raw material was accumulated information on winds, currents, and gales contained in the pilot charts. Simulated drifts were started from every conceivable island, and their "progress" was tabulated. The assumptions that were made as to survival time, etc., were based on actual historical records. We will have occasion to refer to this invaluable and original piece of research again. Suffice it to say here that, while many downwind islands were shown to have been well in the track of accidental voyagers (and we know from other sources that settlement often took place in this way), other stretches of ocean that we know were traversed could only have yielded to purposeful investigation. The Melanesian Trench was one such stretch of ocean.

Yet as early as 1300 B.C. the redoubtable Lapita explorers were already across the Melanesian Trench and established in Fiji. Tonga was colonized before 1000 B.C., and Samoa a few centuries later. The stage was now set for the emergence of the Polynesians, the best-known of the South Sea Islanders. Contrary to most people's assumptions, the Polynesians did not come from anywhere. The brilliant deductions of the young New Zealand prehistorian, Les Groube, have shown that the Polynesians, as we know them today, evolved in Tonga and Samoa from those first Lapita settlers, their direct ancestors. Though the islands further west, including Fiji, were overrun by darker-skinned Melanesians, Tonga and Samoa were never conquered. Their inhabitants remained in relative isolation for something like a thousand years, in which time their language evolved from one of the East Melanesian (probably New Hebridean) tongues. Their characteristic adzes were fashioned, Green thinks, in Samoa, where the central Pacific basalt rocks begin.

As Roger Green has aptly remarked, the Lapita traders had need of their ocean-going outriggers and big double canoes to accomplish what they did. Both types of craft were, as we have seen, familiar to them. In 1975 Green suggested to me that double canoes were favoured above outriggers when it came to crossing the wide Melanesian Trench with heavy cargoes of pottery; the carrying capacity of the double canoes would be almost twice that of the outriggers. A factor that supports this theory is that the big sailing canoes of Polynesia and Fiji were almost all double vessels, while those of Micronesia and Melanesia were mostly outriggers. Moreover, the Mailu of coastal Papua, an East Austronesian people who established themselves on that coast about the time of Christ and made pottery almost indistinguishable from Lapita ware, and whose language and culture has much in common with Fijian and Polynesian, were sailing trading networks to the Trobriands as late as the 1970s. Their outward cargoes were still of pots, their return cargoes of shell; their ships were massive ten-metre double canoes with the claw-shaped sails typical of Polynesia—all in the direct tradition of the Lapita people of so long ago.

Even so, I was not convinced of the correctness of Green's theory until 1976, when I had the opportunity of sailing on two reconstructed ancient vessels: a Micronesian twenty-five-metre outrigger in the Gilberts and a twenty-metre double canoe in Hawaii. The Polynesian double canoe (from Hawaii) proved capable of transporting seventeen of us, with our food, water, domestic animals, and plant specimens for five thousand kilometres to Tahiti. The longer Gilbertese ship had much less carrying capacity.

There is an unsolved mystery that we may puzzle over. Early in the Christian era the Polynesians, who by that time had begun their unbelievable migrations out into the empty mid-Pacific, progressively made less and less and cruder pottery until, in the

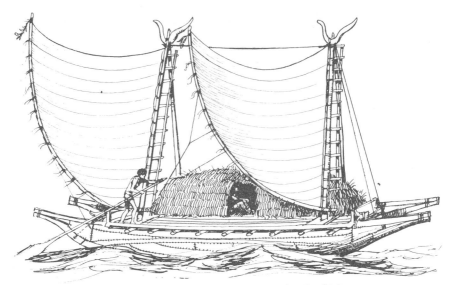

TUAMOTU PAHI

MAORI WAKA TAUA.

WA LAP
MARSHALL ISLANDS

FIJIAN NDRUA

end, they had abandoned pottery altogether. There was no shortage of raw materials on their new islands. We must search for some other explanation. It is pure speculation, but it could be that a revolution in cooking methods from boiling to earth oven took place, after which coconut shells and gourds were found to be unbreakable and easily obtained containers, as good as pots.

We will shortly be following the Polynesians on their mid-ocean saga of expansion, but, before we do so, we will look at those other far from negligible Pacific explorers, the Papuans, Melanesians, and Micronesians.

The Papuans and the Melanesians

Melanesia, which extends from the Solomons to the New Hebrides, New Caledonia, and Fiji, is a racial mosaic whose diversity is still little understood. Melanesians share some physical characteristics with the Papuans of New Guinea and, more remotely, with the Australians. Polynesian traits are evident in Fiji and parts of the New Hebrides. A further complication has been two thousand years of "back migration" from Samoa into the Polynesian outliers—Polynesian islands within geographical Melanesia and Micronesia.

Papuans from New Guinea were living in neighbouring New Ireland and New Britain in 6000 B.C., but from the Solomons eastward the rest of Oceania seems to have been devoid of any human inhabitants until 3000 B.C. or later. The first settlers were mainly Austronesians (who, we must remember, were ancestors of the Melanesians and Micronesians as well as the Polynesians). Lapita traders and their close relatives were probably the first human beings to set foot in a good part of Melanesia—certainly in Fiji, not to mention Tonga and Samoa. But the Lapita potters were not always necessarily the first comers. Long-established speakers of non-Austronesian Papuan languages are found as far from New Guinea as the Santa Cruz archipelago.

An elder cousin of mine, Charlie Cowan, had a trading schooner, *Navanora,* based on Fenualoa in the Santa Cruz Reef Islands in the 1930s. Fenualoa is a Polynesian name meaning "Long Land", and the island is connected by a drying reef to a Polynesian outlier Nufilole. But the language of Fenualoa—I found when I spent the Christmas of 1968 with Gabriel Paikai, ex-bosun to my late cousin (Charlie was murdered on Ndeni in 1936)—is a non-Austronesian tongue, relic of forgotten Papuan voyagers.

Here is another example of Melanesian complexity. The Santa Cruz Polynesian outlier Taumako lies about a hundred kilometres from Fenualoa; here the great *te puke* trading canoes were built. Polynesian is spoken and the sacred Polynesian *kava* is grown, but the Islanders chew betel-nut and use bows and arrows—both Melanesian customs. Moreover, the canoes themselves have Melanesian hulls, Micronesian lee platforms, and Polynesian claw sails, masted after the Micronesian manner.

As seafarers, the Melanesians have received a good deal less than their due. I was told by the Micronesian navigator Hipour in the central Carolines that the west Carolinian people of Sonsorol, Tobi, and Merir had dreaded the west wind lest it bring down New Guinea raiders upon them. The Caroline archipelago is enormous; the victims' islands lie seventeen hundred kilometres from Hipour's home. Nevertheless, his facts were right. Well-documented reports exist of generations of savage raids on these western islands from Irian Jaya (West New Guinea). The aggressors, described as "woolly haired Papuans", must have been notable seamen as well as pitiless killers, because they had to cross at the very least eight hundred kilometres of open sea to come at their prey.

Fijians too must at one time have been among the foremost sea rovers. European explorers found their voyages largely confined to their own islands, but this had not always been so. In the fourteenth century A.D. the Fijians joined the Tongans to form the host that swept eighteen hundred kilometres north through the islands to conquer the Gilberts. Even further afield, there are traditions on Nukuoro of the arrival of canoes from Hiti (Fiji). Nukuoro is in Micronesia, three thousand kilometres north of Fiji, and neither winds nor currents would favour accidental drifts. Yet another pointer to former Fijian maritime ascendancy is that the Fijians, not the Tongans, adapted Micronesian principles of canoe design and introduced them into Tonga about the time of Cook's voyages.

The Micronesians

All Micronesians speak Austronesian languages, though the western ones stem from the Philippines and the eastern from New Hebrides and Polynesia. The Austronesians who first settled the Micronesian island of Saipan in the Marianas were earlier in the field than even their Lapita counterparts. They were "first cousins"; "Marianas Red" pottery is closely akin to Lapita ware.

The open sea distance that had to be crossed was staggering. The nearest big islands were the Philippines, seventeen hundred kilometres away. There were "stepping stone" islands, but the closest of these was still 670 kilometres from Saipan. Yet this ocean waste was traversed and settlement was established at the early date of 1500 B.C.

The Micronesian archipelagos lie mostly north of the Equator, or else straddle it, and they comprise the Carolines, Marianas, Marshalls, and Gilberts. The culture is closely akin to that of Polynesia. Maui Tikitik, for instance, fished up the Micronesian island of Fais just as the identical myth-hero hauled the North Island of New Zealand (the "Fish of Maui") to the surface.

Between the two areas there must have been a great deal of trans-oceanic contact whose details are lost in time. Thus Tahitian and Hawaiian fishooks were not derived from those of Samoa, where the inhabitants came from, but are most like those of Japan. They were almost certainly introduced into Eastern Polynesia by Micronesian sea rovers. We do not know as yet who these were or from which archipelago they came, because the prehistory of Micronesia has been little studied. We do know that the deep-sea navigation of both peoples is virtually identical, practically every concept and technique being held in common. This will become evident when we come to draw on Micronesian voyaging practice in our outline of naked eye navigation. However, more is known about the movements of the Polynesians than those of the Micronesians; it is with the Polynesian saga of discovery that we will open the next chapter.

Islands Under the Stars: the Navigators of Polynesia

*T*HE DIAMOND-BRIGHT STAR-PATHS that appear each night above the trackless Pacific are trusty guides for those trained to interpret them. We will come presently to the arts of the navigators. First, let us see over what vast distances the star-paths led their ancestors.

The story of the great Polynesian expansion has partly been told in my book *Voyaging Stars,* and since I can add to it only in detail, a certain amount of repetition is unavoidable here. I make no apology for this, because the saga of endeavour and high courage behind the bald facts uncovered by prehistorians merits at least a second telling.

The Samoan and Tongan Polynesian heartland (Western Polynesia) includes many fertile islands and well-stocked lagoons. Whatever can have possessed long-established husbandmen-fishermen suddenly to break away from their tropical paradise to seek a perilous destiny on an unexplored ocean? Population pressures may have driven them, or defeat in war, or restless curiosity; many must have been gale-drifted far from their familiar seaways and providentially happened upon land. At any rate, Samoans and people from Vava'u in northern Tonga put to sea in the first centuries after Christ and, well before the end of the first millennium A.D., had colonized the uttermost islands of the ocean that covers a third of the earth. Not one of those islands had ever known the tread of man before. In all the annals of exploration, the world has never seen the like.

LAND OF MEN—THE MARQUESAS

The geographical gulf between Western Polynesia, which includes Tonga and Samoa, and Eastern Polynesia, which includes Tahiti, the Marquesas, and Hawaii among its archipelagos, is an immense one, dwarfing even the Melanesian Trench. The shortest practicable passage between off-lying islands of the two divisions would be in the region of a thousand kilometres; between the main groups, fifteen hundred kilometres. These distances refer to the gap between Samoa and Tahiti. The Marquesas lie an equal distance *beyond* Tahiti, well over three thousand kilometres from Samoa. Only rarely does westerly weather interrupt the prevailing trade winds and open a road eastward.

The first settlement in Eastern Polynesia was in many ways the most remarkable episode of all. To have reached Tahiti from Samoa would have been impressive enough, but the actuality was even more breathtaking. For those venturers from Samoa and Vava'u between the years 200 and 300 A.D. did not go to Tahiti at all, but far past it to the north-east. They straddled all Polynesia and arrived at Nuku Hiva in the Marquesas, 3,300 kilometres upwind of their starting point.

The Nuku Hivans never forgot their origin. Early in the nineteenth century they told an American naval captain that they had originally come from Vava'u. This claim was dismissed out of hand as patently absurd. Then, the anthropologists Y.H. Sinoto and R.C. Suggs, excavating on Nuku Hiva in 1960, found that it had indeed been settled by Western Polynesians, and that the settlement had taken place some time in the third or perhaps fourth century A.D.—long before Tahiti was colonized. Besides adzes of Western Polynesian type that came to light, in the earliest levels there was Lapita pottery—not much, but some. Most of this pottery had been made locally on Nuku Hiva itself, but recent analyses have unexpectedly revealed that a few of the sherds originated in far-away Fiji.

How did the Western Polynesian adventurers reach Nuku Hiva in the teeth of the strong south-east trades and the contrary west-flowing current, and how did they come to miss intervening Tahiti? Certainly they did not drift. The wind and current patterns rule this out absolutely.

What then was the probable course of events? If the voyagers from Samoa-Vava'u had for some reason deliberately pressed eastward, they would most likely have been forced north of their course by the south-east trades into a region of "stepping stone" coral atolls, the Northern Cooks and the Line Islands. Once again Levison, Ward, and Webb's invaluable computer study, referred to in connection with the Melanesian Trench, comes to our aid. Even on the pessimistic assumption that canoes deliberately trying to sail eastward could make good a course of no better than 90° from the wind, 43 per cent would have reached one of these atolls and a further 6 per cent would have come directly to the Marquesas.

I had reached much the same general conclusion on common-sense seamanship grounds before publication of the computer simulation results, when the famous Tongan traditionalist Ve'ehala, governor of Hapai'i, provided startling legendary confirmation. "Here is a story my grandfather told me," he began, as we sat round his coffee table one evening. "Long ago, some men and women of Vava'u set off eastward in search of a new home. They came to eight islands in turn, but none was to their liking. But the next one, the *nuku hiva*, the ninth island, for that is what *nuku hiva* means, did suit them. That was the end of the chiefs' wanderings. They settled on this ninth island and gave it the name that it bears to this day."

One puzzle remains. Why did the pioneers push on so stubbornly from atoll to atoll, a process that may well have taken generations? A reasonable explanation would be that some earlier storm-driven voyager had happened upon Tahiti and had returned to tell the tale. Then the Vava'uans would know for a fact that there was a great high island far to the eastward. The tiny atolls of the Northern Cooks and Line Islands that they came to would obviously not be what they sought, but the valleys and uplands of Nuku Hiva would admirably fill the bill. That they should have by-passed Tahiti on the north would have been only too probable given the direction of the trade winds.

SETTLEMENTS FROM THE MARQUESAS

Nuku Hiva and its neighbouring islands came to be known as the Land of Men. It was certainly a place of daring sea-rover explorers (in whose colonizing ventures the women participated no less than the men), and they soon proved that the spirit of their recent forbears from Western Polynesia was far from dead. In an extraordinarily short space of time they discovered and settled remote and isolated Easter Island, Tahiti and the Tuamotuan atolls, Hawaii, and possibly New Zealand.

What was the driving force for this explosive expansion over thousands of kilometres of remarkably empty ocean (New Zealand, for instance, is five thousand kilometres from Nuku Hiva—the distance from London to New York). In later times visiting Westerners were to see flotillas of great canoes bearing

ASIA

P A C

CHINA

JAPAN

TAIWAN

PHILIPPINES

WAKE
ISLAND

MARSHALL
ISLANDS

O

BORNEO

CAROLINE ISLANDS

NAURU

GILBERT
ISLANDS

OCEAN
ISLAND

PHOEN
ISLAN

INDONESIA

IRIAN
JAYA

PAPUA
NEW
GUINEA

SOLOMON
ISLANDS

ELLICE
ISLANDS

TOK

SANTA
CRUZ
ISLANDS

WALLIS
ISLANDS

NEW
HEBRIDES

FIJI

LOYALTY
ISLANDS

AUSTRALIA

NEW
CALEDONIA

NORFOLK
ISLAND

KER
ISLA

NORTH
ISLAND

NE

SOUTH
ISLAND

ZEA

180

NORTH
AMERICA

C

WAII
OU

AN

EQUATOR

LINE
ISLANDS

MARQUESAS
ISLANDS

TUAMOTU ARCHIPELAGO

TAHITI
SOCIETY
ISLANDS

FRENCH POLYNESIA

TABUAI
ISLANDS

SOUTH
AMERICA

EASTER ISLAND

SOUTHERN

OCEAN

whole sub-tribes putting to sea from Nuku Hiva in search of a priest-chief's dream island. Most, it is surmised, perished in mid-ocean. Some, we know, came to the Tuamotus, where they were slain in the surf. A canoe load that reached Rarotonga met a similar fate. Why the people left their home we do not know. Population pressure after drought has been suggested, but this would not apply to the early period we are considering when the resources of the Marquesas themselves were as yet hardly tapped. So we must leave this mystery unsolved and turn to the new lands discovered by these heroic pioneers.

Easter Island

The object of an enterprise is not necessarily its most important result. Thus the German chemists who synthesized the sulphona-mides were looking for a dye, but actually produced a drug that revolutionized the treatment of infections. Similarly, the object of the *Kon-Tiki* raft voyage was to demonstrate that the Polynesians came from South America. We now have conclusive evidence from archaeology, word analysis, studies of introduced plants and animals, and the rest that this view was wrong. The Polynesian ancestors came, as we have seen, ultimately from South-East Asia, as did their animals—the dog, the chicken, and the pig—and nearly all their food plants. What the *Kon-Tiki* voyage *did* demonstrate in no uncertain manner was something prehistor-ians had always underestimated—the ocean-going capabilities of early sailing craft.

As Easter Island is the nearest Polynesian island to South America, it was there, if anywhere, that evidence of American contact was to be found. It was the last refuge of the *Kon-Tiki* myth, as it were. This solitary, infertile island, thirty kilometres long and four thousand kilometres to windward of Nuku Hiva, was colonized from the Marquesas not later than 400 A.D. There is nothing in the archaeological record to show that the whole Easter Island culture did not evolve from this single landing. There were no mysterious white chiefs from Peru, outer space, or wherever. Introduced food plants (except the sweet potato, discussed below), domestic animals, tools, religion, and language are all Polynesian; maize, pottery, and Amerindian words are absent. There may, of course, have been South American contact, but if it occurred it played no decisive role in the history of this tiny island, named with splendid arrogance by its inhabitants "the Navel of the World".

The famous Easter Island statues were set up in the Middle Ages

STONE STATUES OF
EASTER ISLAND

and cast down in the late seventeenth century by popular revolt
against the tyrannical priest-chiefs. Though the isolation of
Easter Island and the nature of the soft volcanic rock in Rano
Rorakau crater, where the statues were quarried, contributed to
the special development of the islands' monumental sculpture,
the figures are in the Polynesian rather than the South American
tradition. Large stone statues were also carved on Nuku Hiva and
on Pitcairn, among other islands, and massive stoneworks were
constructed in Tonga, Ponape in Micronesia, and by the
Austronesians generally.

   In spite of what has been said above, somewhere along the line
there was prehistoric contact with South America. The sweet
potato was a basic food plant that was carried in the canoes of the
Polynesian voyagers and carefully transplanted at their new
homes. The Marquesas, Easter Island, Samoa, Tonga, Tahiti,
New Zealand, and Hawaii all grew this root vegetable before
Balboa first saw the Pacific. But the plant is of indubitable South
American origin. Its Polynesian name, *kumara,* is the same in
Quechua, the language of the Incas. Whether the sweet potato
travelled in Peruvian *balsa* or Polynesian double canoe we do not
know. There are Polynesian legends of voyages far to the east. The
probability is that the first Nuku Hivan settlers of Easter Island
already had the plant, in which case a far-roving Marquesan

voyager was probably responsible. His archipelago would be a big enough target for a return voyage to be practicable with known Polynesian navigation techniques. The same cannot be said of isolated Easter Island.

Interestingly enough, the sweet potato's history in New Guinea and most of Melanesia is quite different. It was brought to the Philippines from South America on Spanish ships and filtered down through the islands. Several hundred years ago its advent in highland New Guinea created a stone age agricultural revolution and population explosion among tribes unknown to, and unaware of, the outside world.

Tahiti and Hawaii

TANGAROA
THE SEA-GOD
(SOCIETY ISLANDS)

The archipelagos of both Tahiti and Hawaii were settled from the Marquesas around the sixth or seventh century A.D. Tahiti and the intervening Tuamotuan atolls are downwind of the Marquesas, and castaways could well have been the first settlers. Not that return voyages would be impossible. In fact, Tahiti and the Tuamotus remained in close contact down to European times, but by then the Tahitians had lost touch with their original parent archipelago. (They still remembered its existence, however. Tupaia, a Tahitian navigator-priest who sailed with Cook, told the Englishmen the names and correct positions of three of the Marquesas—Nuku Hiva, Fatu Hiva, and Hiva Oa.) As for the Hawaiian settlement, the winds and currents would preclude return. We cannot but speculate that a one-way migration of the kind recorded from the Marquesas in much later times may have been the instrument.

New Zealand

Linguistic evidence suggests a Marquesan element in New Zealand culture. Traditionally the settlers came from Raiatea, near Tahiti, via Rarotonga in the Cook Islands. We have no reason to doubt this, but perhaps the colonizers were Marquesans who had but recently settled Tahiti and had not had time to diverge culturally from the parent stock. The original colonizing of New Zealand is discussed further in the following section.

The Second Centre of Dispersal—Tahiti

The Tahitian chiefs, in the tradition of their Marquesan forbears, pushed out boldly in their high-sterned double-hulled *pahi*, which Cook estimated could sail 170 to 250 kilometres a day with leading winds. Their most significant exploratory voyages were anything but accidental, for they sailed north and south across the trade winds and the current, directions that would facilitate navigated returns. The computer simulation experiments, already mentioned, demonstrate no possibility of drifts reaching the Tahitians' most spectacular destinations—New Zealand and Hawaii.

The Settling of New Zealand

Maori genealogies have been interpreted to mean that the people arrived in New Zealand from Hawaiki, probably the modern Raiatea (formerly Havaiki) in about the fourteenth century A.D., and that an earlier "Moriori" settlement had preceeded the great migration. Recent archaeological discoveries have profoundly modified this concept. We now know that the Maoris arrived much earlier, more like 600 to 800 A.D., and that there were no previous inhabitants. They came from the Tahitian area—very possibly from Raiatea, as tradition suggests—where they may have been recent Marquesan immigrants. The adzes, fishhooks, and weapons of the first Maoris, now called Moa Hunters, were of an early Eastern Polynesian type, identical with assemblages excavated in the Tahitian group. These implements gradually evolved over the centuries into those of the classic Maori, there being no sign of any revolutionary change marking the arrival of a fourteenth century fleet.

However, even many canoeloads of visitors could not be expected to modify significantly the culture of a large settled land. There do appear to have been a number of voyages to New Zealand from tropical Polynesia which, not surprisingly, left little imprint on the big country's way of life. Thus Rarotonga, 850 kilometres south-west of Tahiti towards New Zealand, shares many New Zealand traditions of named canoes that staged in Ngatangia lagoon on their way south. Similarly, the *Tainui* canoe, the biggest ever built in the Tuamotus, which sailed away to unknown lands, turns up again in New Zealand legend— moreover, with the same captain.

Since accidental storm-drifts can be ruled out, the voyages to New Zealand must have been consciously navigated towards the south-west. But this does not mean that the pioneers were necessarily following the tracks of an earlier explorer who had returned home with news of his discovery. The sharp-eyed Tahitians must have observed the direction of the flight path of the annually migrating long-tailed cuckoo. This was a land bird,

so it was obviously making for land to the south-west, the
direction taken by the flocks year after year. Provided with such
absolute proof of the existence and bearing of an unknown island,
the navigators would hardly be deterred by the absence of any clue
as to its distance. They would go out and look, following the star-
path that the birds had taken; in this direction, 2,700 kilometres
beyond Rarotonga, lies the enormous target of New Zealand.
Confirmation that this reconstruction is not altogether fanciful
comes from the ancient Tuamotuan *fangu,* or sacred chant,
whose words it was sacrilege to alter:

> Mine is the migrating bird
> Winging over perilous regions of the ocean,
> Ever tracing out the age-old path of the
> wandering waves. . .

The New Zealand-bound leg from Rarotonga is favoured by
winds and currents, and the objective can hardly be missed—I
myself navigated a catamaran from Rarotonga to New Zealand
without compass or instruments, and arrived only forty-two
kilometres south of my projected landfall. But return voyages to
tropical Polynesia are another matter. In fact, I was at one time
dubious about their feasibility, until recent experience of the
windward sailing qualities of a "performance equivalent" replica
of an ancient Tahitian *pahi* convinced me of their practicability.
The voyage would have taken six weeks at the most, and landfall
on the scattered archipelagos would have been achieved by well-
tried Polynesian navigational techniques—as we shall see later
on in this chapter.

The Settling of Hawaii

The original settlers of Hawaii from the Marquesas were followed
by Tahitians, who reached the northern archipelago some five
hundred years later, around the year 1000 A.D. Voyaging contact
seems to have been maintained for the next few centuries, after
which such very distant voyaging fell into decline and was
ultimately abandoned. Many of the ruling chiefs of Hawaii trace
their descent from these Tahitian immigrants.

Clues to the existence of Hawaii may have been obtained from
some early Marquesan wanderer. They were not really necessary,
however, since northward-migrating golden plovers provided a
signpost exactly analogous to the long-tailed cuckoos for New

Zealand. The voyage between Tahiti and Hawaii is about the longest passage in all Polynesia—4,500 kilometres. The distance is not unbroken, because the Line Islands, uninhabited when the Europeans came, lie to leeward of and half-way along the course. Polynesian ruins were left on all these little islands, which were probably abandoned for lack of rainwater. Malden, for instance, fourteen hundred kilometres north of Tahiti, has stonework built by voyagers from Raivavae, seven hundred kilometres on the *other* side of Tahiti. That the old Tahitians were familiar with these latitudes, so far from those of their home, is attested by the fact that they not only knew of the pole-star, but called it a "pillar of the sky". Yet the pole-star does not become visible until the Equator is crossed into the Northern Hemisphere, seventeen hundred kilometres north of Tahiti (though the star would have topped the horizon rather further south a millennium ago).

As long voyages go, that between Hawaii and Tahiti in either direction is not a difficult one, despite its length. A month would suffice for the passage, which is across the prevailing winds and currents. The targets at both ends are extensive. But until 1976 archaeological proof of contact (as is so often the case) was lacking. Then Dr Kenneth Emory of the Bishop Museum in Hololulu demonstrated unmistakable Tahitian type sails in three rock engravings from the Hawaiian island of Maui. The artist could have been depicting nothing else but ships from Tahiti.

THE VOYAGERS SETTLE DOWN

Well before the Normans conquered Britain, the Polynesian and Micronesian settlement of the Pacific was complete. The explorers could rest. Land-based economies and powerful chiefdoms developed, especially in the high islands, and hazardous long-distance voyaging became steadily more restricted. But it did not cease altogether, and voyages of eight hundred kilometres without intervening land were still being made here and there at the time of European contact (the Carolines to Saipan and Pukapuka to Niue are two examples).

Some scholars, unnerved at the idea of "primitive" people crossing the ocean without instruments, have attempted to depreciate the former Polynesian voyagers. For a time they met with some acceptance, since few scholars have much experience of deep-sea sailing in small boats. But recent research into the nature and accuracy of the star navigation still practised in odd corners of the Pacific, as well as computer studies and the like, have

vindicated the ancient voyagers. Abundant evidence points to
their one-time enhanced range. Let us glance at it briefly.

We saw earlier that today's Santa Cruz Reef Islanders, in
particular the famous navigator Tevake, knew a much smaller
world than their distant Lapita predecessors. Even in the
nineteenth century their range was not very much larger than it is
today. But when Pedro Fernandez de Quiros visited the group in
1606, vastly more islands were known to the inhabitants, for chief
Tumai of Taumako indicated the direction of no less than seventy
islands that he knew, and a "very large land", Manicolo or
Mallicollo, that he told Quiros his people visited. This would
seem likely to have been Malekula in the New Hebrides, which lay
a full thousand kilometres away from isolated Sikaiana, with
which the Taumatoans maintained sporadic contact.

Similarly the Tongans, still daring sea rovers in Cook's day,
told the famous explorer that "Tafeedoowaia" (Tabiteuea), an
island then unknown to the Europeans, had once been under
their sway. Tabiteuea lies 19½ degrees of latitude, or two thousand
kilometres, north of Tongatapu—no mean feat of empire
building.

The famed Raiatean (Tahitian) chief, priest, and navigator
Tupaia—who, as we mentioned earlier, was able to tell Cook of
the existence and position of three of the Marquesas—had a truly
vast sphere of geographical knowledge. Various Fijian, Tongan,
and Samoan islands, far to the west, were included in his list of
known lands. While knowledge of the Marquesas might
conceivably have come from drifters, only purposeful voyagers,
either Tahitian or Western Polynesian, could have carried tidings
of these western islands to Tahiti against the trade winds. Many of
the groups referred to by Tupaia are unidentifiable, but it seems
likely that some islands to the westward that were "10 or 12 days in
going thither and 30 or more in coming back", were as Cook
surmised, in Western Polynesia, most probably Manua in Samoa.

Altogether Tupaia was able to identify every major island
group in Polynesia and Fiji with the exception of Hawaii, New
Zealand, and Easter Island, yet he said that his father had known
and often visited more islands still. Legend has it that Raiatea and
Rarotonga were once united but drifted apart. Similarly, Niue
was said to have been formerly united to Tonga by a mythical
land bridge. How clearly these stories reflect loss of one-time
contact and the once familiar ocean pathways' gradually
becoming barriers.

But though island empires rose and fell over the centuries and the disruptive impact of the Western world almost put an end to voyaging altogether, little pockets of traditional seafaring still lingered on in remote archipelagos that time passed by. Today, with the old skills on the verge of extinction, something of a renaissance has set in—the immeasurably ancient arts of star navigation are being taught once more.

THE STARS OF THE SEA ROADS

In ancient days little was recorded about navigation, for the arts of illiterate seafarers were of scant interest to the kings' chroniclers. Only indirectly, in reference to imports from far-off lands, is something of the enormous extent of the old trade networks revealed. The earliest surviving pilot book, and a good one at that, was written by an unknown Greek-Egyptian trading skipper in the first century A.D. It is called the *Periplus of the Erythraean Sea,* and it describes, not the Red Sea, but the Indian Ocean. Its author shows detailed personal knowledge of open sea passages and anchorages (and greedy officials) to beyond Zanzibar and eastward to India, and adds information about Malaysia and China. Yet he was no trail-blazer. Six hundred years before his time a Phoenician expedition, sent out by Pharaoh Necho, had circumnavigated Africa.

The Arabs, Indians, and Chinese of the Periplus period made great play with stars and winds for direction, and stars for latitude as well—all without instruments. It is a pity that the most scientific of all explorers, Captain Cook, while eagerly questioning Tupaia about new islands, should have missed the opportunity of asking his Tahitian contemporary *how* he navigated.

The origins of Polynesian navigation were undoubtedly the well-tried methods that the Austronesian sea rovers brought with them into the Pacific, for the bold thrusts to Saipan in 1500 B.C. and across the Melanesian Trench to Fiji not much later were no landsmen's hesitant first ventures. It has already been suggested that the monsoon-assisted open-sea passages across the Bay of Bengal and the Arabian Sea were the navigational schooling grounds of the Austronesians. Transmission of techniques could not have been in the opposite direction (*to* the Indian Ocean) because man was sailing the Asian seas aeons before the Pacific.

Before we go on to piece together the fragmentary facts that are all that have come down to us, let us see what comprises the art and science of navigation in general. The first requisite is to be able to steer a fixed course out of sight of land. This may be done by following either a compass direction or, more reliably, a rising or setting star. ("The compass may go wrong, the stars never," said an old Tongan navigator.) The slow-arching sun, the wind, the ranks of ocean swells are all similar direction indicators and are all still used in the Pacific. Speed and distance are matters of experience and informed judgement. Pacific navigators with whom I have sailed could assess distance run as accurately as a ship's patent log. Displacement off course by currents is a particularly thorny problem. Pacific Islanders draw valid conclusions from the observation that open ocean currents are mostly wind driven and follow the prevailing winds. Nevertheless, from Tikopia to the Carolines, the precaution is never neglected of taking back bearings by eye on the receding land to see which way the canoe is being set.

All this amounts to "dead reckoning". Some reference external to the sea's restless surface is needed if a vessel's position is to be confirmed. The "fix" may be a sinuous line of seaweed at a junction of currents, the disturbed sea over a reef, or a star that stands overhead and indicates latitude. All these and many more are Pacific methods, and most crop up as well in Asiatic records.

One other general point should be made. Before the invention of accurate instruments, lunar tables, and ultimately the chronometer—not long before Cook's day—there was no way of determining longitude—the distance east or west. The Spanish explorers, and the Manila galleons that came after them, had to run downwind towards an objective along the parallel of its known latitude, just as the Persians, Arabs, Indians, and Chinese had done centuries before the birth of Christ.

Not all methods of navigation are, of course, equally applicable to different seas. Thus Herodotus around 500 B.C. made passing mention of sounding leads armed with tallow for bringing up samples of the sea bottom—a technique only outdated by the echo sounder. This was off Egypt; it would have been of little use in the abyssal Pacific waters. But most of the methods that have come down to us from the Mediterranean and Eastern seas are identical with those of the Pacific navigators. To mention only two: the Phoenician-Greek "wind compass", the different winds being distinguished by their characteristics, had analogues in the Arabian Sea, Indonesia, Santa Cruz, Tahiti, the Carolines, the Cooks, and many other Pacific groups; shore-sighting birds were carried on shipboard "long ago", according to a fifth century B.C. Indian account, and Tongan and Samoan creation myths refer to a similar practice. It seems probable, however, that this "Noah's Ark" technique would be most appropriate to the early period of exploration. In contemporary Pacific Island navigation, birds are, in the words of a venerable Gilbertese navigator, "our very best friends, for they show us the direction of land".

But this is not the place for a treatise on natural-sign navigation. To simplify matters we will now compare the one-time Indian Ocean "star compass" with the Caroline Islands counterpart, for the Carolines navigation system is the best preserved of any in the Pacific and is still in use for canoe voyages of eight hundred kilometres.

"Star Compasses"

A star-path is a succession of stars that rise or set at a particular point on the horizon and by which one steers. The concept is universal in Polynesia. A "star compass" is a slightly more sophisticated version of the same thing, where certain stars are singled out to indicate named horizon points. Naturally, they will only be in position for a short time, so one actually steers by a series of substitutes, just as with the star path. A peculiarity of the "compass" is that most stars mark two positions, one at rise and the other at set; another is that the points are irregularly spaced round the horizon and so do not fit in with a magnetic rose—a circumstance that must help to account for the star compass's long survival.

In 1553 Ali Re'is ibn Hussain, a Turkish admiral shipwrecked in India, compiled from Indian sources going back to the ninth century A.D. a work called *Muhit* (Ocean). Certain passages in the *Muhit* show that the magnetic compass, then long in use, had been preceded in the Indian Ocean by a star compass. The details of this one-time star compass are brought out even more clearly in an illustration of a thirty-two-point star compass card in the *Majid Kitab,* a later Arab treatise on navigation. The same star names recur to the east and west with the prefixes *mutala* ("rising place"), east, and *majib* ("setting place"), west. The star points, as shown by an unsuccessful attempt to equate them with magnetic points, had been irregularly spaced. The east-west line is indicated by the star Altair, though it actually rises and sets 8½ degrees north of the east-west line. Since the Arab seafarers were nothing if not accurate, this must have been a convention. It is one that is important for comparison, as we shall see.

Caroline Islands navigation also centres on a thirty-two-point star compass. Prefixes meaning rising or east *(daane)* or setting or west *(doloni)* precede the stars' names. The star points are irregularly spaced. Most significantly, the seemingly illogical convention is adhered to of making Altair the east-west marker.

The pole-star did not bear due north when the *Muhit* was written, and many of the southern stars of the Arab compass cannot now be identified, their names being archaic Indian or Persian. Nevertheless, no fewer than eighteen out of the thirty-two star points appear to be identical in the Indian Ocean and Pacific systems. There is a little too much correlation between them, I think, to be due to mere coincidence.

Latitude by Pole-Star

We will continue to take the well-preserved navigation of the Carolines as our Pacific example, but for a second reason. The technique about to be discussed is only practicable where the pole-star (Polaris, or North Star) is visible—that is, north of the Equator. The Carolines, the Marshalls, the Marianas, and Hawaii are the only Pacific archipelagos located, like the long Asian sea routes, in the Northern Hemisphere.

The height of the pole-star above the horizon (or substitute stars in the days before Polaris was where it is now) equals one's latitude. For instance, the pole-star at Puluwat and Satawal in the Carolines stands 7½ degrees high, and at Saipan 15 degrees, so the latitude of Puluwat and Satawal will be 7½ degrees and of Saipan 15 degrees.

The altitude of the pole-star substitutes was estimated in finger-breadths *(isbah)* by the Arabs, 1½ degrees in our measurement, and 2 degree finger-breadths *(chih)* by the Chinese. These could be judged by eye at sea to an accuracy of about a degree, or a hundred kilometres.

On Satawal in the Carolines navigators estimate the height of the pole-star by eye or by the span of the fingers loosely extended at arm's length. This measure is one *ey-ass* and is equal to 15 degrees (an *ey-ass* is a hooked breadfruit-picking pole). The senior Satawal navigators told me that the pole-star was half an *ey-ass* above the horizon at their home island and one *ey-ass* at Saipan, proportions that are exactly right.

The Arabs—and the Indians, Persians, Chinese, and Indonesians before them—used to make their long east-west passages by reference to stellar latitude. Even after instruments had been devised more precise than finger tips, sailing directions for the ports of Ceylon, India, Sumatra, and Malaysia continued to be expressed in *isbah* (or *chih*).

Once again we have a closely equivalent system operating in the two oceans.

The Zenith Star

Two navigational concepts seem native to the Pacific. The first of these is the use of the zenith star. Nowhere in Polynesia, save Hawaii, is the pole-star visible. An alternative method of estimating latitude had to be devised. This was by the overhead or zenith star, the star which night after night passed directly above in the same latitude. Sirius, for instance, passes right above Tahiti (and Fiji farther west); Arcturus (*Hokule'a*), over Hawaii. Looking upwards along the mast, and using a star at or very near your zenith, you can judge whether you are under it or a little north or south by half a degree, or fifty kilometres, on a reasonably calm night—an accuracy not always exceeded by present-day ocean yachtsmen! This technique, which was probably always a restricted one, even a secret one, is best remembered on Tikopia and by one of the hereditary navigator clans of Tonga, but it has been recorded from other archipelagos.

Expanding the Target

The second peculiarly Pacific innovation, made necessary by the tiny size of the individual islands, was "expanding" them. Most islands are part of archipelagos in the Pacific. "You must aim", said the Tongan navigators, "not at a particular tree but at the grove of trees." The Carolinians were expressing the same idea when they spoke of sailing into a "screen" of islands, submerged reefs and bird zones. In other words, the South Seas navigator steers into the middle of an archipelago, which may be hundreds of kilometres across, and then hunts for an island by looking out for land signs.

Not surprisingly, since the coconut palms of an atoll only come into view seventeen kilometres away from the deck of a canoe, land-locating signs are considered of primary importance in the Pacific. Their order of importance naturally varies according to local conditions, but most are known everywhere.

Birds take pride of place in the navigators' repertoire in groups as remote from each other as the Tuamotus and the Carolines. Terns, noddies, and boobies are the most important species, for they all roost ashore, flying out to sea each day to fish and returning home each evening. Their habits vary according to locality, but terns and noddies generally congregate up to forty kilometres offshore, while flocks of boobies may be confidently

WHITE TERN

ARCTIC TERN

TROPIC BIRD

FRIGATE BIRD

STORM PETREL
("MOTHER CAREY'S CHICKEN")

BROWN BOOBY

expected at sixty. The sighting of a substantial number confirms the proximity of land, but only their morning and evening flight-paths indicate its direction.

Ocean swells are distorted and reflected by land far off. Knowledgeable Tikopians, Santa Cruz Reef Islanders, Marshall Islanders, and Tongans are thus enabled to "read the swells" and locate an island from as far as sixty kilometres out at sea.

Cloud signs form another ubiquitous series of pointers towards land. Yet another indicator is the mysterious deep luminescence "like underwater lightning", termed *te lapa* in Santa Cruz. This is familiar in the Gilberts, Marshalls, and Tonga, but not everywhere.

But this is surely enough of analysing. Let us conclude this chapter with something more in the spirit of the great Pacific Islands explorers of the past—an account of how, in 1969, a navigator retraced a course untravelled for three generations, across 750 kilometres of empty ocean.

RETRACING AN ANCIENT SEA ROAD

The Mariana archipelago, whose main islands are Saipan and Guam, was, as we saw, settled about 1500 B.C. by Austronesians from the Philippines. To the southward, 750 kilometres away, lie the far-flung Carolines, home of a closely related people. They were in regular contact with each other until 1686, when the Spaniards massacred most of the Mariana inhabitants. Survivors fled to the Carolines in their canoes, and, not surprisingly, communication abruptly ceased.

After a century, daring Carolinian voyagers began cautiously to renew contact with Guam and Saipan. In 1788 a party landed at Guam. They were seeking to trade for iron, and what they told the Spanish governor (as recorded later by the Russian explorer Kotzebue) leaves little doubt that their voyages were far from haphazard. "They said they had always been trading with the inhabitants of this island [Guam], and only left off when the white people settled here, whose cruelty they themselves had witnessed. . . . the description of the route . . . was recorded in their songs, after which, and the position of the stars, their pilots find their way." From this time onward, until the beginning of the present century, fleets of canoes from Puluwat, Satawal, Woleai, and Lamotrek in the Carolines set out annually for Guam and Saipan.

The seaway to Saipan had, however, been deserted for three

generations when my gaff ketch *Isbjorn* nosed her way into
Puluwat lagoon in 1969. I was intent on finding out whether the
star-path sailing directions for Saipan were still remembered
from the time of the great-grandfathers of the present navigators.
Certainly the 1788 voyagers had been able to retrace the long sea
road after it had been untravelled for a hundred years. But 1969
was the era of space flight and jet aircraft; could the detailed
traditions and skills necessary for the voyage still survive? There
was only one way to find out; the master navigator Hipour was to
provide the answer.

Hipour was one of the most respected of the fifteen practising
navigators of the island. He was unfamiliar with Western concept
and practice and with writing; his long apprenticeship had been
entirely traditional. In his trained memory was stored something
like the equivalent of a nautical almanac and a pilot book
combined. Armed with this knowledge, he had ranged up and
down through the Carolines for a quarter of a century.

"Can you take command of my ketch and take us to Saipan
without instruments, solely by the guiding stars, waves, and
homing birds?" I asked Hipour through his friend, the English-
speaking Ulutak. In anticipation, I had already dismounted the
compass and stowed it away in a locker, together with the sextant,
radio, wrist-watches and charts.

"I think I can," he said simply. Two days later we set sail.

The only intervening island was uninhabited Pik, 170
kilometres to the north, where we would stage. Thereafter there
would be 750 kilometres of unbroken ocean to be traversed. As
Puluwat dwindled astern, Hipour checked the drift by landmarks
on the receding island and duly altered course for a current he
found to be setting across our path. We were heading towards
where Pleiades was sinking in the west, and the constellation
became intermittently visible between scudding clouds when
darkness fell. After Pleiades set we maintained direction by
keeping the Great Bear on a point in the starboard rigging. Then
once Pollux had sunk low enough to steer by, we held our forestay
upon it, for its bearing was the same, Hipour said, as that of the
Pleiades. Once a strange star appeared at which I stared in
surprise; but Hipour merely grinned and remarked, unexpectedly
in English, "Satellite."

After a day on Pik, we continued on a more northerly course so
that we steered on a different set of stars. Hipour made two star
points allowance for current set, as his ancestors had laid down,
and increased this later because of strong winds and rough seas,

again according to their transmitted directions.

The star dome slowly revolving above our heads enabled us to hold our course with compass-like accuracy at night. Day guides were not quite so easy to follow, but each evening when the stars became visible we found we were heading exactly where Hipour said we were. In the daytime, then, the changing angle of the sun and the shadows it cast across the deck, together with the direction of the long Pacific swells, served us well enough.

In these unfamiliar waters Hipour studied the passing ranks of swells for hours on end until their individual characteristics became as recognizable to him as a friend's face. Occasionally he would demonstrate, indicating on the yacht's rail the point at which each wave impinged. Once, five distinct wave systems were detectable.

Five days out from Pik, Hipour judged we were nearing the Marianas. He had deliberately headed upwind of his objective and a little beyond it, for he aimed to cut obliquely through the island chain that stretches north from Saipan, heaving-to at night so not to miss land in the darkness. He made it clear that no individual island but the "screen" of islands and birds was the target, through which only a criminally careless captain could pass unwittingly.

Birds were our guides towards land. First boobies, and later terns and noddies, began to appear and increased in numbers as the day wore on. Towards evening small flocks broke off fishing and headed off in one direction. At almost the same moment Ulutak, red-eyed from scanning the ocean, saw land from the rigging.

Of our hospitable reception in Saipan I best remember Hipour and Ulutak, still uncompromisingly wearing only their scanty breech-clouts, surrounded by a crowd or admirers in one of the town's bars.

At the close of an equally successful return voyage on which we again used birds as a landfall, we crept in through the reef pass at Puluwat in the dark. Suddenly a kilometre-long line of coconut-leaf torches flared in salute, and the water around us erupted with speeding canoes. It was a fitting welcome to the navigator and his helper who had so triumphantly reaffirmed their cultural heritage.

The theme of this book is exploration. But Hipour was not exploring; he was applying sea lore accumulated over millennia. What then, is the relevance of this voyage to the pioneers? It illustrates the efficacy of a navigational system that enabled him to keep his bearings at all times. The discovery of new land must always have been, in the last instance, a matter of chance (apart from bird clues and the like). But only by navigational expertise could an explorer find his way home again and pass on the sailing directions for his discovery. Hipour's return voyage demonstrated skills of this order. His system was probably little altered from that of the first explorers of the Pacific.

3

Peoples of the Pacific Rim

C HINA, LAND OF SILK," wrote the first-century author of the
Periplus, adding with forgivable confusion, "where the
seacoast ends utterly". Certainly the seas about Asia were
familiar waters for the great junks, far and away the most
advanced ships at the beginning of the Christian era (and long
after), whereas the "Boundless Place", as the Chinese termed the
Pacific, remained largely an ocean of darkness. But evidence
exists, tantalizing in its incompleteness, to suggest that parts of
this ocean were not entirely untravelled.

THE THREE-JEWEL EUNUCH

The Chinese admiral Cheng Ho, a eunuch, was born in 1371
and led his first great expedition in 1405 when he was thirty-five
years old, his last twenty-eight years later. His fleets visited the
South-East Asian archipelagos, India, Ceylon, Arabia, Persia,
and East Africa; they may well have touched at Australia.
Humanity and respect for the cultures of the "Western
Barbarians" (even if seasoned with more than a little smug
superiority) characterized the dealings of this great explorer, in
marked contrast to the behaviour of the rapacious Portuguese,
who were to follow him into the Indian Ocean three-quarters of a
century later.

Chinese voyaging reached its golden age with Cheng Ho, its
ultimate flowering before it was abruptly cut off. For the
mandarinate, representing feudal landed interests, achieved
power at the court of the emperor at the expense of the more
outward-looking imperial eunuchs. For complex economic and
social reasons foreign trade and contacts became anathema. Only
forty years after Cheng Ho's death the official records of his
expeditions were burnt by the vice-president of the war Office,

CHINESE JUNK —
THE PECHILI TRADING VES[S]

and by the turn of the century it had become a capital offence to build a seagoing junk with more than two masts.

The eminent scholar Joseph Needham has pointed out that there was nothing new in Chinese semi-governmental trading missions with the South Seas and the lands at the far border of the Indian Ocean. They had been undertaken for a thousand years before Cheng Ho's time. Lists of return tribute missions exist for as early as the second century A.D. A fleet of twenty-five Chinese ships reached Ormuz on the Persian Gulf in 1301; seven years earlier, one of a fleet of fourteen junks had deposited the returning Marco Polo at the same Persian port. It was the scale and scope of Cheng Ho's operations that were unprecedented.

Thus the first expedition, and it was typical of the other six made by Cheng Ho, consisted of thirty-seven thousand men and no less than sixty-two great ships. The largest "treasure ships" were 147 metres long and 60 metres wide, had nine masts and carried upwards of five hundred men—ocean giants indeed. (These dimensions received unexpected confirmation in 1962 with the discovery at the site of the Ming shipyards near Nanking of the twelve-metre-long rudder post of one of Cheng Ho's ships.) In the course of two years the fleet visited Indo-China, Java, Sumatra, Ceylon, and the west coast of India.

Most interest attaches to the last three expeditions, the fifth, sixth, and seventh. While the Pacific squadrons visited Java, Borneo, and Okinawa, other elements of the fleet cruised the East African coast to Zanzibar and beyond, bringing back giraffes to Peking, while others again called at Mecca. Hosts of embassies from all over the Eastern world and the Asian Pacific islands flocked to the Celestial Empire bearing tribute (a form of imperial trade in this context). Not least in importance were exotic herbs and drugs, and it is of interest that no fewer than 180 doctors accompanied one of the expeditions.

If we turn our attention to the Pacific archipelagos of South-East Asia, Indonesia, and the Philippines, we find evidence of widespread and prolonged Chinese trading contact in ubiquitous remains of Chinese porcelain, only equalled in East Africa. Needham has pointed out that in Borneo, for example, the Chinese traded ceramics, beads, and metal tools for edible birds' nests, hornbill ivory, and rhinoceros horn, and that this trade was already ancient at the time of a Chinese treatise on trade with Indonesia, including Borneo and Timor, written in 1225.

Most significant of all ceramic finds has been that of a Chinese porcelain statuette of Shou Lao, the god of longevity, unearthed in 1879 at Darwin, from four feet below ground, among the roots of a banyan tree at least two hundred years old. The date of the figure is consistent with Cheng Ho's time. It is reasonable to suppose that the statuette was deposited in the fifteenth or sixteenth century, but who brought it? Chinese ships had been trading with Timor ever since the seventh century, and Timor is no more than 650 kilometres from Darwin. The alternative would be one of the Indonesian proas that visited the northern Australian coasts for the sea-slug known as bêche-de-mer or trepang—significantly enough, for the Chinese market. Aboriginal traditions have been cited to the effect that the Indonesians were preceded by a much lighter-skinned people called the Baijini, who had looms and set up temporary agricultural settlements—not implausibly the Chinese.

Leaving aside early trepang fishers, what other motives could the Chinese have had for visiting Australia? Professor Chiao-min Hsieh has suggested that part of one of Cheng Ho's expeditions may have travelled there from Java to offer sacrifices to Canopus, the star of the South Pole, which governs longevity. We remember that it was the god of longevity whose statuette was dug up at Darwin.

While the evidence remains inconclusive about early Chinese visits to the Australian mainland, the same cannot be said about New Guinea. The north coast was within the sphere of the Chinese seafarers and traders, who long ranged through Indonesia and the Philippines. This early trade did not differ in principle from that with Borneo. Nor did it come to an end with the Dutch occupation of Indonesia, as the following account shows.

Captain Thomas Forrest of the East India Company was sent on a voyage to extend the company's trade into "the unfrequented parts of Asia", and found himself in 1771 in Geelvink Bay on the north coast of New Guinea. Here, he discovered, the Chinese controlled the trade with the outside world, and were also in the habit of sailing a week's journey further east in search of turtle shell. Not surprisingly, in view of the generally high standard of Chinese trading ethics, the savage inhabitants were "said to deal honestly with the Chinese". They "advance their goods for several months before returns are made," said a contemporary account. According to H.T. Fry, to whom I am indebted for this account, the Chinese exchanged iron implements, basins, and beads for massoy bark, ambergris, sea-slug, turtle shell, small pearls, dried birds of paradise, and, less worthily, for slaves.

THE INDONESIANS AND AUSTRALIA

The Indonesian trepang fishers were no fly-by-nights, for the industry flourished on the Australian coasts from about 1700 until the last proa came in 1906-7. The Australian National University prehistorian Campbell Macknight estimates that two thousand men each season were scattered in temporary processing camps from Coburg Peninsula, near Melville Island, to the Gulf of Carpentaria. The Dutch historian Le Roux points out that "the most favoured grounds of all were Broad Sound and Shoalwater Bay". These last are between Mackay and Rockhampton, inside the Great Barrier Reef, beyond Torres Strait on Australia's east coast. It is salutory to realize that the little proas

were berthing there regularly half a century before Cook
"discovered" that coastline.

It is intriguing to speculate how the Aborigines reacted to these
"Malays" from another world. Relations were good, it seems;
much better than with the later colonists from Europe, who
ruthlessly expropriated the land. Baron Van der Capellen wrote
in 1824:

> The annual voyage to those parts [New Holland] seems to have
> taken place for a very long time, even before the establishment of
> Dutch power in Macassar.... every year a number of young men
> from those parts accompany them to Macassar out of curiosity,
> subsequently returning to their own country. These men, whom I
> have seen in Macassar, are of a type quite distinct from the other
> peoples which one encounters in these regions. They are very black,
> tall in stature, with curly hair, not frizzy like that of the Papuan
> peoples, long thin legs, thick lips and, in general, are quite well
> built.

Not all these young men returned home to Australia. In 1876 a
pearling lugger skipper reported there were then about seventeen
Aborigines settled in Macassar with local wives.

The voyage to Marege, as Australia was called, was begun from
Macassar (now Ujung Padang) at the southern tip of the Celebes
(now Sulawesi). The outward journey made use of the north-west
monsoon, which begins to blow in December; the return, the
south-east monsoon from the end of April. To the landfall on the
Coburg Peninsula after rounding Timor was an open sea stretch
of 650 kilometres, across which the proas seem to have averaged
about four knots. These trading proas belonged to small
entrepreneurs, who relied upon long-term credits. Crew and
captain worked for shares in the proceeds of the enterprise, just as
do the crews of the tiny lateen-rigged fishing proas from Madura
that come to the Kimberley coast of Western Australia today. And,
then as now, the hard-worked crews generally remained in a
permanent state of indebtedness.

The trading proas, or *paduwakang*, that made these voyages to
Arhem Land and beyond were 20–50-ton vessels; their crews
numbered twenty to forty. The great English naturalist Alfred
Russel Wallace, who took passage on one from Macassar to an
island off New Guinea in 1856, said he had never "made a twenty
days' voyage so pleasantly". His description of the ship is worth
quoting:

The deck sloped considerably downward to the bows, which are
thus the lowest part of the ship. There were two large rudders, but
instead of being placed astern they were hung on the quarters. . . .
Our ship had two masts . . . which were great movable triangles. . . .
The mainyard, an immense affair nearly a hundred feet long, was
formed of many pieces of wood and bamboo bound together. . . .
The sail carried by this was of oblong shape, and was hung out of
the centre, so that when the short end was hauled down on deck the
long end mounted high in the air.

Wallace's proa averaged some one hundred miles a day. The
sails, as he so graphically describes, were canted square sails, the
most ancient of all fore-and-aft rigs and—together with boomed
lateens, primitive lateens, and claw-shaped sails—hallmarks of
the Austronesian legacy.

Who were these seafaring traders who came so regularly and
confidently to the Great South Land? They were Macassarese and
Bugis from the Macassar region, with a sprinkling of of Bajau
Laut—Sea People—from further north. They were not always
peaceful traders, however; they had the reputation of occasionally
reverting to another trade—some of the fiercest piracy the world
has ever known.

Oddly enough, up to the sixteenth century the Bugis and
Macassarese were mostly farmers. What trade there was from
Macassar was mostly in the hands of "Moors" (Arabs and
Indians), Malays, Javanese, and latterly Portuguese. The
Javanese were then the great sea traders of Indonesia and had been
for two centuries before the era of Cheng Ho's voyages. This
Javanese preponderance ended when the Dutch clamped their
rule over western Indonesia. "There is nothing in this world",
wrote an official to the directors of the Dutch East India
Company, "that gives man better right than might and power
added to right", and in accordance with this principle, the good
burghers used their right and power effectively to stifle Javanese
trade.

The men of Macassar were not slow to fill the gap. Kareng-
Pattingalloang, for instance, who became chief minister of the
sultanate in 1636, collected a notable library of European charts as
well as Chinese treatises and a "gigantic terrestrial globe". The
Bugis were fascinated by charts and soon began to make their own
after European models, the more so as their range expanded to
Siam, Cambodia, Manila, and Australia.

In the middle of last century a South-East Asian chart, drawn in
black and red on cowhide and labelled in Buginese characters,

was taken by Captain Jordens of the paddle-driven warship *Merapi* from a pirate kampong. A very similar one was found on the ship of a Philippine Bajau Laut pirate captured in 1847. The Buginese inscription relating to yet another such chart gives us a clue as to how the European models, upon which they were based, were obtained (the Dutch were understandably reluctant to oblige). It reads: "...given to me by Captain Thomas Forrest".

We have encountered this English East India Company captain before—in Geelvink Bay, New Guinea, in 1771. Forrest held the highest opinion of the intelligence and enterprise of the Buginese and Macassarese seamen, whom he termed a high-spirited people ... fond of adventures, emigration, and capable of undertaking the most dangerous enterprises". "They are fond of sea charts," he wrote; "I have given many to certain noquedas (commanders of prows) for which they were very grateful, and often wrote the names of places in their language." This was especially true of Forrest's esteemed friend, the *noquedali* Inankee, to whom the Englishman presented charts of his New Guinea voyage.

Buginese and Macassarese sources of navigational information were by no means limited, of course, to Forrest's charts. Their proas were constructed and rigged in traditional fashion, with European features increasingly incorporated; their wave and star navigation was their own and ancient; charts were acquired through piratical raids and bribery of the Dutch company's servants. No wonder these daring seamen not only visited Australia in passing but occupied seasonal settlements for two hundred years.

But to return to our earlier question; were the trepang traders from Macassar preceded in Australia by the Chinese? From the beginning, the market for trepang was exclusively Chinese, as was that for sandlewood, turtle shell, pearl shell, bird-of-paradise plumes, and shark fins from New Guinea and the Eastern Archipelago. All these products, says Forrest, were sold "to the annual Chinese junk at Macassar".

The Darwin statuette of Shou Lao seems too precious an object to have been carried aboard a rough *paduwakang;* indeed, the Macassarese earthenware deposited in considerable quantities in northern Australia is all of rough quality. Moreover, the circumstance of the finding of the figure among the roots of the ancient banyan tree suggests it was placed there not later than 1600, a century before the Macassarese, while its style is more or less contemporaneous with Cheng Ho. So whether the god's enigmatic representation was left by one of Cheng Ho's captains on an astronomical/astrological mission or by some questing trading junk, we must, I think, award the palm of Australian discovery provisionally to the fifteenth-century Chinese. This holds whether or not we accept the evidence, outlined in the next chapter, suggesting early Portuguese contact, for this would have taken place in the following—sixteenth—century and would have constituted a rediscovery.

There remains one piece of evidence of prehistoric contact with Australia, probably by way of New Guinea, from Indonesia and the Philippines. This is the provenance on both sides of Cape York Peninsula of more than one variety of introduced but Aboriginal-built outrigger dug-out canoe. As the indigenous Aboriginal canoes of Australia are bark-built, the Cape York craft clearly bespeak outside influence. But where from and how long ago? To obtain even a tentative answer, we must first separate double-outrigger canoes—those having an outrigger on each side—from those with an outrigger on one side only.

The single outriggers were used along five hundred kilometres of coast, including Cooktown and extending southward to Palm Island, while the double outriggers were found on both sides of Cape York Peninsula further north. Single-outrigger canoes, one of which was described by Captain Cook, were called in the neighbourhood of Cooktown *wangga*. This is an Austronesian word for canoe, not an Australoid one; in this context, it is Melanesian. Like the Cooktown canoes, the Melanesian ones are single outriggers, so this most ancient of outrigger imports into Australia probably came from that part of the Pacific.

Double-outrigger canoes are now generally considered to be more recent than single outriggers and to have evolved, like the former, in the Indonesia-Philippines region, perhaps two thousand years ago. (Pacific Island canoes, incidentally, are all single outriggers or else are double-hulled canoes.) The double outriggers from the tip of Cape York Peninsula have features that show them to have been derived from Torres Strait Islands models, which in turn owed their inspiration to Indonesia. The anthropologist A.C. Haddon, basing his conclusions on types of outrigger attachments, considers that other Cape York double outriggers were derived from an island in the northern Solomons whose water craft are of Indonesian type, and also from the Philippines. We can only speculate about the dates and routes of this flow-on of double outriggers from Indonesia and the

Philippines to northern Australia, or the long-forgotten epics of the castaways and voyagers who brought them to the southern continent. Only the canoes themselves bear witness that such contact occurred.

CHINA AND SOUTH AMERICA

Transpacific voyages or drifts, if they occurred at all, took place in the remote past before the dawn of the Christian era, at a time when Chinese documentation of such events was scanty and ambiguous. The evidence at best is circumstantial, but in sum it is a little too striking to be glossed over altogether. By way of introduction, I shall quote from Joseph Needham's monumental *Science and Civilisation in China.*

> "The ambassador of the Han, Chang Chhien," wrote Chang Hua about 285 A.D., "won through across the Western Seas to reach Ta-Chhin (the Roman Empire) . . . but the Eastern Ocean is yet more vast, and we know of no one who has crossed it." Perhaps this was because no one ever came back. . . . once any group of people sailed from Asia to America on primitive craft there was very little chance of their ever returning, since before relatively modern times no general understanding of the regime of winds and currents could develop. Of those who made the journey, within the span of the 1st millennia B.C. and A.D., many were probably fishermen or traders, involuntary carriers of culture to the Americas, but assuredly sometimes the great voyage was undertaken purposively for one reason or another, though not with knowledge of the landfall.

During the Ch'in Dynasty, in the third century B.C., and the Han which followed it, the rulers of China were convinced that plants that conferred longevity or even immortality were to be found on islands out in the Eastern Ocean (the Pacific), and many expeditions went in search of them. The only one of the commanders whose name has come down to us is Hsu Fu. With three thousand young men and girls, Hsu Fu set forth eastward in 219 B.C. to found an empire on what is believed to have been the island of Honshu in Japan.

Needham speculates that some of the many other captains who set out on the same quest were driven eastward by the prevailing westerlies that blow along the track of the Kuroshio current and ultimately survived to reach the Americas. That such drifts are by no means impossible is shown by the fact that East Asian junks were driven onto the American shores about once every five years

during last century, and out of sixty nineteenth century drifts of
Japanese junks out into the Pacific, twelve or more were blown
right across, to end up in places ranging from Alaska to Mexico.
Survivors of such accidents were common; in fact, the first white
men to encounter the Salmon Indians of north-west America
found them to be holding Japanese slaves.

No less an authority than Needham has been so struck by the
similarities of the high cultures of China and Central and South
America as to be convinced that over the centuries the far older
Chinese civilization has made repeated contributions to the
American. Excavations in Ecuador have revealed house types, net
sinkers, and coolie yokes, radio-carbon dated to about 200 B.C.,
that were in all respects similar to artefacts in Han Dynasty China
about the same date—the very time, we remember, when Chinese
expeditions were being sent out into the Pacific in search of the
islands of longevity.

But if we accept that such one-way transpacific journeys were
probably made so long ago, why were they not continued, and
return voyages accomplished, in later centuries when more able
craft were available? Probably because by the time Chinese
shipping had developed to a technical level that made it fully
capable of crossing the Pacific back and forth, the agrarian tone of
the civilization had set hard. The cold isles of the far north were
unattractive and the Pacific seemed quite empty.

All the foregoing would be tenuous indeed were it not for the
circumstance that the type of craft presumed to have conveyed
these voyagers is unique in certain of its features and is found
nowhere else in the world except *Asia* and *Ecuador*. All the
evidence points to the Asian models, especially the Chinese, being
the earliest. The craft in question is an advanced type of sailing
raft steered by a remarkable system of inserting and withdrawing
daggerboards in place of the familiar rudder.

While it is not certain all the Ch'in "ships" came into this
category, it seems likely that at least some of them did. Professor
Needham cites a good deal of circumstantial evidence, while the
Taiwanese scholar Professor Ling Shun-sheng has concluded
from a study of Chinese documents that seagoing sailing rafts
were in common use off China by the fifth century B.C. and
probably much earlier. At first sight rafts seem unlikely craft for
major transoceanic voyages, but before we reject the idea let us
examine the build, capacity, and performance of these strangely
sophisticated and able vessels.

First and most important comes the principle of dagger-board or "insertion" steering. This can be applied only in sailing vessels, for it depends upon the interplay of wind pressure on the sail and water pressure on the hull. Thus if a board is thrust down into the sea between or alongside the logs (or a paddle likewise inserted) towards the *stern,* the force of the wind on the sail causes the craft to pivot *downwind.* Conversely, if the board is inserted forward, the craft turns up into the wind. Three or more boards were used in rafts steered in this way, and a very accurate course could be maintained by their manipulation and fine adjustment. It is obvious that the whole principle involved is quite distinct from the one to which we are accustomed, the use of a rudder or angled steering oar.

A secondary effect of dagger-boards (or leeboards) in sailing rafts has nothing to do with steering at all. It is the reduction of leeway or sideways drift under sail, and in this role they function exactly as does the centre-board of any sailing dinghy—and just as effectively, for racing dinghy and clumsy looking raft alike skim lightly over the surface with only their immersed boards hanging down. The conquistadores of Ecuador and Peru expressed their amazement at how effectively the big Inca *balsas* (dagger-board sailing rafts), even laden with cargoes of pottery and foodstuffs, outstripped the Spanish caravels to windward. A good description of these South American rafts is given by Miguel de Estete, a member of Pizarro's expedition:

> They saw coming over the sea a raft under sail which had the appearance of a ship. . . . These balsas are of some very thick and long wooden logs, which are as soft and light on the water as a cork. They lash them very tightly together with a kind of hemp rope, and above them they place a high framework so that the merchandise and things they carry will not get wet. They set a mast in the largest log in the middle, hoist a sail, and navigate along this coast. They are very safe vessels because they cannot sink or capsize, since the water washes through them everywhere.

It is evident from the date of the above and a number of other early Spanish accounts that these dagger-board sailing rafts (their sails, incidentally, were lateens, not unlike Pacific island ones) were actively trading off Ecuador and northern Peru in pre-Columbian times. But what is particularly significant is that this seems to be the *only* part of aboriginal America where sail was ever used (Brazilian *jangarda* are so like their Ecuadorian cousins that they could be derived from them, possibly in Portuguese times; on present evidence it is doubtful if the Caribs or the Maya used sails on their canoes). Thus here we have not only the single known instance of American sail, but also a method of steering and reducing leeway found elsewhere only on the sailing rafts of China, Taiwan, Vietnam, and India. Moreover, some at least of these Asiatic dagger-board rafts were plying the sea long before Columbus first sighted the New World. Consequently the possibility of transpacific "borrowing" looms large.

To turn now to the *balsas'* Asiatic counterparts. The sailing rafts of southern India are known as *kola maram* and are used for catching flying fish. They are semi-boat-shaped log rafts carrying two lateen sails and are steered by two dagger-boards and an inserted paddle. The Vietnamese, Taiwanese, and Chinese dagger-board rafts are of more interest to us. They belong to a single tradition, and it is from this culture area, especially from China proper, that the presumed prototypes of Inca *balsas* will have come, if they were not developed independently.

All the three eastern Asiatic varieties are made of bamboo. Some very elaborate two- and three-masted cargo-carrying sailing-rafts with slim dagger-boards were trading along the coasts of Vietnam late last century, while the fishing rafts of Taiwan, with their three dagger-boards, still ply the sea today. There is general agreement that the Taiwanese rafts originated in mainland China, but there is no consensus as to how long ago. One authority insists that the ancestors of the Taiwanese fishermen came over from Fukien about three hundred years ago, but there is mention in Chinese literature of raids by Taiwanese aborigines in sailing-rafts on Chinese coastal villages four hundred years before that. Regardless of when rafts were introduced into Taiwan, they were, as we have seen, in use in China itself very much earlier— certainly well before the Christian era.

Apart from the present-day Taiwanese survivors, many varieties of large rafts were, until recently, a common sight on the turbulent Chinese rivers. One type, though laden with seven tons of cargo, drew no more than seventy-five millimetres of water. No wonder the big rafts of yesterday were so easily driven under sail! Rafts in general are, of course, as Miguel de Estete pointed out of the Peruvian *balsas*, virtually unsinkable because they do not rigidly oppose the force of the waves. Furthermore, damaged lashings can readily be replaced at sea. Many raft types, including those of Taiwan, India, and some Chinese varieties, are partially boat-shaped, and this helps protect their occupants and cargo from spray and improves their "streamlining".

There is every reason to believe that the Chinese junk, which is square-ended and compartmented by a series of watertight bulkheads and has no keel, is a direct descendent of the bamboo raft. But as to when this development took place, we are quite ignorant. Chinese literary sources are ambiguous and unhelpful.

To return now to the Ch'in and Han explorers in their hopeful search across the eastern seas for drugs of longevity; how could any of them have possibly reached the distant shores of America and bequeathed their raft technology to the Incas? We have already given a clue about their likely route: driven before the east-going currents and winds that prevail off Japan, they would pass north of Hawaii, like generations of disabled junks long after their time, and ultimately into the current that flows southward along the California coast to Mexico.

Cold would have loomed a good deal larger as a problem of this northern traverse if we did not know that the big Inca *balsas* (and no doubt their assumed prototypes) had platforms to keep their cargo and passengers dry. Also Chinese quilted clothing is about the best insulated material known—as the West has recently realized. Nor is a downwind passage across the North Pacific comparable in terms of inclement conditions to the windward crossings of the North Atlantic accomplished by the Vikings in spray-swept open boats. As to food, innumerable Pacific Islanders adrift have demonstrated that expert fishermen can do a good deal more than supplement their rations from the sea. Rain-water would have been abundant.

We have traced our hypothetical Asiatic sea rovers as far as Mexico and perhaps to the off-lying Galapagos Islands, where, incidentally, Ecuadorian pottery has been found, although it is very difficult to date. But from here on the current and often the wind become contrary. How would the battered sailing rafts have fared? Clinton Edwards, who has studied aboriginal American water craft more closely than anyone else, points out that the *balsas* "regularly made long voyages carrying large cargoes, *both with and against the set of the current and the prevailing wind*" (my italics). If the *balsas'* prototypes were as weatherly, Ecuador would have been far from unattainable from Mexico or California. There remains the problem of why, if Asiatic raftsmen came that way, their vessels were not copied by North or Central Americans. One can only suggest that there was no niche in the economy of the day into which cargo-carrying sailing-vessels could usefully fit.

A possible alternative route between Asia and America that has been suggested is via the tropical Pacific, the way the Polynesians came during their millennia-long expansion. The motivation for such a voyage in a single generation would have to be strong indeed, for it would be in the teeth of the trade winds and the currents (except the narrow and at times tenuous equatorial counter-current). Then, some trace of the advanced dagger-board rafts of China could be expected if they had ever passed that way. In fact, there is none. Although sailing-rafts were common throughout Polynesia, the dagger-board was unknown.

This circumstance deserves a little amplification, for there is every reason to ascribe the dagger-board steering *principle* to our old friends the Austronesians; like the outrigger, the double canoe, and the reversing-ends manoeuvre, the dagger-board is found along the track of the Austronesians' sea-borne wanderings. It was used on the *sailing-rafts* of southern India, Vietnam, Taiwan, and China, and it was used on the large *sailing canoes*, though not the rafts, of the Pacific Islands—specifically, the big double canoes of Tahiti and Fiji and on the present-day seventeen-metre outriggers of Ninigo.

But speculation about whether the sailing-rafts of the New World derived, by way of transpacific voyage, from the Old, admits of no certain conclusion. We can only note that the combination of sail and dagger-boards represents a technical package that seems too complicated to have been invented more than once. Neither the Spaniards nor the Portuguese understood the function of dagger-boards. All the evidence points to the Chinese as having been the originators of such devices, and we know that the Chinese sailing-rafts were so steered.

INCA BALSAS AND POLYNESIA

The famous *Kon-Tiki* raft voyage demonstrated the ability of such craft to cross the Pacific. Though archaeological and linguistic evidence has disproved the theory of the Polynesians' South American origin, the probability remains strong that there was some contact between the continent and the island world (we have already cited the South American sweet potato in Polynesia). The intriguing question is whether this took place by Inca *balsa*, Polynesian canoe, or both.

Balsas certainly made off-shore trading voyages of hundreds of kilometres, perhaps as far as the Galapagos, and their crews were obviously supplied with sufficient maize cakes and water for their journeys. There is little doubt that, if blown out into the south-east trades, they could have survived the passage to the Tuamotus or the Marquesas quite as well as the heroic little band on *Kon-Tiki*.

We have been speaking rather loosely about the Incas, but their empire was a comparatively recent one, only some three hundred years old when the Spaniards came. Unfortunately, Inca traditions effectively blotted out those of their precursors, the coastal empire of Chimu among them. But a few intriguing legends have come down to us. For instance, Gieza de Leon, who, from 1535, was fifteen years a conquistador, relates the story of Tici-Viracocha, "Foam-of-the-Sea", who ultimately "moved over the waves and never again appeared". There were also Inca traditions of one Tupac Yapanqui who made long voyages to the west.

Similarly, there are Polynesian legends, as of the Marquesan canoe *Kahua* sailing eastward to the great land of "Te Fiti". On balance, effective contact through Polynesian sea rovers seems more likely. It is to be feared that the usual tragic fate of Pacific castaways awaited Tici-Viracocha or Tupac Yapanqui if they did reach Polynesian shores, for neither maize, the staple food of the *balsa* sailors, nor the dagger-boards that steered their craft, ever found a home in Polynesia.

This uncertainty should not obscure the high probability of Polynesian–American Indian communication. By one means or another the broad Pacific was spanned long before the white man came. Nor were the newcomers indifferent to the traditions of their predecessors. Tupac Yapanqui's was but one of the legends that inspired the Spaniards to sail out into the unknown South Sea, and Cook's Tupaia was but the most famous among many who pointed the direction of distant islands.

In subsequent chapters we will be leaving the shadowy realm of prehistory for the documented stories of European explorers. It is no denigration of their achievements to recall that they were every one after-comers; the original discoverers of the Pacific were Islanders and dwellers along the ocean's rim. Their names are for ever lost, but we should never forget that these nameless seafarers were once living men; perhaps the greatest maritime explorers the world has ever known.

TWO
The Westerners

16ᵀᴴ CENTURY CARRACK

The voyages of Magellan, Mendaña, Drake, Quiros and Torres are shown on the front endpaper map; those of Schouten/Le Maire, Tasman, Dampier, Woodes Rogers, and Cook are shown on the back endpaper map.

4

"We will eat the leather from the yards"

AGELLAN'S CIRCUMNAVIGATION OF the world, and, incidentally, the first European crossing of the then-unknown Pacific Ocean, was without question the greatest voyage of all time. Whether it should be classed as a Spanish or a Portuguese achievement, the reader must judge for himself. For my part, this epic of unmatched determination is the property, not of any single nation, but of all mankind. Indeed, among the 240 men in Magellan's armada there were, apart from Spaniards and Portuguese, Basques, Flemings, Frenchmen, Greeks, Genoese, Neapolitans, Germans, Negroes, Malays, and one Englishman, Master Andrew of Bristol, the flagship's gunner.

The time was the opening of Western Europe's age of expansion, a period of rapacity, high courage, and technical advance unparalleled in human history. Magellan began his voyage in 1519, less than thirty years after Columbus had discovered America, twenty-one years after Vasco da Gama had reached India round the Cape of Good Hope, and only five years after the Pacific Ocean itself had first been discovered (by Europeans). The circumnavigation's full impact on geography can only be appreciated in the context of medieval Europe's awakening with a fanatical purpose that spanned the world, and in which the rivalry of Spain and Portugal was prominent.

No time was lost in dividing up the known and unknown worlds between the two Catholic powers (to the exclusion of all heretics). Less than two months after Columbus's return, on 4 May 1493, a papal bull was issued laying down that all discoveries westward of a line one hundred leagues west of the Azores belonged to Spain, and all east of it to Portugal. By the Treaty of Tordesillas, signed a year later, the line of demarcation was moved further westward, to 370 leagues west of the Cape Verde Islands. This line was the Great Meridian which came to be accepted as 51° west. The coastline of Brazil, the only Portuguese territory in South America, still terminates at this meridian.

But what was to be decided about the Great Meridian's continuation on the other side of the world? That this was 129° east there was little (though there was some) dispute. But just where on the real world it ran was another question altogether. Before Magellan's voyage the size of the world was still very much in doubt and was generally grossly underestimated. The outstanding question at issue was whether the fabulous Moluccas—the Spice Islands—which the Portuguese were rumoured to have reached, were on the Spanish or Portuguese side of the line. Magellan's objective was to find the answer, one which he was convinced would be favourable to Spain.

Actually Magellan was wrong in this. The important Spice Islands (Halmahera, Tidore, Ternate, Ambon, and others) and the Philippines, which he discovered for Europe, were on the Portuguese side of the Great Meridian. Four years after the death of Magellan the matter was resolved between the kings of Spain and Portugal at the junta of Badajoz, when Portugal retained the Spice Islands but ceded the Philippines to Spain. But long afterwards the Great Meridian continued to leave its mark on world political geography. It is surely no coincidence that, soon after England's capture of Manila in 1763 and inheritance of Spain's sphere of influence, Captain Phillip should fix the western limit of the newly founded colony of New South Wales at this very 129° east meridian, now the boundary of Western Australia.

MAGELLAN'S APPRENTICESHIP IN SOUTH-EAST ASIA

MAGELLAN

Fernão de Magalhães (anglicized as Ferdinand Magellan) was a member of the Portuguese petty nobility who spent his youth at the court of King Emanuel. It was a heady atmosphere for an impressionable boy—tales of the Congo, of Diaz pushing round Africa, of the Cortereal brothers' heroic death off Greenland, of Juan de Solis with his sixty companions eaten by Indians on the Rio de la Plata, and, above all, of the fabulous East, now open to conquest by Europeans by right of their superior cannon and in the name of the Holy Cross.

However, it was not until 1504 that Magellan, then twenty-four years old, was able to obtain permission to leave court. In that year, only seventy-one years after Cheng Ho's last voyage to Africa, he set out for India under Francisco D'Almeida, the most enlightened of any of the Portuguese viceroys. Not much is known about Magellan's seven years in the East, although it is enough to reveal the tough, stocky little man to have been a field commander of decision and courage, as the following incident shows.

Albuquerque, who had succeeded d'Almeida as viceroy, dispatched two ships from Cochin in 1510—

> and at night they both struck on the shoals of Padua, which are opposite the Maldive Islands, and remained aground, upright and without breaking up. Upon this they prepared the boats as well as they could, and raised their sides, and put inside water and biscuit, and victuals which did not require cooking. The captains and pilots and as many men as could, got into these boats and returned to Cochym. The people who remained in the ships set shores on each side of the ships, with the yards, which they cut. All this was arranged and commanded by an honourable gentleman, who remained as overseer, named Fernan de Magalhaes, who had been much wounded in Calecut.... [The captains] reached Canor in eight days, from whence they sent a message to the governor, who at once sent Gonzalo de Crasto in a caravel, with two pilots; and they went to the ships and put the best things on board the caravel, until they could not load it any more, and having recovered all the men, they set fire to the ships, as they were already full of water. In this Fernan de Magalhaes worked hard, and did much service, and attended well to everything.

From other accounts it is clear that Magellan had volunteered to stay behind with the anxious and suspicious sailors when the other officers left in their boats.

The previous year Magellan's personal initiative and bravery had led to the rescue of a Portuguese contingent trapped ashore during an abortive attempt on Malacca. (Malacca, which is on the Malay Peninsula opposite Sumatra, should not be confused with Maluco—the Moluccas, or Spice Islands—which is nearly three thousand kilometres further east.) One of those who owed his life to Magellan was a man named Francisco Serrão (generally written Serrano), whose enduring friendship was to have important consequences.

Of much more negative import for Magellan's career was his bluntness in expressing his opinions without fear or favour in a semi-feudal society that demanded servility to the powerful. Thus

Magellan was not afraid to stand up to even the formidable Albuquerque. The occasion was a council of war on the eve of Albuquerque's attack on Goa, called to persuade the captains of vessels then loading to delay their departure for Portugal and join the invasion fleet.

One of these captains was Magellan. The ships of burden, he said, ought not to be taken to Goa, "inasmuch as if they went thither they could not pass this year to Portugal", since "it was not possible to lay the fleet before the port of Goa before the end of November, as the winds were now contrary for that place: and with respect to the crews, let his worship say whether it was well that they should go, that it seemed to him that he ought not to take them, since there did not remain time for them to lay out their money, nor to do anything of what was necessary for the voyage; and thus said Fernan de Magalhaes."

Albuquerque was a vindictive man to those who opposed his designs, and his unfavourable report to King Emanuel certainly helped promote the virulent antagonism to Magellan that the king was to show. There was another and even more significant reason for the king's attitude, however, and it is linked indirectly to that same Francisco Serrano whom Magellan rescued in Malacca in 1509.

Malacca, the great emporium of the Indies, was taken by the Portuguese in 1511, and thence three ships, under Abreau and Serrano, promptly set out for the Moluccas. These fabled Spice Islands had exerted a magnetic attraction on Europe as far back as the days of ancient Egypt. Western travellers had visited further Indonesia in Arab, Indian, Javanese, Siamese, Cambodian, and Chinese vessels, but no European ship had penetrated so far before the Portuguese.

The expedition coasted Sumatra, Java, Bali, Lombok, and the Lesser Sunda Islands, and then turned north to Ceram and Banda, where a junk was purchased to replace Serrano's ship, which had been lost. From here the ships sailed for Malacca again, laden with priceless cargoes, but Serrano was wrecked again and, after a series of extraordinary adventures, including the capture of a pirate junk, he and six or nine surviving Portuguese arrived in Ternate in the very heart of the Spice Islands. And there the remarkable Serrano remained for nine years until his death in 1521, living as a semi-royal potentate with a harem. He wrote to his friend Magellan that he had discovered "yet another new world, larger and richer than that found by da Gama".

Magellan, meanwhile, was stationed in Malacca from mid-1511

until the end of 1512. There is some evidence that he went off on an unauthorized exploring expedition which may even have reached the Philippines. Whether he did or not, he undoubtedly accumulated a good deal of information from Serrano's correspondence and from Asian pilots about the Spice Islands and the Philippines. The conclusion he came to—that both archipelagos were in Spain's half of the world—while erroneous, was perfectly reasonable in the light of current misconceptions about the circumference of the earth and the near impossibility of accurately determining longitude. What was not reasonable, or at any rate tactful in Portugal, was the forthright assertion of his opinion.

By the middle of 1512 Magellan was back in Portugal and at court again, having been shipwrecked and losing his "small property" en route. His record had been a distinguished one, and he deserved well of his royal master. Instead, we find him dispatched to Morocco within the year with a punitive expedition against the Sultan of Azamor, where he was wounded in the knee and acquired a permanent limp. Magellan had already survived seven years in the East, where the death rate was five out of six adventurers. Now at least he could have expected to win favour. He returned to Portugal, "bringing before the king his services", but Emanuel's hostility was implacable and quite beyond reason. In insulting terms he refused Magellan promotion and either present or future employment and contemptuously gave him leave to denaturalize himself and seek employment in whatever service he chose. The shaken captain asked for the privilege of kissing the king's ring at parting; even this request was brusquely denied.

With but little alternative, Magellan transferred his allegiance to Spain. In 1517, at the age of thirty-seven, he crossed the border together with the astronomer Ruy Faleiro. His great scheme of sailing *westward* to reach the Moluccas in the Far East must already have been worked out in his mind, for he wrote to Francisco Serrano in the Spice Islands that he would be with him soon "if not by way of Portugal, by way of Spain". He fared very differently in Spain. As the chronicle puts it, he "had much knowledge of the art of navigation, and enterprise, and devoted himself to that, he came to an understanding with the directors of the House of Trade of Seville, so that the emperor [Charles I of Spain became the Holy Roman emperor Charles V] gave him a fleet of five ships, with which he navigated, discovering a new way to Moluco". Thus Emanuel lived to regret his spitefulness.

But before we follow Magellan in the preparations of his great voyage, let us digress very briefly to speculate about some Portuguese voyages which are not as well documented and which may well have led to the first European discovery of Australia.

The Portuguese and Australia

While the Portuguese were strengthening their hold on the Moluccas, they also mounted several voyages from Malacca towards the south-east in search of certain fabled Ilhas do Ouro—Islands of Gold. The most important was a full-scale expedition comprising three caravels. This was a major flotilla; Vasco da Gama, Christopher Columbus, and Abreau and Serrano had no more. Moreover, it was commanded by a full naval captain in Albuquerque's armada, Cristavao de Mendonça (James Cook, by comparison, was a lieutenant). They sailed from Malacca in 1522, touched at Pedir in Sumatra, and after that—nothing, until the fleet's return. Nor are there surviving records of this important expedition. In accord with the "policy of silence" imposed by King Emanuel, they were swallowed up in the Casa da India in Lisbon, the compulsory repository, on pain of death, of all exploration journals, logbooks, and charts. And the Casa and its contents were totally destroyed in the great Lisbon earthquake of 1755. Thus, though Mendonça is generally credited with having reached *India Meridional*—Australia—hard proof is lacking.

When, early the following century, the Dutchman Frederik Houtman discovered the islands off Western Australia now known as Houtman's Abrolhos, he had with him Portuguese maps he had stolen in Lisbon. It seems strange that a Dutchman should bestow on a discovery this apt and idiomatic Portuguese name, for Abrolhos is a contraction of *Abra Olhos* (Open your eyes! Watch out!), unless the islands already bore that name on the Portuguese chart he had before him.

One other named navigator is credited in Portugal with a voyage to Australia. In 1525 Gomes de Sequeira was storm-driven off course on a voyage from Ternate. Accounts differ widely as to the direction in which he went and the whereabouts of the land where he stayed for four months. Palau or Yap in the Carolines, say some authorities. Others point to a 1554 map where is written, opposite some islands shown in the position of Arnhem Land, *"Ilhas que achou Gomez de Sequeira"*.

In support of Portuguese claims to European primacy on the southern continent, it should be mentioned that the Portuguese colony on Timor probably dates from very soon after the Abreau-Serrano expedition, perhaps from 1516—and Timor is only 475 kilometres from Australia. And if "India Meridional" did indeed become known to the Timor colonists, its arid coasts were unlikely to appeal as Ilhas do Ouro—any more than the vast Australian Antarctic Territory is considered by Australians today.

It is ironical that the very centralized security system that characterized Emanuel's "policy of silence" should have led in the Lisbon earthquake to the destruction of all definitive evidence of early Portuguese contact with Australia. The documentary loss was ultimately as complete as was the deliberate vandalism of Cheng Ho's records nearly a century before.

MAGELLAN'S VOYAGE ROUND THE WORLD

Spain's reception of Magellan and the astrologer-astronomer Ruy Faleiro (who, though learned, was more than a little mad and reputed to be in league with the devil) was as warm as Portugal's had been frigid. The two expatriates had been deeply engaged in the study of Martin Behaim's globe, portolan charts, the declination tables of Regiomontanus—all the navigational treasures of the Casa da India—before they left Portugal. The result, their unheard-of project of sailing west to reach the East, was already fully formulated and their arguments marshalled.

Magellan was fortunate in winning the friendship of an influential Portuguese, Diogo Barbosa, Alcalde of the Arsenal. He took the navigator into his home, and his daughter Beatriz later became Magellan's wife. Duarte Barbosa, a nephew of Diogo, was to be one of Magellan's most trusted captains—and to lose his life very soon after the death of his general. (The commander-in-chief of a fleet in those days was a *general,* it was his flagship that was the *admiral*).

No time was lost in approaching the Casa de Contratación in Seville, the Spanish equivalent of the Casa da India, whose officials, led by Juan Aranda, interrogated closely the two Portuguese about their revolutionary proposals and sought confirmation (which was amply forthcoming) of their world standing as geographer-navigators. Aranda, not without an agreement for a commission on the profits of the voyage, escorted them personally to the court of the young King Charles. There Magellan explained his plan to reach the Moluccas by sailing westward round South America and affirmed his conviction that these most desirable Spice Islands lay within the legal territory of

Spain. The rather lukewarm Council of State was swayed in the
navigator's favour by the powerful Bishop of Burgos, Juan de
Fonseca, and the decision having been made, the king became and
remained a staunch supporter of the enterprise—despite the
heavy pressure, amounting to blackmail, of the Portuguese
ambassador.

The role of the bishop was ambiguous, to say the least. There is
more than a little suspicion that he was using Magellan for his
own designs; that there was from the beginning a plan to mutiny
and murder the commander. Whatever his secret intentions, Juan
de Fonseca publicly promoted the preparations for the expedition, his designs unsuspected by Magellan until a dramatic
warning reached him in the Canary Islands after the fleet had left
Spain. This we will come to later.

An agreement was drawn up whereby Charles promised to fit
out five ships, with two years' provisioning, under the command
of Magellan as captain-general (Faleiro's increasing madness
ultimately prevented his sailing as joint leader). There was to be
no trespass on the territories of the king of Portugal—the Spice
Islands were, of course, assumed to lie within the Spanish zone.
The leaders were to receive a twentieth of the long-term profits, a
fifth of the profits from the current expedition, and, if they
discovered more than six islands, a fifteenth of the profits of the
trade with any two of them. The captain-general received the title
of *adelantado,* and the Order of Santiago, Commander of St
James of the Sword, was conferred upon him.

We know far too little about the ships Magellan used. They
were certainly more powerful than those of Columbus thirty years
earlier, for the *Santa Maria,* the flagship of the great Genoese
discoverer, was the only one of his three ships to be completely
decked-in. The others were semi-open boats with gaping
undecked holds amidships (into which in bad weather the sailors
used to defecate, rather marring the pleasures of tropical
cruising). The medieval designations *nao,* simply meaning
"ship", and *caravel,* a smaller, shallower, more handy version, are
uninformative as to rig or number of decks. A "great carrack" like
Magellan's *Trinidad* was probably three-masted. The foremast
and mainmast each carried a square sail, whose area could be
increased by lacing to it a "bonnet". Above these fore and main
courses were set small single topsails. There were no staysails or
jibs; the cocked-up bowsprit served mainly as a point of
attachment for the fore rigging. The after, or mizzen, mast set a
lateen sail.

The tonnage of the ships can be misleading. But, ten *toneles de porte* in Magellan's time would be roughly equivalent to twelve tons burden (capacity) today—and near double that number of tons displacement. The five little ships commissioned by the king, with the aid of the banker Christopher de Haro, were the *Trinidad*, 110 *toneles* burden, the flagship; the *San Antonio*, 120 *toneles;* the *Concepción*, 90 *toneles;* the immortal *Victoria*, 85 *toneles,* to which Magellan afterwards transferred and which was to be the first to sail round the world; and the *Santiago*, 75 *toneles.* The Portuguese factor in Seville, Sebastian Alvarez, wrote his master King Emanuel that the ships were "very old and patched up. . . . I should be ill inclined to sail in them to the Canaries." Alvarez seems to have distrusted his own pessimism, for he went to unbelievable lengths, as we shall see, to sabotage the fleet's preparations or, failing this, to organize shortages, mutiny, and murder.

The full complement of the tiny fleet was 240, with 55 to 60 aboard each of the "great carracks", *Trinidad* and *San Antonio.* The carracks were "high-charged" ships, with tall narrow steeply sloping poops and lofty forecastles, features that were soon to be abandoned on the sleeker galleons. Massive outside timbers, or

SPANISH CARAVEL

TWO MASTED CARRACK

"wales", stiffened the already stout hulls, resplendent in black and gold. The *Trinidad,* being of some 110 medieval tons burden, probably displaced 200 tons. She was 26 metres long on the waterline, 7½ metres broad, and drew nearly 3 metres. Her best speed downwind was around four knots. Steering was by tiller, to which relieving tackles were rigged in bad weather, for the steering wheel was far in the future—even the whipstaff, a kind of vertical tiller extension, was a product of later Elizabethan times.

Nominally, the fleet was well stocked and equipped. The food comprised biscuit, flour, rice, dried fish, salt pork, cheese, chick-peas, lentils, broad beans, wine, vinegar, olive oil, mustard, garlic, capers, honey, sugar, salt, almonds, raisins, prunes, figs, quince preserves, six cows, and three pigs. The main meal at sea was at midday, the salt pork first having been soaked in a "steep tub" and softened up by being trampled under foot by a sailor for an hour. The water allowance was a litre and a half a day, and the daily ration of claret a surprisingly generous one litre.

In addition to foodstuffs there were looking-glasses, beads, knives, fish-hooks, red caps, cloth, ivory, quicksilver, brass bracelets, and twenty thousand bells for trade and presents. And should encounters prove less than friendly, the five ships carried between them seventy-one small cannon, fifty muskets, sixty crossbows (still the more reliable weapon), a thousand lances, as well as swords, shields, daggers, and personal armour.

The needs of navigation were served by seven astrolabes, twenty-one quadrants, thirty-five magnetic compass needles, eighteen sand clocks, and twenty-three hand-drawn parchment charts (no prudent captain would undertake the same voyage today with less than a thousand infinitely more accurate ones). Latitude could be determined with reasonable accuracy to half a

ASTROLABE

DUTCH GALLEON 1570

degree (50 kilometres). Magellan was well in the forefront of navigators of his age in attempting to measure longitude by lunar distances, lunar eclipse measurements, and magnetic variation, but the instruments and tables at his disposal were far too crude for the first two methods, and the third was based on a misconception about the earth's magnetism. So, while Magellan was very far from being one of those pilots who, in the words of his companion-biographer Antonio Pigafetta, were "so proud that they will not hear speak of longitude", his longitude error across the Pacific was *more than fifty degrees.*

I have said the armada was *nominally* well equipped. Magellan had powerful enemies; Portuguese intrigues, mainly directed by the factor Alvarez, never ceased; hostility to the foreign upstart commander (and his thirty-seven sea-hardened fellow countrymen, the backbone of the fleet) was openly shown by aristocratic proteges of the Bishop of Burgos. Like many a wise commander after him, Magellan was constantly on guard against the chicanery of corrupt port chandlers, and personally supervised, as far as he was able, the loading of stores. Despite all his efforts, however, Alvarez's bribes were so effective that a fair amount of the rations of the five ships found their way back on shore again. The ingenious Alvarez also fomented a riot against the captain-general and is even believed to have tried to have him poisoned.

The ships' captains were appointed directly by King Charles and so did not come within the powers of life and death (literally "cord and knife") that had been accorded Magellan. Thus in their case the ultimate sanctions of discipline were legally denied their commander. And Juan de Cartagena of the *San Antonio,* Gaspar de Quesada of the *Concepción,* and Luis de Mendoza of the *Victoria* were in league with the Bishop of Burgos and probably with Alvarez as well. This left but a single loyal captain, Joao Serrano of the little *Santiago,* a relative of Magellan's friend Francisco Serrano, who was busily trading spices in the Moluccas.

It would seem that the dice were so heavily loaded against the armada's commander that his enterprise never should have succeeded. Nor would it have gone even half way had he not had the courage to act decisively without fear or favour when the time came.

But this was still in the future. Preparations went ahead despite sabotage, until the day came for Magellan to receive the royal standard and for his captains to pledge allegiance to him at a solemn mass at the church of Santa Maria de Victoria in Seville. Then the ships dropped down-river under foresails to complete their loading at San Lucar.

On 20 September 1519 the company made their last confession, anchors were broken out, square sails hoisted, and with the wind fair and pennants flying, the armada crossed the bar of the Guadalquivir into the open Atlantic. With them went Alvarez's pious hope that "God Almighty grant them a voyage like that of the Cortereals"—a reference to the brothers who had perished in 1501 and 1502 on successive arctic voyages. King Emanuel's contribution to the proceedings was to order Portuguese ships to the River Plate, the Moluccas, and the Cape of Good Hope to intercept the explorers, but he was too late.

With *Trinidad* in the van, the fleet sailed southward towards the Fortunate Isles—the Canaries. During the week they spent at Tenerife loading pitch there came to them a swift, lateen-rigged caravel, flying the flag of Castile, Leon, and Aragon. As it luffed to anchor a boat was put over and rowed quickly to the *Trinidad* with an urgent dispatch for the captain-general. It was from his father-in-law, Diogo Barbosa. The Spanish captains, he wrote, especially Cartagena, had boasted to their indiscreet relatives of their intention of killing Magellan if they had any trouble with him. There was nothing Magellan at this moment could do. No matter whether the men were good or evil, he replied, he would do his duty to the king; and to this end he had offered his life. But not for a moment did he ignore the warning; he prepared to act with speed and decision should the necessity arise.

The log of the pilot Francisco Albo has survived, as have several shorter journals of the voyage, but by far the best account is by Antonio Pigafetta, Knight of Rhodes, from Vicenza on the Venetian plain. Wanting to see with his own eyes, "the very great and awful things of the ocean", he had made his way to Seville during the outfitting and petitioned Magellan to be included in the company. It is fortunate for posterity that the request was granted, for Pigafetta was a keen and interested observer—though a little too credulous of old salts' yarns. He was also loyal and very brave.

The fleet weighed from Tenerife on 3 October 1519 and stood southward into the ocean-sea. At first the trades blew fair. Magellan in the *Trinidad* went always in the lead, displaying on the poop, to maintain contact at night, "a torch or faggot of burning wood, which they called a farol". Pigafetta details the combinations of lights that signalled to the following vessels to close up, reduce sail, tack, heave-to, and so on.

Then came the doldrums and calms, then head-winds and fierce squalls, which drove the yard-arms under. Several times Saint Elmo's fire appeared at the masthead, "which comforted us greatly," says Pigafetta, "for we were in tears, only expecting the hour of perishing". No storm-tossed vessel that is visited by the saint's light is ever lost, he goes on to explain.

The calms were made noteworthy for Pigafetta by the visits of "large fish called *Tiburoni*"—sharks—"which have teeth of a terrible kind, and eat people when they find them in the sea". In lighter vein are the sailors' tall stories about sea-birds which the Knight of Rhodes solemnly set down, thus bequeathing us some of the most delightfully inaccurate natural history ever written. For instance, there was one kind of bird with no fundament; another which laid its eggs on the back of its patient mate; yet another named the *"Cagaselo"*, idiomatically translated as the "crap-eating bird", which chased other birds and swallowed their excrement. Not bad observation this last, for there is no doubt from Pigafetta's account that he is describing frigate-birds' piratical dive-bombing of other sea-birds. The purpose is to make them disgorge their last fish meal, which the frigate-bird swallows. No doubt the panic-stricken victim often voids as well as vomits, giving rise to the Italian gentleman's understandable mistake.

During this trying period—in the three weeks that they were in the doldrums the ships progressed no more than twenty kilometres—the second-in-command of the fleet, Juan de Cartagena, began to show his hand. Ranging close to the flagship, he publicly queried the course being steered and, upon being ordered to steer where he was told, replied insultingly and for three days failed to salute the flagship. Magellan called the captains together in his cabin, where the arrogant Cartagena upbraided him openly. He had misjudged his man; he was promptly arrested and confined in the *Victoria* under the guard of Mendoza. There was no support for mutiny as yet.

Now the armada picked up the south-east trades beyond the Equator. The coast of Brazil was sighted towards the end of November, and on 13 December they anchored where Rio de Janeiro now stands. With bottoms fouling, the average speed of the fleet had been reduced for the last two thousand kilometres to three knots with wind fresh and free. After two weeks trading with the friendly Indians, they set out again, partly because the villagers had not food enough for such a multitude, but also because Rio bay was in the king of Portugal's sphere and their right to remain there was debatable.

The explorers examined the La Plata estuary, where de Solis, its discoverer, had perished. Investigation soon proved that this was not the hoped-for passage into Balboa's "South Sea", and they pushed on into utterly unknown seas, examining every inlet, in daily peril of shipwreck, down the bleak coast of Patagonia. For the first time Western seamen experienced the furious *pampero*, which howls down off the desolate treeless pampas out of jet-black towering clouds laced with lightning. The *sudestada* too, the "devils dribble", was often their portion; terrifying storms these, as I have good reason to know, for they drive the mariner, lying helplessly ahull, towards a lee shore.

Exposed and dangerous anchorages were time and again their lot as they investigated each of the great shoaling inlets that indent this coast for hundreds of miles. They were six days confined in the Bay of Toil, and only escaped into the open sea with difficulty. Great tides—the rise and fall was now eleven metres and increasing—added to their danger. Once, at anchor in a violent gale, the *Trinidad* broke all but one of her cables. It was autumn now and bitterly cold. Provisions were eked out with "geese", which were black and could not fly—the first European description of penguins—and with "sea wolves", which had "a head like that of a calf, and the ears small and round. They have large teeth, and have no legs, but feet joining close on to the body, which resemble a human hand: they have small nails to their feet, and skin between the fingers like geese"—an excellent description of seals.

Still Magellan pressed on southward along this storm-swept coast, where even today you can sail for days without ever a sight of the works of man. On clear nights a cross of stars mounted in the southern sky, as if warning the faithful to go no further. On one night of tempest the crews had given themselves up for lost when they again saw the fires of Saint Elmo, this time accompanied by Saint Nicholas and Santa Clara, at the masthead, and knew they were saved; as if by a miracle a narrow opening in the land to their lee offered hope of haven.

Under shortened sail, with the best leadsmen in the chains, the *Trinidad* stood in through the swirling tide race of the unknown channel. Two miles from the sea a landlocked lagoon opened out, towards the head of which the fleet came thankfully to anchor. The date was 31 March; they had been three months exploring the dreary coast, and the southern winter was approaching. Magellan named this haven in 49°20′ south latitude Port St Julian and determined to make it his winter quarters.

A smithy was set up on a small island and preparations set in hand to careen the ships, burn off the heavy weed, and re-tar the worm-eaten hulls. Fish and fowl were abundant, and the captain-general reduced rations from the ships' stores. The expedition had been half a year on the way with no visible result except privation and danger. Murmurings arose, fanned by the Castilian high officers, that Magellan the Portuguese had deliberately led the fleet into a trap and that they were doomed to perish in these frigid solitudes. Magellan marvelled that Spaniards could be so unmindful of the king's orders that they should even consider giving up. Would not their privations be a measure of their future glory? He himself had made up his mind to go "as far as seventy-five degrees towards the antarctic pole", where, adds Pigafetta, "in the summer time there is no night, or very little". Magellan insisted that a strait must exist. He was determined to die rather than shamefully turn back. The men were temporarily silenced, but the officers continued their secret plotting.

On Palm Sunday, following the celebration of High Mass at an altar on shore, Magellan invited his captains to dine with him. Alvaro de Mesquita, who had replaced Juan de Cartagena on the *San Antonio*, was the only one to attend. Next night Cartagena, released by his custodian Luis de Mendoza, joined Gaspar Quesada from the *Concepción* and the faithless pilot Sebastian del Cano of the *Victoria*. With thirty armed followers they boarded the *San Antonio* and imprisoned Mesquita. The ship's master, Juan de Elorriaga, who heroically refused to yield, was stabbed four times by Quesada.

Magellan discovered the revolt next morning when he sent a boat to the *San Antonio* to pick up men for a watering party. The ship, they were told, was under command of Quesada, not Magellan. From the *Victoria* and the *Concepción* the answer was the same. Only the little *Santiago* under Serrano, whose crew was but half Spanish, remained loyal. The three mutinous ships were anchored across the narrow channel with their guns trained on the *Trinidad* and the *Santiago*. Return to Spain forthwith was the mutineers' demand, brought in a letter from Quesada. Magellan suggested a parley aboard the *Trinidad*, but this suggestion was, not surprisingly, refused out of hand.

It was now, with the most powerful grandees in the fleet and overwhelming fire-power ranged against him, that the captain-general showed his mettle. The skiff bringing Quesada's message was seized and six picked men under Gonzalo Gomez de Espinosa, the master-at-arms, were substituted for the crew. With weapons concealed, they rowed to the *Victoria* (whose largely non-Spanish crew might again be won over to the captain-general) with a message for Mendoza. Meanwhile, Duarte Barbosa, Magellan's relation by marriage, with fifteen men, lay ready in the flagship's longboat. As anticipated, the message was scornfully rejected by Mendoza, whereupon the master-at-arms, on Magellan's orders, leapt upon him and cut his throat. At Espinosa's hail, his men swarmed aboard, with Duarte Barbosa's hard on their heels and, in a moment, without the loss of another life, resistance was at an end.

The three loyal ships now in Magellan's possession were warped out and anchored across the harbour mouth, for it was thought the mutineers would attempt to steal out under cover of night. The *Trinidad* cleared for action and, soon after midnight, the *San Antonio* appeared. The *Trinidad* poured in a broadside, grappled and boarded, and the mutineers gave up at once—again without loss of life. The odds, now four to one, were too much for Cartagena, and he too surrendered, to join his fellow conspirators in irons. The mutiny was over.

Given the circumstances of planned and premeditated mutiny, the punishment inflicted on the mutineers cannot be considered severe. The body of Mendoza was drawn and quartered and hung on a gibbet on the little island. Forty men were found guilty of treason and condemned to death, but pardoned under penalty of working in chains until the fleet sailed. Sebastian del Cano was among their number. He was not to forget the lesson and subsequently redeemed himself by sailing the *Victoria* on to Spain after Magellan's death. Quesada, however, could receive no mercy; the life of his servant was spared on condition that he beheaded his master. Then Quesada's body too was quartered and joined that of Mendoza on the scaffold. Cartagena and a priest were sentenced to be marooned. When the fleet set sail they were put ashore on the windswept pampas, never to be heard of again.

Now the refitting of the ships could go ahead in earnest. During this time the voyagers encountered Patagonian Indians, whose enormous stature so impressed Pigafetta that he described them as giants. Then Serrano's *Santiago,* on a scouting expedition to the south, was wrecked, fortunately without loss of life. Soon the fleet moved on to another anchorage, Rio de la Cruz, which Serrano had discovered, and there passed the remainder of the winter catching and drying fish. Spring came, and with the warmer

weather and longer days, the armada put to sea on the 18 October
1520. Magellan in the *Trinidad* was again in the van. Serrano now
had the *Concepción*, Duarte Barbosa the *Victoria*, and the loyal
but indecisive Mesquita, the *San Antonio*.

The dreary routine of heaving-to at dusk, so as to be able to pick
up marks ashore next morning and not risk missing the longed-
for channel, was resumed. But not for long. Four days out from
Rio de la Cruz they passed beneath the mighty Cliff of the Condor,
and five kilometres further on came to a headland that was named
Cape Virgins, in Saint Ursula's honour. Beyond was a wide bay
whose further shore could barely be distinguished. The latitude
was 52° south by Magellan's reckoning; it was in fact 52°18′—
only thirty kilometres out. Perhaps this was at last what they were
seeking. Strait or deceptive bight? The fleet stood in to the
westward.

A brief description of the famous waterway that the ships were
now entering is necessary if we are to comprehend the full extent
of their undertaking. The strait that connects the Atlantic with
the Pacific near the bottom of South America is five hundred
kilometres long. It passes through two worlds. The eastern or
Atlantic side is treeless, rolling pampas, over which the wind
howls and dust devils swirl. The brown expanse is broken only by
a *frigorifico*, a few scattered corals. Nowadays at night one sees the
flaming gases of oil wells, like a row of monstrous street lights—a
wry commentary on Magellan's name, Tierra del Fuego, Land of
Fire, for the Alacalufe campfires he saw were but pale reflections
of the flares of today.

And yet, little else has changed. Inside Cape Virgins the tide
ranges a colossal fourteen metres. Beyond the two narrows, where
the passage constricts to three-quarters of a kilometre wide, the
rise and fall is not much more than one metre.

Then, two hundred kilometres towards the Pacific, one enters
another world. Snow-capped mountains rise on every side,
cloaked in tangled antarctic beech to the water's edge. Westerly
gales follow each other without let, whipping white the waters
with hail and driving snow showers. The kelp streams out below,
and the low clouds scud by overhead. Here nothing has changed
since Magellan's day. Here and there the framework of a deserted
wigwam; that is all. The furious squalls called williwaws
continue to howl down the mountainsides into the lonely
anchorages (deceptively named "port" or "harbour"). It is one of
the most savagely beautiful places on earth, but hardly a

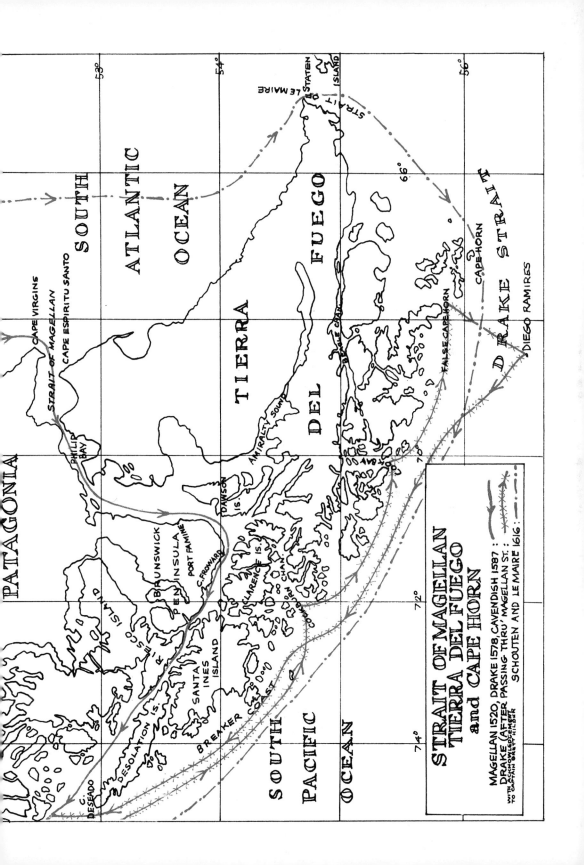

STRAIT OF MAGELLAN
TIERRA DEL FUEGO
and CAPE HORN

MAGELLAN 1520, DRAKE 1578, CAVENDISH 1587 :
DRAKE (AFTER PASSING THRU' MAGELLAN ST. :
WITH ACKNOWLEDGEMENT
TO CAPTAIN SALT HILDER
SCHOUTEN AND LE MAIRE 1616 :

PATAGONIA

SOUTH

ATLANTIC

OCEAN

TIERRA

DEL

FUEGO

SOUTH

PACIFIC

OCEAN

DRAKE STRAIT

CAPE VIRGINS
CAPE ESPIRITU SANTO
STRAIT OF MAGELLAN
PHILIP BAY
BRUNSWICK PENINSULA
PORT FAMINE
C. FROWARD
DAWSON IS.
CLARENCE IS.
AMIRALTY SOUND
DESOLATION IS.
RIESCO IS.
SANTA INES ISLAND
BREAKER COAST
C. DESEADO
COCKBURN CHAN.
BEAGLE CHAN.
BAY
FALSE CAPE HORN
CAPE HORN
DIEGO RAMIRES
STRAIT OF LE MAIRE
STATEN ISLAND

53°
54°
56°
66°
68°
72°
74°

yachtsman's paradise. I know, for I spent two months there under sail.

Five miles inside the entrance the armada came to anchor off a line of breaking shoals on the southern shore. No sign of a further passage as yet. That night came a howling *sudestada* which caused them to weigh anchor hurriedly and tack to and fro between the invisible shores, guided only by the cries of the leadsmen in the chains. Day broke, and the *San Antonio* and the *Concepción*, unable to weather a headland to the west, ran desperately into a narrow opening which, to their inexpressible relief, soon opened out into a wide bay, on the far side of which could just be discerned a second narrows. Meanwhile the *Trinidad* and *Victoria* stood to and fro across the entrance. At dusk the other ships seemed to be returning, their topsails black squares against the sunset. Then suddenly they began to recede as if caught by a giant hand and swept back out of sight.

Had some whirlpool sucked them down? A long anxious night, a day of foreboding, and one more night of diminishing hope. Then the wind shifted into the west and a shout came from the lookouts. The *San Antonio* and *Concepción* appeared beyond a point in the First Narrows, spewed by the racing tidal stream, which here runs at eight knots (I was myself carried through those same narrows backwards before I had time to get up sail) and driving before the wind. The *Concepción* was the faster sailer and reached the admiral first. "The strait!", Serrano called and discharged his artillery. At which, says Pigafetta, "all together, thanking God and the Virgin Mary, we went to seek further on".

Through the two narrows they sailed into near tideless waters where the shores fell back thirty kilometres from each other. Here the fleet again split up, the *San Antonio* and the *Concepción* being sent to explore a wide opening to the east (now known as Useless Bay) while the flagship and the *Victoria* continued south-westward beneath the beetling crags and hanging glaciers of the encroaching mountains. They rounded Cape Froward, the southernmost point of continental America, a frowning headland only two hundred kilometres north of its more famous counterpart, Cape Horn. Some distance further on ancorage was found (with the aid of thirty-fathom cables tied to trees on shore) in a bay which has never been identified, but which the explorers named the River of Sardines. The Cape Horn skipper Felix Riesenberg thinks it may have been Bahia Cordes.

From here a boat was sent on to reconnoitre while the crew

fished, collected mussels, and hunted stringy kelp geese and the flightless birds now known as *patos vapores*—motorized ducks— with their crossbows. One anchorage is very like another in the straits; if the River of Sardines was indeed Bahia Cordes, it abounds in kelp-covered rocks and has still, according to the *Pilot,* "not been thoroughly examined". Above towers a three-peaked mountain, whose snow-streaked precipices plunge down into the rain-saturated forest below. Seals and penguins swim through the kelp; the most surprising inhabitants of the gloomy woods are the tiny green humming-birds that the Alacalufe called *Sinu-k-Tain*—the Daughters of the Wind.

In six days' time the boat returned. They had found the "cape of the other sea" and "the sea great and wide". The news was too much for the composure of Magellan, perhaps the toughest explorer of all time. "He began to cry," says Pigafetta, "and he gave the name of Cape Desire to this cape, as a thing which had been much desired for a long time."

Now all that remained was to collect the two other ships. The *Concepción* was soon found, but though the ships searched as far as Cape Virgins and left messages under cairns, the *San Antonio* was never sighted again. Nor could she have been. The pilot, Esteban Gomez, a Portuguese much envious of Magellan, had overpowered the good-natured Mesquita and was well on his way back to Spain. The fleet's astrologer opined that this was what had happened, as well he might have guessed, since Gomez had openly urged returning at a council of war held before the First Narrows.

The loss of the *San Antonio* was a grievous blow indeed, for she was the heaviest ship of the armada and carried the bulk of the provisions. Food was woefully short now. The crew had been finding meagre sustenance on the fish they caught and "a sweet herb named appio [celery]". More than one counselled retreat. But the captain-general was adamant. "If we have to eat the leather from the ship's yards," he said, "we will still go on and discover what we have promised the Emperor. I trust God will aid us and give us good fortune."

The loyal captains Joao Serrano and Duarte Barbosa were behind their commander. The fleet set sail, and a week later the three gallant little ships left the gaunt rock slabs of Cape Desire to port and became the first European vessels to enter the ocean that Magellan named "Pacifico". They had been five weeks beating against wind and current in about the most difficult waters in the world, yet the proud-spirited Pigafetta, undeterred by misfortune and hardship, could write: "We found by a miracle, a strait which we called the Cape of Eleven Thousand Virgins . . . and it issues in another sea, which is called the peaceful sea, it is surrounded by very great and high mountains covered with snow. . . . I think that there is not in the world a more beautiful country, or a better strait than this one."

With high hopes, Magellan shaped course north-west. Soon Pigafetta was delighting in "swallows"—flying fish—"that fly more than a crossbow-shot, as long as their wings are wet". But neither the most learned cartographers of Europe, much less anyone aboard the tiny specks of the armada, had the remotest inkling of the enormous span of the ocean they were attempting so boldly to traverse.

By some extraordinary mischance the little ships managed to avoid almost every one of the multitude of South Sea Islands among which they threaded their way. Pigafetta sums up with terrible restraint:

> Wednesday, the twenty-eighth of November, 1520, we came forth out of the said strait, and entered into the Pacific sea, where we remained three months and twenty days without taking in provisions or other refreshments, and we only ate old biscuit reduced to powder, and full of grubs, and stinking from the dirt the rats made on it when eating the good biscuit, and we drank water that was yellow and stinking. We also ate the ox hides which were under the main-yard, so that the yard should not chafe the rigging: they were very hard on account of the sun, rain, and wind, and we left them for four or five days in the sea, and then we put them a little on the embers, and so ate them; also the sawdust of wood, and rats which cost half-a-crown each, moreover enough of them were not to be got.

Scurvy soon began to take its toll. Besides those who died twenty-five or thirty fell ill. Through it all the trade winds blew free and the Pacific for once lived up to its name. In those three months and twenty days they saw no land except two uninhabited islands, where there was no place to anchor as there was no bottom. The first isle was in "fifteen degrees of austral latitude, and the other island . . . in nine degrees". These they not unnaturally named the Unfortunate Islands.

The identity of these islands must be of interest to all students of Western exploration in the Pacific as being the very first South Sea Islands ever discovered. Professor H.E. Maude, of the

Australian National University, Canberra, by a masterly analysis of Albo's log of the voyage and other evidence, informed by his personal acquaintance with the whole area, has identified them as Pukapuka in 14°50′ south, an isolated outlier of the Tuamotus (not to be confused with another Pukapuka in the Cooks) and Flint in the Line Islands.

Disappointed in their hopes of refreshment, the fleet sailed on and on, never guessing that this ocean they were crossing covered a full third of the earth. The "upper and lower gums of most of our men grew so much that they could not eat"—even of the scanty fare available, related Pigafetta. Among the nineteen who died on this passage were an Indian from Brazil and a "giant" who had been kidnapped in Patagonia.

North and west they continued, with the commander demonstrating his mastery of the theory and practice of navigation by correcting the course for magnetic variation, wherein all his pilots had gone astray. They crossed the Line and pressed on into the Northern Hemisphere, where the familiar *Tramontana*, the pole-star, greeted the weary wanderers as an old friend. The armada was a thousand kilometres north of the latitude of the Moluccas (well known to Magellan) before he altered due west on 23 February 1521; a powerful argument that the commander had learned of the existence of the Philippines or even visited them when he had disappeared east from Malacca in 1511 and 1512, for he was now in the latitude of that supposedly unknown archipelago.

The awful ordeal of the Pacific was now almost at an end. On 6 March, ninety-eight days out from Cape Desire, the look-outs sighted two high islands ahead. These were Guam and Rota in the Marianas. Soon, outrigger proas, painted red, black, and white, with lateen sails of matting, were darting in and out among the ships "like dolphins bounding from wave to wave". The men were bearded and had hair down to their waists. The women—those fabulous women of the South Seas for the first time seen by Europeans—were "beautiful and delicate, and whiter than the men, and have their hair loose and flowing, very black and long, down to the earth". They made beautiful mats and their provisions included sweet potatoes, sugar-cane, coconuts, and "figs a palm long"—bananas.

But this idyllic scene was very soon marred by tragedy. As was to happen over and over again in the South Seas, the Islanders perceived the newcomers as totally alien beings to whom the normal usages of society did not apply, particularly regarding possessions. Moreover, Polynesians and Micronesians (unlike Melanesians) were never trading people. Even today, should you express admiration for an object in someone's home, it will immediately be presented to you. To offer payment would be unthinkable. In some other way, perhaps at another time, you may proffer a gift or service in return. This is the system of *gift exchange*, incomprehensible and misunderstood by the European explorers.

Thieves was Magellan's reaction, and for long the Marianas were to bear his designation of "Ladrones", or Islands of Thieves. "They robbed us, in such a way that it was impossible to preserve oneself from them," wrote Pigafetta. "They stole away with much address and diligence the small boat called the skiff, which was made fast to the poop of the captain's ship, at which he was much irritated, and went on shore with forty armed men, burned forty or fifty houses, with several small boats, and killed seven men of the island; they recovered their skiff." A terrible vengeance, in part explained if not condoned by the commander and his men being in extremity.

Pigafetta continues: "After this we set sail suddenly, following the same course. Before we went ashore some of our sick men begged us that if we killed man or woman, that we should bring them their entrails, as they would see themselves suddenly cured." Such were the half-civilized Europeans—brave, bigoted, and superstitious—that history was about to unleash on the free peoples of the Pacific.

On 9 March, the day the fleet sailed, Master Andrew of Bristol succumbed to scurvy. For the others, relief was at hand. In a week the armada came to Samar in the Philippines, where the sick were taken ashore and speedily returned to health with fresh food—coconut milk, bananas, fish, and palm oil. And here at last the material objects of the voyage, gold and spices, were in evidence. Spanish armour and Spanish gifts and trinkets impressed the inhabitants, who readily embraced acts of conversion to Christianity. Enrique, Magellan's personal slave, whom he had brought from the East Indies eight years before, was here able to act as interpreter.

From Samar the fleet moved on to the greater kingdom of Cebu, where again the rajah and many of his subjects were converted and swore allegiance to Spain. Success, complete and absolute, was in the expedition's grasp, when Magellan, who had stood firm through all adversity, at last showed a chink in his armour.

Religious fanatacism seems to have caused him to overestimate the power of Western arms.

The rajah of Macatan, a little island off Cebu, was in revolt. Magellan decided "to bear further witness to the omnipotence of God, and to consolidate the power of his ally, and hence the power of Spain", by bringing the rebels to heel by Spanish might alone. He firmly rejected his friend the rajah of Cebu's offer of men and insisted on leading the assault in person. The result was disaster. The thin wooden shields of the Filipinos served to deflect or slow down both musket balls and crossbow bolts. The vulnerable limbs of the Spaniards were not protected by armour. The Europeans fell back before overwhelming assaults. For upwards of an hour Magellan, Pigafetta (who was himself badly wounded), and a handful of others made a fighting retreat back to the boats, which were cravenly about to abandon them. Here, while the boats stood too far off to be of real assistance, Magellan, like Cook in like circumstances 250 years later, was cut down and killed.

With the death of their leader, on 26 April 1521, the expedition fell to pieces. Enrique, the slave and interpreter, who had been wounded at his master's side, was spoken to harshly by the tactless Duarte Barbosa. In fear at Barbosa's threats, he told the rajah falsely that the Spaniards were preparing to attack and advised him to get in first. Twenty-seven of the crew, including Duarte Barbosa, were massacred, and the wounded Serrano was abandoned by his comrades when the expedition fled in disorder. The now-rotten *Concepción* was scuttled, and for seven months the *Trinidad* and *Victoria* wandered about the archipelagos from Mindanao to Borneo, eventually reaching the Moluccas.

Francisco Serrano, Magellan's friend, had died that same year. Nevertheless, they were able to load the ships with spices, and with the one-time mutineer del Cano in command of the *Victoria* and the staunch master-at-arms Espinosa of the *Trinidad,* they set sail for Spain via the Cape of Good Hope. The *Trinidad* soon developed a leak and put back to the Moluccas, whence she unsuccessfully attempted to recross the Pacific. Several more islands in the Marianas were discovered as well as some of the Carolines before the worn-out ship was forced to return to the Moluccas again, where she surrendered to the Portuguese. Only four men of her complement ultimately reached Spain.

The *Victoria,* under del Cano, successfully circumnavigated the globe, to cast anchor in San Lucar on 6 September 1522, where it was discovered that, in the course of their west-about voyage, a day had been lost. Out of the 240 who had set out from this same port with banners flying three years before, only thirty-one in the *Victoria* returned to Spain.

So was accomplished the most daringly conceived of all Pacific voyages made by Westerners. Magellan died in the attempt, but his name is rightly acclaimed in the accomplishment. It is fitting that it should be commemorated in the steely waters of that grim southern strait and, above it, in those two hazy constellations that the Polynesians call *Rua Mafu* and we know as "Magellanic Clouds".

5

Spain Challenged

C HRISTOPHER COLUMBUS, WITH a genius all his own, solved the wind patterns of the North Atlantic on his very first voyage. He made the outward passage before the Portuguese trades and the north-east trades and the return via the Gulf Stream and the brave west winds of the north. The accomplishment of a corresponding feat in the Pacific—a successful west-east return from Asia to America—was to take forty-four years.

CHRISTOPHER COLUMBUS

Not that the will was not there. Espinosa struggled mightily in 1522 to recross the Pacific in the *Trinidad*. Sensibly realizing that the only practicable route was through the west wind belt beyond the easterly trades, he pushed north as far as 42° or 43°, opposite northern Japan, where twelve days of storm, bitter cold, and recurrence of scurvy at length forced the stalwart soldier-captain to accept defeat. This was no dishonour; many a tall Manila galleon, in infinitely sounder condition than the much-abused *Trinidad,* was to fare no better in those harsh North Pacific seas.

On the way back to the Moluccas the *Trinidad* anchored at what is now Maug Island in the northern Marianas to obtain provisions. The battered *Trinidad* at this stage must have been in a sorry state—it was not long afterwards that she fell to pieces on the beach at Ternate while being unloaded after surrendering to the Portuguese. Here on Maug Island a mariner named Gonzalo de Vigo deserted with three companions. They were the first of a group of men who were to play a major part in introducing the customs and technology of the West to the Pacific Islanders—the beachcombers.

The cloves brought back to Spain by del Cano in the little *Victoria* were valuable enough to wet the appetites of the emperor Charles and his Antwerp bankers. A large fleet was at once fitted out; no less than seven ships, of which the biggest, the *Santa Maria de la Victoria,* was a full three hundred tons. In command was Fra Garcia de Loaisa with none other than Sebastian del Cano as pilot-major. They sailed with high hopes in July 1525. Only four of the ships succeeded in reaching the Pacific end of Magellan's strait, and soon these were separated by storm: the *San Lesmes* was never heard of again; the *Santiago* turned north and ultimately fetched up in Mexico; the flagship and the *Santa Maria de Parral* set out across the Pacific. The *Parral,* after a mutiny and fighting with the inhabitants, was wrecked in the Philippines. The *Santa Maria de la Victoria* passed through the Marshall Islands and called at Guam, where she picked up Gonzalo de Vigo, the lone survivor of the three who had deserted the *Trinidad* in 1522. Both Loaisa and del Cano by this time had died. The ship ultimately struggled on to the Moluccas.

No more ships sailed from Spain for the Pacific. Mexico was now firmly in the hands of Cortes, and Pizarro was soon to destroy the Inca empire in Peru. Henceforth, Spain's Pacific fleets were built on that ocean's shores.

The first Mexican expedition of three ships, the *Florida* being the flagship, sailed under command of Alvaro de Saavedra in October 1527, to ascertain the fate of the *Trinidad* and Loaisa's expedition. Only the *Florida* reached the Moluccas, rescuing several survivors of the *Parral* en route. Saavedra made two determined attempts to return across the ocean, on the second of which he died. On the way, however, much of the north coast of New Guinea, discovered two years earlier by the Portuguese Meneses, was examined and the Admiralty Islands were discovered.

We will pass over the 1537 expeditions of Grijalva, who was slain by his mutinous crew before his ship finally fell to pieces on the coast of New Guinea; and Villalobos, who, after passing through the Carolines and discovering Iwo Jima, was, like the others, unable to return from the Moluccas.

It was not until 1565 that two ships that had been with the fleet of Miguel Lopez de Legaspi in the conquest of the Philippines at last succeeded in recrossing the Pacific back to New Spain, as Mexico was then called. The pilot Urdaneta, who had been with Loaisa, planned the route and sailed with Felipe de Salcedo in one of the ships, the *San Pedro.* They were preceded by a month by Alonzo de Arellano in their consort, the *San Lucas.* Urdaneta's plan, the same as that attempted by Espinosa in the *Trinidad* nearly half a century before, was to make a wide sweep north to about 40°, where westerly winds drove them to California, down which they coasted to Mexico. This was the route that would be followed by those fabulous treasure ships, the Manila galleons, for the next 250 years. Loaded deep with the spoils of the Orient, they left Manila usually in June and reached Acapulco in New Spain five or six months later (the outward, west-bound journey took only half as long). The treasure was carried across the Isthmus of Panama to Nombre de Dios, whence the treasure fleet, with a strong escort called the Indian Guard, sailed for Spain.

The triumph of Spain in the South Seas was complete. The Pacific was a private lake—until a stocky little captain from Plymouth first plundered the treasure-laden mule train on the isthmus and then had the impudence to erupt into Spain's own sea. But before we come to Drake's story, there is one more Spanish expedition that cannot be passed over. This was Mendana's first expedition, in 1567, the earliest exploration voyage into the Pacific Islands proper.

THE ISLES OF SOLOMON

An article of faith among European geographers that persisted down to the time of Cook was that the earth's symmetry demanded that the Northern Hemisphere land mass had to be balanced by an equal area in the south. Thus arose the idea of *Terra Australis Incognita*—the Unknown Southern Continent. A firm believer in its existence was one Pedro Sarmiento de Gamboa, an able mathematician, a dabbler in heresies who walked a tightrope with the Inquisition, and a commander whose competence was marred by brutality. When at length an expedition was approved to search for the southern land, Sarmiento was made second in command to the viceroy's nephew, Alvaro de Mendaña, a young man of twenty-five and a surprisingly good and humane leader.

The expedition set out from Callao in Peru in 1567 in the *Los Reyes*, 250 tons, and the *Todos Santos*, 107 tons, inexplicably provisioned for only a short voyage, only two years after Arellano had found the route back across the Pacific. This was the first expedition to sail westward *south* of the Equator. It was not until they reached the western part of the ocean that land was sighted, which was Nui in the Tuvalu group. Contrary winds prevented a landing. A few days later the ships had to sheer off hastily from the reefs of Ontong Java. Then, on 7 February 1568, eighty days out from Callao, the lofty ranges of Santa Isabel rose over the horizon and it seemed that Sarmiento's southern continent was at hand.

Two days were needed to come up with the land, where suspicious but not unfriendly bow-and-arrow-armed warriors in graceful crescent-shaped canoes were beguiled with caps and bells. A chief named Bilebanara exchanged names with Mendaña and promised to supply food. However, there were 250 men in the expedition, and the Islanders, despite their flourishing sago and yam patches, coconut groves, and pigs, were subsistence agriculturists who had no surplus available to feed so many strangers. Any substantial trade in foodstuffs meant starvation for their own people. So began the melancholy sequence that was to bedevil relations between explorers and islanders in every part of the Pacific—initial wary good will, the captains' need to feed their crews, the total inability of the Islanders to comply, and the situation finally resolved by means of the newcomers' firearms.

This is what happened on Santa Isabel and afterwards on Guadalcanal, Florida, New Georgia, Malaita, Ulawa, and San Cristobal. Mendaña and the Franciscan friars accompanying the expedition tried to restrain the excesses of Sarmiento, but the need for provisions was paramount and his brutalities were condoned. One item of sustenance that was offered the Spaniards profoundly shocked them, however: the quarter of a boy, garnished with taro. "We were all struck with great wonder and pity to see so much cruelty and so strange a thing," one of the company recorded.

A brigantine, an open boat of five tons or so, was built on shore in a space of fifty-four days, and in this tiny craft virtually the whole of the Solomons, containing some of the largest islands in the Pacific, was examined in the six months that the expedition remained.

San Cristobal was the last stop. Here again the initially friendly Islanders were soon antagonized. A stockade was built to protect the crews while the ships were careened, scraped of sea growths, and recaulked. A planned settlement was abandoned, largely on account of the Solomons' notorious malaria and the absence of significant amounts of the gold the explorers so diligently sought. Foraging parties were ambushed. Solomon Islanders could glide through the densest rain forest silent as deadly ghosts, and Sarmiento's war dogs and arquebuses were no more a match for them than Japanese bayonets were to prove against Sergeant Vouza and Silas Sitai, guerilla leader of the Solomons, 375 years later in the Second World War.

On 17 August 1568 the repaired ships set out to return to Peru.

The route they were to take was subject to dispute, but eventually they followed Arellano into the north and came back to South America via New Spain. So little was understood of longitude that the archipelago they left behind was thought to be more than a thousand leagues nearer America than it really was. Subsequent voyagers, including Mendaña himself, were to seek for it in vain, and two hundred years were to pass before Europeans visited the Solomons again.

On the way home Namu in the Marshalls and Wake Island were discovered. Then the ships were separated by a hurricane-force gale. This was followed by calms and the ravages of scurvy, from which thirty men died. Eventually, by a remarkable coincidence, both ships within a week of each other crept into the same little port in Baja California. In one respect Mendaña's feat was unprecedented; after two years and thirteen thousand kilometres, more than two-thirds of the expeditioners came back alive.

The Peruvian authorities were not impressed. Mendaña had to mortgage his own fortune to bring the ships again to Callao, where a new viceroy wrote to the king that Mendaña's islands were of little importance, since there was no gold, silver, spices, or merchandise to be got from them. With the typical conquistador "humanity", he allowed that "the advantage that might be derived from exploring these islands would be to make slaves of the people". It was to be twenty years before Mendaña could gain support for a second expedition. Long before this an event occurred that was to signal the beginning of a new era in the Pacific and the world. The dreaded corsair El Draque, Drake the Dragon, penetrated Spain's private sea. Just nine years after Mendaña's return he seized the *Los Reyes*, renamed *La Capitana de Moriel* in honour of her service as flagship on the Solomons expedition, in Valparaiso Bay.

THE WORLD ENCOMPASSED BY FRANCIS DRAKE

In Drake we have something like a modern man—fiercely individualistic, a strategist whose thinking was little circumscribed by outworn tradition, a very human man not above snobbery and avarice; yet the one who enunciated and enforced the revolutionary doctrine—"The gentleman must hale and draw with the mariner, and the mariner with the gentleman." Perhaps Drake's strong Calvinism and fervent patriotism smack to us of an earlier age. His record is certainly stained by his early slaving voyages, but his mercy to his bitterest foes is legendary; moreover,

FRANCIS DRAKE

Drake's friend the Cimaroon chief Pedro said Drake had shown friendship that between white man and black passed all understanding. It is ironical that Drake and Dampier, equally humane and more scientist than buccaneer, should to this day be regarded up and down the west coast of South America as little better than devils incarnate. Centuries long have been the shock echoes at Drake's unthinkable eruption into the Peaceful Spanish Sea!

Drake's school of seamanship was akin to that of Cook's—a small bark trading along the English east coast and the ports of Zeeland—narrow waters where racing tides sluice between hidden sandbanks and seas break short and merciless beneath the fog banks. He graduated to the wider shores of the Atlantic under his kinsman John Hawkins. Before he was twenty he was on his first voyage to the Spanish Main. The Spanish Main was, of course, the Spanish *mainland*, the north-east coast of South America from the Orinoco River to the Isthmus of Darien, what is now the Caribbean coast of Venezuela, Colombia, and Panama. This was the meaning of the term in Drake's time as it was in Dampier's. It was only romantic Victorian poets who misapplied it to the Caribbean Sea.

It was a period of extraordinary attrition between the world empire of Spain and the half of the British Isles ruled precariously by Elizabeth, when only the young queen's bewildering diplomatic footwork and courage saved the nominal peace and the growing independence and power of the upstart nation. English ships could be seized and their crews burnt at the stake by the Holy Office; the ever more confident English seamen could challenge Spain's monopoly in the West Indies, but still open warfare was avoided. Thus, while Elizabeth herself and some of her closest counsellors were shareholders in Drake's circumnavigation voyage, and she said to him on its eve: "I would be gladly revenged on the King of Spain for divers injuries that I have received", this involvement was strictly secret; the expedition that set sail from Plymouth on 15 November 1577 was officially bound for Alexandria to buy currants.

There were five ships, ranging in size from the *Pelican* (afterwards renamed the *Golden Hind*) of 100 tons, to the 15-ton *Benedict*. Smaller they were than Magellan's of fifty-eight years before, but mere tonnage obscures the revolution in ship design that had occurred in the interval. Magellan's *Victoria* had been a carrack; Drake's vessels were galleons. Carracks were essentially mobile fighting platforms for soldiers, with immensely high fighting castles at the bows and lesser "summer castles" at the sterns. These upperworks were added to the hulls and supported on arches as in a building, whereas galleons were designed all of a piece as tall-sterned ships, manoeuvrable and seaworthy, whose fighting teeth were increasingly to become their long-range guns.

Like his predecessor, Drake passed the southern winter in the same desolate Port St Julian in Patagonia. And here the similarities between the two master navigators, themselves very much alike physically and in character—stocky, innovative, immensely competent and tough—become almost bizarre, because Drake too was here faced with mutiny, in this case by a well-born soldier, his second-in-command and erstwhile friend, Thomas Doughty.

The true rights and wrongs of this episode probably can never be untangled, particularly since Drake's log is lost and the only full account is by the parson, Fletcher, his enemy. What is beyond dispute is that a jury of forty seamen found Doughty guilty of mutiny; that given the choice of marooning or execution, he chose the latter and was duly beheaded beneath Magellan's mouldering gibbet.

The long-term effects are less in doubt. Drake's torment of mind at the dissension that had brought his company to this pass comes out vividly in his own words: "For by the life of God it doth even take my wits from me to think on it. Here is such controversy between the sailors and the gentlemen, and such stomaching between the gentlemen and the sailors, that it doth even make me mad to hear it." Drake's remedy, already referred to, ushered in a new era at sea: "I must have the gentleman to hale [haul] and draw with the mariner, and the mariner with the gentleman."

A further result of this fatal clash was to settle once and for all on English ships the question of divided authority between soldier and sailor. The vessel's captain was paramount. The opposite principle obtained in the fleets of Spain. When the Spanish Armada was sent to attack England ten years later the military commanders in each galleon had orders from Medina-Sidonia to hang any captain who lost station (some did so), so contributing in no small measure to the Armada's defeat.

Two unseaworthy ships were destroyed in Patagonia and the rest careened and rerigged. On 17 August 1578 the *Pelican (Golden Hind)*, the *Elizabeth*, and the little *Marigold* set out again and three days later came in sight of Cape Virgins. Nuno da Silva, a Portuguese pilot captured by Drake in the Cape Verde Islands and

DRAKE'S GOLDEN HIND

later released in Mexico, had this to say about the *Golden Hind:*
"She was in great measure strong, with two sheathings . . . well
furnished and fitted with very good masts, tackle and double suits
of sails." She mounted eighteen cannon, was watertight running
free but leaked on the wind. The two sheathings referred to were
an innovation by John Hawkins. A layer of horsehair and pitch
was laid over the hull and held in place by thin outer planking, a
not inneffective protection against ship-worm.

Just within the second narrows the ships were provisioned with three thousand penguins at what is today still known as Elizabeth Island. (It is uninhabited and as desolate as when Drake was there; only the penguins are fewer.) The ships made the passage of Magellan Strait in the remarkably good time of fifteen days, and on 6 September the *Golden Hind* and her consorts, with the grim grey slabs of Cape Desire (Deseado) abeam to larboard, were breasting the swells of the open Pacific. The serious seagoing difficulties should have been over; instead they had only just begun. The immortal saga of Cape Horn was about to open.

Two days out from the Evangelistas at the Pacific exit from the strait (where a lonely lighthouse now stands) the *Mare Pacificum* proved, in Fletcher's words, more of a *mare fusiosum,* for an "intollerable tempest" arose which was to last, with but momentary intermissions, no less than fifty-two days. For two weeks the ships, lying ahull in enormous seas, were driven helplessly towards the south-west, and somewhere in this waste of Southern Ocean the 30-ton *Marigold* was overwhelmed and lost with all twenty-nine hands. A slight easing allowed the remaining two vessels to hoist reefed topsails and stand north-east towards the coast.

A full month after the gale broke they recovered the land some little way north of Cape Desire. Fearful mountain squalls, the williwaws, exposed the very sea bottom where they tried to anchor—in Fletcher's words: "sending us headlong upon the ... swelling waves of the seas, over the rocks at the sight thereof at our going in was as fearful as death itself, at the last in this miserable state we were driven as though through the eye of a needle into a great and large bay by a most narrow passage of rocks." Incredibly, Drake had led his ships through this needle's eye at night. They came to anchor, surely deserving of respite, yet the williwaws swept down from the heights again with such violence that the "cables brake ... the ankers came home", and the ships were driven back out to sea.

They were never to meet again on that voyage, for the *Elizabeth* regained the straits, where her captain, John Winter, in an extraordinary parallel with the *Trinidad's* desertion of Magellan, "full sore against the mariners' minds", hauled his wind and sailed back to England. Drake's solitary flagship was left alone as a "pellican in the wildernesse".

Now, as the little galleon was driven south-east towards Cape Horn, a desperate battle began to find shelter, repair the storm-battered ship, and rest the exhausted and half-frozen crew. On 14

October, six days after losing the *Elizabeth,* the *Golden Hind*
came to anchor fourteen kilometres off the spouting cliffs of
Tierra del Fuego in the great depth of fifty fathoms (ninety-one
metres). Next day some shelter was found closer in, where they
stayed two days before being driven out to sea again. At another
dubious anchorage among the heaving streamers of kelp, very
close to the Horn, Alacalufe Indians came out in their crescent-
shaped bark canoes, almost decked in, the seams stitched with
sealskin thongs, and of "such comely proportion and excellent
workmanship" that they might have been made "for the pleasure
of some great and noble personage, yea, of some prince".

During the five days spent here the ship's pinnace was lost with
seven or eight men aboard. On its own in the most remote and
stormy seas of the globe, an open boat would seem to have no
hope of survival. But survive it did. Through unknown channels
into Magellan Strait it sailed, back up the coast of South America
to where Buenos Aires now stands. The heroic seamen died one by
one; the sole survivor, Peter Carder, gave himself up to the
Portuguese in Brazil and reached England nine years later.

Now the last flick of the terrible gale forced the *Golden Hind*
out to sea for the final time. She drove south for a day; then, in 57°
south according to Da Silva, she came to anchor at an island.

The identity of this island has aroused much controversy, one
rather fanciful theory holding that it was a land that has since
sunk. It may well have been Cape Horn Island itself, but the
latitude given of 57° is too far south by a degree. More likely it was
Diego Ramirez islets, which lie in 56°30' (not an unreasonable
discrepancy in those stormy seas and cloudy skies and with the
instruments of the day), ninety-seven kilometres south-west of
Cape Horn. These small islands are the very last land before the
islands fringing the Antarctic Peninsula, 750 kilometres further
south. This conjecture of Drake's position is at any rate the
opinion of the distinguished Australian navigator Captain Brett
Hilder, and I for one concur, having plotted da Silva's positions
on the chart and obtained the same result.

But whichever island it was, Drake realized its enormous
significance—the continent of South America could be turned.
Casting himself down and reaching his body out over the furthest
cliff, he told his people that he had been on the southernmost land
in the known world, "without which there is no maine nor iland
to be seene to the Southwards, but that the Atlanticke Ocean and
the South Sea, meete in a most large and free scope". It is
appropriate that those wild waters which Drake gazed upon,

where the Cape Horn "greybeards" that roar around the world are compressed between the jut of Antarctica and the horn of the Americas, should bear the name Drake's Passage.

From this point on the weather relented, and the *Golden Hind* was able to make good speed up the coast of Chile into somewhat warmer waters, there to uphold the doctrine that the "Ocean by right is the Lord's alone, and by nature left free for all men to deale withall". But before we follow the great navigator northward, let us spare a thought for the heroic men and women who had long preceded him to Cape Horn. For the Canoe Indians, or Alacalufe, whose craft so aroused Drake's admiration, were accustomed to paddle out to Cape Horn island itself, there to hide under the rocks and scanty bushes until, at night, they could seize sleeping cormorants for food. These extraordinarily daring coastal seafarers are gone from Cape Horn now. A fragment of the tribe yet remains at Puerto Eden in the Patagonian Channels (there were forty-eight when I encountered them in 1965), but the courage and hardihood of these first of Cape Horn seamen should not be forgotten.

We have dwelt long on this remote region because Drake's discovery that here the Atlantic and South Sea met "in a most large and free scope" opened the main doorway into the Pacific for those who came after him from Europe and later America. After the route round the Horn was pioneered by the Dutch, the tortuous Magellan Strait fell into disuse for sailing ships. The other entry point into the ocean was round Africa via the Cape of Good Hope. Thus, while Drake was to explore a good deal more of California than of the South Seas proper, he did much to serve later explorers. His superb seamanship in the involuntary epic of Cape Horn was significant not only to the English but to all Western nations—and to the Islanders yet unknown by the West, who had lived hitherto free from its rapacious clutches.

Drake's first Pacific landfall was a far from happy one. Running north in the Humbolt Current with a fair wind, the *Golden Hind* came to the island of Mocha off Chile, where Drake hoped to obtain fresh food and water. The Indians, apparently friendly, made a surprise attack on a watering party. Two sailors were slain and Drake received an arrow in his cheek before the boatload could withdraw. The crew thereupon begged Drake to open fire on the beach with his guns. It is a measure of his humanity and understanding that he would not. The Indians had taken them for their persecutors, the Spaniards, he said, and had bestowed upon them a Spaniard's reward. The misunderstanding was natural, since the Indians knew of no other Europeans and some of the crew, strictly against orders, had used the word *agua* when asking for water. So, without firing a shot in revenge, Drake put to sea again, leaving the Araucanian Indians to continue their historic struggle against Spain, which they were to wage for the next 250 years, with ultimate success.

Nevertheless the expedition's luck had at last changed. Here was no Indian Guard to protect the Spanish merchantmen and treasure ships, which indeed were mostly unarmed until the frantic messengers of the viceroy warned the city governors of Chile and Peru to mount cannon with all speed. Drake captured ships at will, sometimes several in a single day. He took from them what he wanted before returning them to their owners, for he sank not a single prize, nor did he fail to treat his prisoners with consideration and courtesy before releasing them. As has already been related, Mendaña's old flagship with a cargo of wine and gold was captured in Valparaiso roads, when the first Englishman over the bulwarks cried *"Abajo perro!"* ("Down dog!") and hit the nearest crewman over the head with a stick. The rest promptly surrendered.

The richest prize was taken on March 1579 after a long hide-and-seek chase. She was the treasure galleon *Our Lady of Conception,* known familiarly if rather rudely to the Spaniards as *"Cacafuego"* ("Shit-fire"), and she was *en route* to Panama (for transhipment of her cargo to Spain) heavy laden with the spoils of the silver and gold mines of Peru. The action when it came was short and decisive. A chain shot carried away the *Cacafuego's* mizzen; Drake grappled, and his boarders loosed a flight of arrows and arquebus balls. The Spanish crew fled except for the commander, San Juan de Anton, who, though wounded, resisted until overpowered. Drake, who was removing his armour when this gallant enemy was brought aboard the *Golden Hind,* embraced him saying: "Be patient. This is the usage of war."

In gold and silver alone the *Cacafuego* yielded 400,000 pesos—perhaps six million dollars in our present money—with pearls, emeralds, and silks besides. No wonder, when this hoard was being transferred to the *Golden Hind,* a Spanish ship boy called out, with humour that doubtless earned him a cuff over the ear, that their ship should be renamed the *"Cacaplata"* since she was voiding silver instead of fire. Five days it took to loot the Peruvian galleon, prudently hove-to well outside the shipping lanes, then her crew were returned aboard loaded with gifts, which might have been better appreciated had they not so recently been the property of the recipients, and the *Golden Hind* disappeared across the horizon.

This incident smacks superficially of the piracy of which the Spaniards were to accuse Drake and his colleagues. But the *Golden Hind* was a *privateering* ship in which the queen herself had an investment. Among her cargo, as the observant San Juan de Anton noted, were agricultural implements for the possible founding of a colony, for Drake's foray into the South Sea was part and parcel of England's aggressive commercial expansion in face of the Iberian monopoly of half the world. As Raleigh pointed out at his trial, this was war between the nations; whereas the harbours of Cadiz and Lisbon had once been crowded with shipping, after decades of English attrition these great ports were nearly empty.

"The wind commands me away. Our ship is under sail," Drake had written to Elizabeth. And now the wind commanded him home—by way of the Strait of Anian (Bering Strait), which was presumed to exist between Asia and America, and the legendary North-west Passage. Meanwhile, Pedro Sarmiento, in the West Indian phrase "lacing his stays up when his character gone", went to plant a colony in Magellan Strait to block it against any other impudent intruder. What became of this colony, the City of King Philip, will be seen when we discuss Cavendish's voyage in a later chapter.

Drake did not press on toward Bering Strait. Although it was early June, fog and gale and bitter cold decided him to take the alternative course, to cross the Pacific and return home round the world. So, about the latitude of present-day Seattle he turned south again, seeking a haven where his ship could be careened and made ready for the long homeward passage. A little north of what is now San Francisco he found a suitable bay. New Albion he named it, because the white cliffs reminded him of England. Having established the most friendly relations with the Indians and nailed to a post a plate engraved with the queen's name and a record of the country's accession to her kingdom, Drake set off for home on 25 July.

Sixty-eight days later the ship reached an island in the Carolines; we do not know which one because Drake's log, which he presented to Queen Elizabeth, was subsequently lost. It is worth noting that the crew of the *Golden Hind* did not suffer from scurvy. This was no accident. The captain took every opportunity to refresh them with vegetables, fruit, and green herbs. In this,

Drake was ahead of his time as far as English ships went, though in fairness it must be pointed out that the Spaniards by this date had come to recognize the antiscorbutic value of green plants. It is a tragedy that when at last the Lords of the Admiralty followed suit they should have chosen the juice of the lime, the least antiscorbutic of all citrus fruits. Scott and his men who died in the Antarctic were the most famous victims of this error.

Whichever Caroline island it was where the *Golden Hind* touched, the explorers met with the same reception as that which had so incensed Magellan in the Marianas further north; Drake, like his predecessor, named his first South Sea Island the Island of Thieves. However, Drake was a good deal more merciful than Magellan had been and contented himself with shooting off "a great peece, not to hurt them, but to affright them . . . at the noise thereof every one lept out of his canow".

Notwithstanding this unhappy reception, the visitors' admiration was aroused by the perfection of the Islanders' outrigger sailing canoes. Indeed, those of the Carolines, and formerly the Marianas as well, are probably the most beautiful and effective outrigger craft ever built. Even today, thirty-footers, different in no important respect from those seen by Drake, are sailing without instruments to Saipan, well over seven hundred empty kilometres away. Interestingly enough, there is a tradition in these islands that in former times when stone and shell tools only were available, the finish of canoes was rough. This is not born out by Drake's description of their hulls as bearing "a glosse, as it were of a horne most daintily burnished". Plainly, the present-day Carolinians underrate the craftsmanship of their progenitors.

After the Carolinian interlude, the English galleon touched at Mindanao in the Philippines to take on water before proceeding to Ternate in the Moluccas. Resisting the temptation to proselytize in the manner of Magellan, Drake traded for spices with the sultan. The inspiration for the formation of the English East India Company is said to have owed much to this initiative.

The expedition sailed in mid-December, the *Golden Hind's* hold bearing a virtual king's ransom. In this moment of supreme accomplishment the ship ran full upon a submerged reef. The water was too deep to kedge. Guns, provisions, and some of the precious cargo were jettisoned. Divine service was held, and parson Fletcher preached a sermon. It would be intriguing to know just what he said, for he was no friend of Drake's. There can be no doubt it was uncomplimentary to the commander, because when a change of wind rocked them clear shortly afterwards, the infuriated Drake had the parson chained by the leg to a staple in the deck and, with but dubious authority, pronounced sentence of excommunication upon him.

A pleasant fortnight was spent in Java. After that the *Golden Hind* touched land only once, at Sierra Leone, before dropping anchor in Plymouth Sound, a ship full of "joyful minds and thankful hearts" after an eventful voyage of nearly three years. With her usual skill, Elizabeth rode the storm of protest from Spain and its powerful English sympathizers against Drake's impudent plundering. His detractors, however, had little hope against the queen's high favour. Besides, the little captain was the popular hero of England. In the spring Elizabeth knighted him at Deptford, on the deck of the *Golden Hind.*

6

Mendaña's Swan Song, Quiros, and Torres

"THE BITCH OF England" was the Spanish poet Lope de Vega's description of Elizabeth I of England, and doubtless the queen's feminine subtleties could be aggravating to her enemies. Dona Isabel de Barreto y Mendaña, who could well qualify for the title of "The Bitch of Spain", was in a different category altogether. For sheer unfeeling avarice Mendaña's beautiful young wife, the first Western woman "explorer" to cross the Pacific, stands on her own, even in that age of colonial brutality.

For years after his return from the 1567 expedition, Mendaña kept petitioning to be allowed to lead another voyage to the Solomons. The young man of twenty-five who had led that earlier venture was an elderly fifty-three before the request was granted. The Pacific was no longer a Spanish lake, and Spain had need to consolidate her claim to the unknown southern continent of which the Solomons were believed to be outliers. In the interval between Mendaña's two expeditions, Drake had come and gone, Cavendish had wreaked even greater havoc eight years later, and Hawkins had followed in 1593.

This was to be a colonizing venture, so there were wives and children among the 378 people who sailed from Peru, with banners flying and music playing, on 16 June 1595. But even before the start, the seeds of disaster were only too apparent. Mendaña, never a strong leader, had little control over Doña Isabel and her three brothers, nor yet over the quarrelsome campmaster and his soldiers. The one admirable figure in the expedition was the Portuguese pilot (Portugal was now united with Spain), Pedro Fernandez de Quiros. He was disgusted by the bickering and greed that marked the preparations and was only persuaded with difficulty to remain. On Mendaña's orders the five charts Quiros drew showed only a short stretch of Peruvian coast and two of the Solomon Islands, laid down fifteen hundred Spanish leagues (ten thousand kilometres) from Lima; if more were shown, Mendaña believed, the ships might desert.

The expedition was privately financed, and this was part of the trouble. Provisions were so skimped that the would-be colonists, down-and-outs and the sweepings of Callao, were forced to bring their own rations. One ship had been bought with Doña Isabel's dowry, but it was in such poor shape that it was forcibly exchanged for another, the *Santa Ysabel*. The other vessels were the *San Gerónimo*, flagship, the frigate *Santa Catalina*, and the galliot *San Felipe*.

The fleet proceeded a little north of Mendaña's previous track, and on 21 July came to "The Land of Men", the Marquesas, the first archipelago in Eastern Polynesia to be settled by the people of Vava'u and Samoa, and now the first major group in Polynesia to taste, to their cost, Western Christian civilization.

By way of entr'acte, seven or eight Islanders were shot on minimal provocation the first day. The following morning a watering party of twenty soldiers going ashore on Tahuata Island were hemmed in by curious sightseers in canoes—obviously not a war party, since they included women and children. Just to establish proper relationships of "respect" with the "Indians" the soldiers wantonly opened fire. One Marquesan jumped overboard from his canoe with a child in his arms, and a soldier killed them both with a single shot, "lest he should loose his reputation as a good marksman". What would such fame serve him, exclaimed the disgusted Quiros, if he entered into hell!

Twice in the days that followed, unarmed Islanders bringing food to the ships were shot and killed, and three of their bodies were hung from a yard-arm. In answer to Quiros's protests one soldier explained that he killed "because he liked to kill". Mendaña had little say over these atrocities. A camp was established ashore; he urged that a colony be established, but despite the richness of the fertile island and the beauty of the pale-skinned women, who were said by Quiros to outrival even the famed beauties of Lima, no colonists were forthcoming. They preferred to wait for a land where their magic loadstone, gold, was to be had in abundance. Farming was very far from their taste.

The soldiers encamped ashore began to quarrel among themselves, and there were more murders of the patient Marquesans. To set against this, at least in the eyes of the vicar and two priests with the expedition, one Marquesan learned to make the sign of the Cross and say "Jesu Maria". Before the ships mercifully resumed their voyage on 5 August, three crosses were raised ashore—poor compensation, said the humane Quiros, for the estimated two hundred Islanders who had been slaughtered, both through deliberate policy and wanton blood-lust. Such evil deeds, he added, "were not things to do, nor to praise, nor to allow, nor to refrain from punishing if the occasion permits". Sadly there was no one in authority with the will or strength of character to punish.

The Marquesas lie no more than half-way to the Solomons from Peru, but so vague were the ideas of longitude at this period that Mendaña expected to sight the Solomons from day to day. Irritation, dissention, and incipient mutiny spread among the cut-throats and dubious women who made up the expedition; feuding broke out between the murderous old camp-master and Doña Isabel's no less criminal, if aristocratic, brothers. The ships passed the atolls of Pukapuka in the Cooks (not to be confused with Pukapuka in the Tuamotus, seen by Magellan) and Niulakita in the Tuvalu Group, but at neither place could an anchorage be found. This increased the discontent.

The *Santa Ysabel* became short of water (which was carried in earthenware jars that were readily broken at sea) and of wood—to the extent that her crew began to burn the galleon's upper works. She was crowded with 130 or more people and was underballasted so that she was liable to capsize and could carry but little sail. Thick weather was encountered, and when on the night of 7 September the black silhouette of high land reared ahead, the lights of the *Santa Ysabel* were no more to be seen. The land they had reached was Ndeni, largest island of the Santa Cruz group. Though Mendaña never knew it, San Cristobal in the Solomons lay barely three hundred kilometres further on. As the remaining three ships drew closer to the forested slopes of Ndeni, the perfect cone of the active volcano Tinakula, seven leagues on their right, came into view. Then, the flotilla entered a deep bay on Ndeni, to this day known by Mendaña's name of Graciosa Bay, at the head of which they anchored and prepared to found their colony.

Before we go on to look at the happenings that occurred on Ndeni, let us consider what had happened to the lost *Santa Ysabel*. Before 1971 this question could not have been answered, but in that year Professor Roger Green found evidence of a fair-sized sixteenth-century Spanish settlement, which had probably been inhabited for a year or more, on a hillside near Pamua village on San Cristobal. Both here and at Graciosa Bay, where excavations were also carried out at the site of Mendaña's settlement, were found masses of Peruvian-made Spanish style pottery—mostly the remains of ships' water jars. There is little doubt, then, that Pamua in San Cristobal was where the *Santa Ysabel* ended her voyage, and that a good many survivors lived for some time in a settlement overlooking the empty sea. What became of the settlement is not hard to deduce. Judging by the known behaviour of their compatriots, they would have lost no time in antagonizing the already warlike Melanesians. Tetanus-poisoned arrows, aided no doubt by malaria, would have done the rest.

Back at Graciosa Bay the melancholy sequence, familiar from the Marquesas, was being re-enacted. There were wanton acts of butchery for amusement and "in order that, by means of the chastisement inflicted on them, it might have the effect of preventing greater evils". Only Quiros had the courage to protest, and he did so at the risk of his life. By now the soldiers, sailors, and would-be colonists had become a leaderless rabble. They insisted on building the settlement, against Mendaña's advice, at the head of the bay. Then they complained that the site was ill chosen. Indeed it was, for the fevers for which Ndeni is still notorious began to take their toll inside the stockade on the river flats. "Let us go on to Manila", a Christian country, demanded the malcontents.

The feuds and animosities among that shoddy company cannot readily be disentangled, but they appear to have polarized between the camp-master and Mendaña's brothers-in-law. It was Doña Isabel who put forward the obvious solution: the camp-master and his friends should be murdered. In this she may have had reason. Certainly, the veteran camp-master was among the foremost in ordering the killing of "Indians". On the fatal day, Mendaña, who was now ailing, Don Lorenzo, his eldest brother-in-law, and Lorenzo's two brothers led a party ashore bearing the royal standard to "do justice on the camp-master". Meanwhile a foraging party of soldiers had set out from the camp to the village of chief Malope, who had all along been the Spaniards' staunch friend.

When the camp-master came out of his hut, he immediately took in the situation and called for his sword and dagger. It was too late. At a signal from Mendaña he was stabbed to death and his body stripped. Lorenzo stabbed and killed a friend of the dead man and only Quiros's protests prevented a general massacre.

Doña Isabel came on shore with her sister, the vicar, and an armed party of sailors to where the heads of the two men had been set up on stakes. All were called to mass, where the vicar exorted the company to be obedient and not to be scandalized at the deaths, "for these were ordained". Soon afterwards the file of soldiers returned from Malope's village with the news that a soldier had, for no reason whatever, murdered the friendly chief. This was too much even for Lorenzo and Mendaña, not so much because of the wanton cruelty of the act, perhaps, but because dire trouble for the colonists was likely to ensue.

The ensign in charge of the party was seized and beheaded, his wife's entreaties being disregarded. The murderer of Malope was surprisingly only placed in the stocks, Quiros having pointed out that they could hardly do without any more men. In an extraordinary sequel, however, the murderer of the chief was so upbraided by his comrades that he gave up his will to live. "He left off caring for himself, and died very suddenly after a few days."

The ensign's head was given to Malope's kinsmen, but this last atrocity had been too much even for these long-suffering people. Arrows, spears, and ambushes greeted the Spaniards on every hand, so that they were hemmed in within their stockade. Fever increased its ravages, and Mendaña himself, weakened by worry and disappointment, fell victim. He died on 18 October 1595 and was buried to the rhythm of muffled drums.

The command of the whole expedition now devolved upon Mendaña's widow, Doña Isabel, assisted by her brother Don Lorenzo. However, they would not have seen civilization again had it not been for Quiros. Not that his advice was often heeded at this stage; his protests at breaking faith with the "well ordered" Islanders, who "themselves kept faith", were met by threats of death. But the Melanesians had now been so affronted that all supplies were cut off. Starvation, as well as malaria, faced the colonists. Men, women, and children died every day. Many, the vicar found, had not confessed for years. One dying wretch admitted that he did not know if he was a Christian or a Moor. A poisoned arrow wounded Don Lorenzo in the leg, and he died at the beginning of November. The vicar contracted fever and soon followed him. With only fifteen healthy men left in the camp, the decision was taken to abandon the enterprise and sail for Manila.

On 18 November, seventy-two days after first sighting Ndeni, the defeated expedition set sail, leaving behind the bodies of forty-seven of their compatriots. The ships were in poor repair now, the crews starving; the pilot of the *Santa Catalina* had no chart, nor had he the ability to use one. Not surprisingly, his ship was later lost with all hands on an unidentified coast. Ndeni was left "in the hands of the devil", says Quiros's chronicle. Perhaps it would be fairer to say that the devils departed. Today Craciosa Bay, with its clear streams, little beaches and quiet gardens, is peaceful. The descendants of the murdered Chief Malope retain no vestige of a legend about the Europeans' traumatic visit. Like a forgotten nightmare, the memory of that first encounter with "civilization" has passed utterly from the collective memory of Solomon Islands man.

Quiros laid course north-westward to avoid New Guinea. The galliot *San Felipe* parted company and eventually reached Mindanao. The flagship *San Gerónimo,* soon to be completely alone, continued north across the line. Her gear was rotten, she leaked freely, and every day men and women died of starvation and were fed to the escorting sharks. Daily rations were reduced to half a pound of flour, mixed with salt water and baked in embers, and a quarter of a litre of foul, stinking water. They prayed for rain. Mothers' milk dried up and their nursing infants died. The survivors barely had strength enough to carry the dead up on deck.

But Doña Isabel, the commander of the expedition, had her private stores of water, wine, vinegar, pigs, and olive oil. Her response to Quiros's plea on behalf of the dying company that she make available some of her resources was met by the suggestion that a couple be hanged. The precious water was used by her to wash her hair and clothes, and when Quiros protested, she replied that she could do what she liked with her own property. To this Quiros bitterly responded that she was washing her clothes in the crew's life-blood. Doña Isabel's response to this insult was in character. She began plotting with her remaining brothers to kill Quiros, the one competent pilot who could save them. Fortunately, her plans came to nothing. And Quiros's very gentleness and mistaken loyalty prevented him from dealing with the lady in the effective manner employed by Magellan and Drake at St Julian.

The desperate voyage continued. Both Ponape in the Carolines and Guam in the Marianas were sighted, but landing was prevented in the one case by reefs and in the other by lack of serviceable boat tackle. The *San Gerónimo* struggled on to reach the Philippines in January 1596. Here at last food was forthcoming, though Doña Isabel, ever jealous of her supposed rights and her purse, did her best to discourage purchases from the Filipinos. More than a month was needed to thread the complicated archipelago to Manila. Four Spaniards who boarded the ship at the entrance to Manila Bay were appalled at the misery of the still destitute company, the more so when they saw that Doña Isabel still retained two of her original pigs. "Is it a time for courtesy with pigs?" they asked, with studied understatement, and the animals were reluctantly given up.

Virtue and vice ideally should receive their just rewards, but this does not necessarily happen in real life. Doña Isabel married the cousin of the governor of the Philippines, and the subservient Quiros was persuaded to sail her and her new husband in the refitted *San Gerónimo* back across the Pacific to New Spain.

That Doña Isabel was the first *European* woman Pacific explorer should not blind us to the fact that she was far from being the first *woman* explorer of that ocean. Paintapu, the strong-minded Gilbertese navigator of a war fleet, was a notable predecessor, and the names of heroic Polynesian chieftainesses are preserved in legend. Throughout the ages, steadfast women, side by side with their men, explored in Stone Age vessels and successfully colonized the farthest reaches of the Pacific.

THE LAST GREAT SPANISH EXPLORATIONS—QUIROS AND TORRES

We already know of Quiros's humanity and brilliance as a pilot and navigator during Mendaña's fated voyage. We have also seen that he was hesitant and indecisive in assuming the responsibilities of leadership. This weakness was to become more pronounced towards the climax of his own great voyage. Quiros's letters and reports to the king show him, on the one hand, to be sincerely committed to the overt aim of all Spanish expeditions, the conversion of the heathen and the saving of souls, and on the other, obsessed with a more immediate purpose, the finding of pearls and gold. The accepted method of locating such treasures was to torture the local inhabitants. Quiros abhorred and fiercely rejected such behaviour. He was left with an irreconcilable conflict between his humanitarian ideals and his compatriots' aims and methods.

It is a measure of Quiros's spirit that, even while he was navigating the wretched *San Gerónimo* to the safety of Manila, he should be planning a new expedition to seek for the unknown southern continent. He concluded rightly that the Santa Cruz Islands (Ndeni and its neighbours) were near the Solomons and confidently assumed that the continent he sought lay close at hand. His determination to find it and convert its heathen inhabitants became an obsession. The efforts Quiros made to bring his plan into fruition were extraordinary. His initial approaches having been blocked in Peru, he went to Spain, to the Pope in Rome, to any who might aid his cause. Indifference, shipwreck on his voyage back from Europe, the discouragement of jealous officials—all were overcome. In 1605 he was granted three ships by the Viceroy of Peru and prepared to sail.

The *San Pedro y Paulo* of sixty tons, the *San Pedrico* of forty tons, and the handy little "launch" *Los Tres Reyes Magos* made up the fleet. The company, which numbered nearly three hundred, included six Franciscan friars and four nursing brothers. There were provisions for a year and agricultural implements and domestic animals for new settlements. The deeply religious character of the enterprise from Quiros's viewpoint emerges in the solemn service of dedication before sailing, when the officers were forced to abandon their finery in favour of Franciscan habits. Of Luis Vaez de Torres, the captain of the *San Pedrico,* who was later to assume independent command, we know little. He was a Galician, and his subsequent achievement proved him to be a very fine seaman and an able commander.

Quiros was aged forty when his fleet left Callao on 21 December 1605. His strain of mysticism was to intensify until it was to dominate all his thinking to the exclusion of common sense and the power of decision; nor was his health equal to the recurring crises of the expedition. The plan was to follow a course of large zigzags between the parallels of 30° and 10° south to be certain of coming across the unknown southern continent. Had it been followed consistently many large archipelagos, and perhaps Australia itself, would have been discovered.

As it was, despite stern orders on morality (Quiros had all card tables thrown overboard), discipline, and general behaviour, the crew and pilots soon began to murmur about the cold and the wintry weather. All except Torres, who stoutly maintained that he could see no reason for departing from plan. Nevertheless, Quiros weakly gave in and altered course northward just beyond the position of then undiscovered Easter Island and, after sighting two uninhabited islands near Pitcairn, passed safely through the dangerous Tuamotu archipelago. Here unpredictable currents set between low atolls that rise out of the sea as dark horizon smudges on starlit nights, scarcely distinguishable from rain squalls at five kilometres—and in overcast conditions, are indistinguishable altogether until one feels the fatal scend of the surf. Neither Quiros nor the imperturbable Torres had lost their art, and they came through safely to bring up in the lee of the big atoll of Hao on 10 February 1606.

The Tuamotuans carried spears and clubs, but they did not harm the four sailors who swam in from the break of the surf. Water was the expedition's great need, but they failed to find any and had to content themselves with coconut water. A friendly chief was kidnapped but later released loaded with presents. He showed no animosity, sending Quiros his feather head-dress. This custom of seizing unsuspecting Islanders, resorted to often by Quiros, marred his generally kindly behaviour. In fairness, his motives were generally to convert these ignorant heathens—but also to bring them back as examples of Spain's new "Indian" subjects. In this, Quiros was acting in the tradition of all Spanish explorers from the time of Columbus.

Leaving Hao, the ships continued to thread through the Tuamotus, passing several atolls but failing to find an anchorage anywhere. The acute water shortage was temporarily relieved by the surprisingly modern expedient of distilling salt water with an apparatus they had brought with them. Fifty jars of fresh water were obtained; then the procedure had to be given up for lack of fuel.

Mutinous bickering became rife, a state of affairs the commander was too weak to control. One of his recurring bouts of sickness aggravated his wavering as to decisions about the course. A deviation away from the supposed site of the unknown continent brought the flotilla to uninhabited Caroline Atoll on 21 February, where an abundance of fish and coconuts was found, but no water. (The Spaniards were clearly unaccustomed to subsisting on coconut water and "bleeding" the palm fronds for toddy, as all atoll dwellers long ago learned to do.) The Caroline Atoll is not to be confused with the Caroline Islands, thousands of kilometres away in the north-west Pacific; 370 years later it was to prove a navigational hazard for the uninstrumented Polynesian double canoe *Hokule'a,* described in the last chapter.

The stay at Caroline Atoll did nothing to improve the mutinous spirit of the crew and some of the pilots. All manner of wild tales circulated—that Quiros was deliberately leading them to their deaths, for reasons unknown, or because he was a Portuguese. Let us abandon the voyage, they said, and head towards Manila. The commander made matters worse by issuing threats of confiscation of goods and hanging that he had not the will to carry out; nor would he listen to Torres, who could see no reason whatsoever for abandoning their stated objective, when all that was needed was firmness and consistency.

The ships were now proceeding in the approximate latitude of the Santa Cruz Islands, still far over the horizon to the westward. On 1 March a long line of coconut palms were sighted ahead, and next day graceful mat-sailed double canoes, beautifully inlaid with mother-of-pearl, came out to them. The beauty of the Islanders so impressed Quiros—one boy was "so beautiful and with such golden hair that to see him was the same as to see a painted angel"—that he called the island "Gente Hermosa", the Land of Beautiful People. It was Rakahanga in the Northern Cooks. The beauty of the people and the excellence of their mats, shell adzes, and canoes did not prevent the usual bloodshed, and the expedition left, still without water (the surf was too high), in a worse mood than ever.

It was 7 April before land was sighted again, and the ships came to anchor off a fringing reef in the lee of the wooded hills of the Polynesian outlier, Taumako. Here at last they could water the ship from the fresh mountain stream that enters the sea behind the village. The village, the same now as it was then, is built on an artificial island on the fringing reef, where brilliantly coloured sea snakes writhe at low tide; on the flood the outrigger canoes come surfing in a full kilometre to the base of the village embankment. The Polynesian inhabitants have adopted certain customs from the neighbouring Melanesians, notably the chewing of betel-nut and the use of the bow and arrow. Walking through that sago-thatched village among the loincloth-clad, tattooed men and bare-breasted women, watching an islander shoot fish in the lagoon with his bow and arrow, was an uncanny experience for me—so little seemed to have changed since Quiros's visit so long ago.

The best relationships with any Islanders on the voyage were established on Taumako. The chief was a fifty-year-old man called Tumai. He had "a good body and face, handsome eyes, well-formed nose, colour rather brown, beard and hair turning grey". The volcano Tinakula and "Indeni" (Ndeni, in the Santa Cruz group, where Mendaña had died) was five days voyage away to the south-west, he said. The Taumakoans had heard of the killing of chief Malope on Ndeni and of the head Mendaña had sent his people in attempted expiation. "It was understood", writes Quiros, "that this was the reason why he [Tumai] and all his people showed themselves to be so alarmed when they saw arquebuses, and explained their knowledge of ships and people like us."

Tumai was able to point out the direction and distance away of seventy named islands, ranging from "Guaytopo" (Vaitupu in the Tuvalu group) to "the great country of Manicolo", or "Mallicollo" (Malekula in the New Hebrides) far to the southward. The sixty-foot *te puke* canoes, with their claw-shaped sails and palm-leaf houses on their outrigger platforms, which were staked out in the lagoon, helped explain the three thousand-kilometre range of the chief's largely first-hand geographical knowledge.

TE P

Now at last the expedition resumed its proper course to the southward. The ships coasted past Tikopia and the Banks Islands, all of which Tumai had described. Tumai's "Mallicollo" was never reached, but on 29 April high hills that reared up into the clouds were sighted. This, decided Quiros, must be the long-sought continent. He marvelled that it was for him that God had reserved so great a discovery. A fortnight later he named it Austrialia del Espiritu Santo (*Austrialia*, not *Australia*, named for King Philip III of Spain, a prince of the House of Austria). It was only an island, Espiritu Santo, the largest of the New Hebrides. Torres was sent ahead and found a sheltered harbour bordered by a fertile plain. Here the ships furled their sails and the company prepared to found a settlement.

Quiros's orders were to treat the inhabitants kindly, but when a chief indicated the limit of the land to be occupied by the Spaniards, open war broke out. The Melanesian warriors, defeated by musket fire, retired into the woods, from which they continued to wage guerilla warfare. The disappointed Quiros nevertheless decided to go on with his plans for a city.

The dispositions of the commander were curiously elaborate, and more than a little mad. A Ministry of War and Marine was set up. Calling together the ships' companies, Quiros announced that he was founding the Order of the Knights of the Holy Ghost, in which they were all enrolled and given a blue cross to wear on the breast. After the ceremonials and masses, in which the crews enthusiastically joined, Quiros appointed magistrates, a chief constable, an accountant, and a treasurer. A stockaded church cum fort was built, melons and maize were planted, and all the "region of the south as far as the Pole" was claimed for the crown of Spain. Daily, foraging parties went abroad to gather pigs, poultry, and yams from the Melanesian gardens, and always they clashed with the affronted New Hebridean jungle fighters. Then, quite suddenly, when the expedition had been at their "New Jerusalem" barely three weeks, Quiros announced to an incredulous company that Austrialia del Espiritu Santo was not to be settled after all. They were to sail the next day.

What now occurred is one of the most confusing and controversial episodes of the whole voyage. Departure was delayed until 8 June by food poisoning from eating poisonous lagoon fish. But no sooner were the ships out of shelter and bucking the strong south-east trades than Quiros changed his mind again and decided to return to the bay they had just left and winter there. The *San Pedrico* and the launch made shelter, but the flagship, *San Pedro y Paulo,* was set down to leeward. Next morning she was gone.

For three days Quiros strove to regain the land to windward. At the end of that time the vacillating sick man gave up the fight and sailed for the north and ultimately Mexico. Torres felt he had been deserted, not an unreasonable conclusion. But the weight of the evidence points to the scarcely responsible Quiros having lost all will of his own, of being in the hands of his single-minded pilots, who were minded to do only one thing—to return home.

The Viceroy of New Spain received Quiros kindly. Astonishingly enough, the dream of discovery and colonization, which the explorer had thrown away when almost in his grasp, was far from dead. At his own expense and in dire poverty, Quiros went back to Spain, where he agitated ceaselessly to be sent out again. At his death in 1614 he was still trying.

TORRES DISCOVERS HIS FAMOUS STRAIT

Mystified by the extraordinary disappearance of the flagship, Torres searched the shoreline for wreckage, and finding none, returned to the original anchorage, where he waited for two weeks. At the end of this time he opened the sealed orders of the Viceroy of Peru. They were to search for land as far as 20° south, and if none were found, make their way to Manila. Here Torres showed his calibre as a leader. He was determined to carry out these orders, he wrote, "although contrary to the inclination of many, I may say the greater part; but my temper was different from that of Captain Pedro Fernandez de Quiros."

So the *San Pedrico,* with the gallant little launch in attendance, duly set off into the south-west, though they had at that time "nothing but bread and water" and it was "the height of winter, with sea, wind and ill-will against us", as Torres wrote. They were right to follow this course, he added, for these were not voyages performed every day. The ships proceeded to 21° south; then, as no land had appeared, they steered north-west towards the eastern tip of New Guinea and the road to Manila.

On 14 July in 11½° south, a long line of breakers ahead barred the passage. Torres realized that this was the eastern extremity of New Guinea, for he wrote with his usual taciturnity, "I could not weather the east point, so I coasted along to the westward on the south side." Did he have any foreknowledge that the unknown south coast of New Guinea, which was universally assumed to link up with the dimly rumoured southern land mass not yet labelled New Holland, was really one side of a strait? It seems unlikely. On the other hand, Torres's confident persistence in pushing forward into the unknown along that reef-fringed coast suggests the intuition of a great explorer—an intuition made up no doubt of real clues like the run of tides, which added up to an inspired hunch that here was a way.

Just what route Torres took through the tortuous tide-swept waters of the strait that bears his name has never fully been worked out. However, Captain Brett Hilder has plotted all the information available (there are three accounts) against the Admiralty chart to arrive at some high probabilities. The barrier reef that fringes the south coast of New Guinea a few kilometres off shore is penetrated by many reef passes opposite the mouths of rivers and bays. One would hesitate to try to pilot such clumsy ships in and out among the uncharted coral, but this is what Torres did, for three weeks, during which he obtained wood and water in the bays and estuaries. Then on 2 September "a storm of wind" parted the *San Pedrico's* cable and she ran off to the westward, at first under bare poles. Two days later she came over the edge of a *placel*, or shallow sandy bank, of six to eighteen metres, studded with innumerable reefs and islands, and anchored.

The Spanish word *placel* survives today in English as *placer*, a word used in alluvial mining. The *placel* of Torres was the shallow continental shelf that connects New Guinea and Australia, and the place where he encountered it and anchored can be identified as Bampton Island in 9° south, off the mouth of the Fly River. Torres named the island Maladanza, because of the evil dance he had been led around the coral reefs. These reefs forced the determined navigator to abandon the Papuan coast and head south-west with the predominantly west-flowing current that indicated an eventual opening into an ocean.

This opening into the Arafura Sea and the Indian Ocean was still far off, however. Torres awaited a favourable tide and then sailed under foresails only, trusting that the stream would sweep the ships through the deeper channels; he would anchor on the turn of the tide. A daring manoeuvre with razor-sharp coral on every side, but by its aid the explorers ran safely down what is now the Great North East Channel to come to anchor in Endeavour Strait in 10°48′ south latitude by astrolabe. Cape York, ten kilometres to the south, appeared from this anchorage to be just one more of the mass of islands that surrounded the ships instead of the tip of the great southern continent that they had sought so long.

Endeavour Strait is a good deal more free from dangers than is the deeper passage further north, which is used by modern deep-draught ships. Once Torres had crossed the bar he turned north until he came to the *placel* again, the narrow continental shelf that fringes what is now Irian Jaya. The expedition had been thirty-four days among the shoals. From then on, Torres's account continues, "the sea was clear with good depths. We ran before the East wind which blew fresh, proceeding westwards along the shore and at nightfall we stood out to sea and lay without sails."

The ships were now in open waters, approaching the western cape of New Guinea. They encountered Muslim traders who wore flowing robes and carried muskets, in contrast to the almost naked feather-bedecked Papuan warriors further east. The Spaniards managed to trade a little, especially for a "biscuit called sago", but they were severely hampered because all the beads and bells and knives, as well as the medical supplies and tools, had been on Quiros's ship.

But now this remarkably well-conducted voyage was nearly over. Torres helped the Sultan of Batjan in the Moluccas quell a revolt, but managed to avoid the fate of Magellan. A little further on he found the Portuguese-Spanish colony at Ternate in conflict with its Muslim neighbours and lent his aid, leaving behind twenty men and the launch. On 22 May 1607 the *San Pedrico* anchored in Manila.

So Torres briefly enters into history and, after showing himself to be one of the world's most competent explorers, disappears into obscurity again. More than that, the Spanish authorities, ever jealous of divulging information that might encourage encroachment into their preserves, suppressed the news of his discovery. It was not until 1762, when the British captured Manila, that the English geographer-explorer Alexander Dalrymple found there a copy of Torres's letter to the king. Then at last Torres found due recognition. The strait, one of the most geographically important in the world, was named after him on Dalrymple's suggestion, 160 years after the date of its discovery.

With Torres and Quiros closes the heroic age of Spanish exploration. One of its greatest achievements had been, not the conquest of new lands and unhappy peoples, but the almost unheralded conquest of scurvy, the age-old scourge of mariners.

Just what this meant can be realized when we contemplate the awful death-rates among the crews of Magellan and his contemporaries and learn that both Torres and Quiros lost only one man each.

There was to be one more brief burst of Spanish activity in the Pacific, stimulated by English and French discoveries in the late eighteenth century. These were three expeditions from Peru to Tahiti between 1772 and 1776. It is noteworthy that these Spanish voyages, unlike the British and French, spilled no Tahitian blood.

7

Spain Overtaken

THE ECLIPSE OF Spain as an active Pacific power was an aspect of the struggle of her medieval empire to survive in an increasingly "modern" commercial world. Spain's possessions were immense; the great Micronesian archipelagos of the Marianas, Carolines, and Marshalls, the Philippines, and all Central and South America. Madrid had a hard enough task to hold onto what she had in face of Dutch and English attrition; there was no energy for new adventures. The challenge to Spain's hegemony opened with Drake and continued for more than two hundred years.

CAVENDISH AND THE SHIP "DESIRE"

The annual galleon from Manila to Acapulco was the greatest treasure ship ever to ply the Pacific, perhaps any of the world's oceans. Three times the Manila galleon was captured by the enemies of Spain, each time by Englishmen. They were Cavendish, Woodes Rogers and Dampier, and Anson.

The handsome young court gallant, Thomas Cavendish, was an unashamed imitator of Francis Drake; surprisingly, he proved an able commander in his own right. His ships, the *Desire* and the *Content*, with the small "barke" *Hugh Gallant*, were fitted out at his own expense. They sailed from Plymouth in July 1586, nine years after Drake had set out and with several Drake veterans in the crews, with the object of harassing the Spanish. Cavendish wintered in a sheltered bay not far from the ill-fated Port St Julian; he named it Port Desire after his flagship, a name—Puerto Deseado—that is still retained. The flotilla entered Magellan Strait on 6 January 1587.

The Spanish authorities had not been idle since Drake's unwelcome visit to the South Sea. Pedro Sarmiento, the same

who had been Mendaña's second-in-command in the discovery of
the Solomons, was immediately dispatched to the Strait of
Magellan to intercept the corsair should he return that way.
Sarmiento continued on to Spain after carefully surveying the
passage and reported to Philip II that the strait could be fortified.
A huge armada of twenty-three ships carrying 3,500 people, of
whom 500 were to be colonists, left Spain in 1581. Never again
would heretics be permitted to penetrate to Spain's great treasure
coast. However, shipwreck, the English raider Edward Fenton,
and the vacillation, cowardice, and eventual desertion of the
commander Don Diego Flores reduced this mighty fleet to four
ships under the gallant Sarmiento, before Magellan Strait was
finally entered *two and a half years* after the start of the
expedition.

Further shipwreck and desertions plagued the unhappy
company, but eventually a strong fort was built beside the last
good anchorage before Cape Froward. Here something like 430
men and women, with stores for only six months, attempted to
form a settlement—La Ciudad del Rey Felipe, The City of King
Philip. By now Sarmiento had only one small pinnace left. He
sailed to Brazil for help, was shipwrecked, and both his relief
ships were likewise lost. The colonists at the bottom end of the
world by that time must have been starving. Desperate to obtain
help, Sarmiento sailed for Spain, but was captured by the
English. It is good to learn that Elizabeth, on hearing his story,
had him immediately released. But the unlucky man's troubles
were not yet over. He was taken prisoner and held for ransom by
the French.

Meanwhile, the overcrowded Rey Felipe could not support its
population, and two hundred men were turned out into the bleak
Patagonian winter to fend for themselves. The gardens that were
planted were failures; the abundant fish, fowl, and mussels of the
strait seem to have eluded the settlers; while the Tewelche,
Alacalufe, and Ona Indians, who already had bitter scores to settle
with the Spaniards, gave them no rest.

It was three years after Rey Felipe had been founded that
Cavendish dropped anchor off the now silent and deserted
fortress. One of the handful of survivors, Hernando, was taken
prisoner. The chronicler of the voyage recorded the melancholy
story.

> [Rey Felipe] had four forts [or bastions] and each fort had one cast
> piece in it, which were all buried, and the carriages left standing in

their places. They dug for these pieces and recovered all [taking them aboard the *Desire*]. The city had several churches in it, and seemed to be very well contrived, especially as to its situation, which was the most happy place in all the Streights, for the convenience of wood and water. But miserable was the life which this forlorn remnant of Spaniards had lived there for the space of two years, having hardly anything but a few shell-fish to support nature withal, except they had the good luck to take a deer, at any time, that came down from the mountains to drink in the streams. Their design in coming to this town was to fortify the Streights, so that all other nations besides themselves, should be debarred of passage into the South Seas.

At last they died like so many dogs, in their houses, in great numbers; and the stench of the putrefying carcasses infecting those that survived, they were forced to quit the town with one consent, and go rambling upon the sea coasts living upon leaves and roots and sea herbes, or what animals they at any time happily caught.

Cavendish renamed the place Port Famine. Today nothing remains of King Philip's erstwhile city; dark beech woods sweep down to the shores of the rocky bay. It is still called Port Famine on Famine Reach, but nobody goes there now; it broods alone with its memories.

The Englishmen themselves had a far from easy passage of the rest of the stormy strait. They too were short of food, and the incessant westerly gales, which time and again stopped the flotilla in its tracks, brought driving sleet and bitter cold. It took forty days of incessant striving to reach the Pacific.

Unwisely, an attempt was made to land at Mocha Island, where Drake had fared so badly against the Araucanian Indians. Cavendish did no better. "Arauco is full of wonderful rich gold mines," he wrote, "yet the Spaniards never could subdue it, but always returned with the greatest loss of men. For these Indians are marvellous desperate and careless of their lives, to live at their own liberty and freedom." The expedition was much more successful against the Spanish ships and towns, which they looted and burnt all along the long coastline of Chile and Peru. There was one outstanding difference from the earlier English enterprise: Drake made a point of avoiding unnecessary destruction; he sank no ships and burnt no towns. But the situation was quite different now. England and Spain were openly at war, and Cavendish carried the Queen's commission.

All along, the expedition's hoped-for prey was the galleon from Manila to Acapulco, which was due in Mexico towards the close of the year. The end of September found Cavendish careening his ships, so that they might sail faster in chase, at a little island off Mazatlan, Mexico. Here the *Hugh Gallant,* which was no longer seaworthy, was abandoned. On the evening of 9 October the remaining two ships sailed. Cavendish knew that the treasure galleon, on its way to Acapulco, always made in towards Cape San Lucas, the southernmost tip of the peninsula of Baja California, and it was there that he lay in wait.

On 4 November 1598 their patience was rewarded. They were beating up and down off the headland of California when the trumpeter of the admiral (the *Desire*), "going into the top, espied a sail bearing in from the sea with the cape, whereupon he cried out with no small joy, to himself and the whole Company—'A Sail! A Sail!'" Immediately cracking on all sail and working their way up to windward, the English ships gave chase.

The galleon was the *Santa Anna,* "Admiral of the South Sea", "whereof the King of Spaine was the owner", described by the Bishop of the Philippines as "the richest ship to leave these isles". She was a huge vessel, 700 tons burden as against the 160 tons of the *Desire* and 60 tons of the *Content,* but against their combined crew of nearly a hundred seasoned fighting seamen, the *Santa Anna* carried barely twice that number, of whom a good part were passengers, some of them women. Nevertheless, Tomas de Alzola, captain of the *Santa Anna,* was a brave and determined man. This was to be no easy victory.

The five-hour battle that ensued is best described in the words of Francis Pretty of the *Desire:*

> In the afternoon, we got up unto them, giving them a broadside with our great ordinance, and a volley of small shot; and presently laid the ship aboard. . . . Now as we were ready at the ship's side, to enter her, being not past fifty or sixty men at the uttermost in our ship, we perceived that the Captaine of the said ship had made fights [screens to protect the crew and repel boarders] fore and after, and layd their sailes close on their poope, their midships, with their forecastle, and having not one man to be seene, stood close under their fight with lances, javelins, rapiers, and targets, and an innumerable sort of great stones, which they threw overboard upon our heads and into our ship so fast, and being so many of them, that they put us off the shippe again, with the loss of two of our men which were slaine, and with the hurting of four or five.

Cavendish now tried the tactics that were soon to be so effective against the Spanish Armada. The account continues:

[We] gave them a fresh encounter with our great ordinance and also with our small shot, raking them through and through, to the killing and maiming of many of their men. Their Captaine still, like a valiant man with his company, stood very stoutly unto his close fights, not yeelding as yet. Our General encouraging his men afresh with a whole noise of trumpets, gave them the third encóunter with our great ordinance and all our small shot, raking them through in divers places, and spoiling many of their men.

The *Santa Anna* now being "in hazard of sinking by reason of the great shot, whereof some were under water, she set out a flag of truce."

In the tradition of Drake, the prisoners were well treated. They were put ashore inside Cape San Lucas with a store of provisions, including wine, sails for making tents, and planks to build themselves a pinnace. Before departing, Cavendish provided them with arms.

Fifteen days were needed to despoil the *Santa Anna*. The first choice of the hungry Englishmen fell not on the riches, as might have been expected, nor even on the wine, but on crystallized fruits and sweetmeats from China. But the more serious plundering of the cargo soon took all their attention. The gold coin alone was worth the equivalent of at least four million dollars in present-day money. There were also pearls, 562 pounds of musk as well as other priceless perfumes, and oriental silks and damasks literally by the ton. When the holds of the *Desire* and the *Content* were at last full to overflowing and the *Santa Anna* was put to the torch, there were still five hundred tons of goods aboard her.

Cavendish was a generous commander, and the shares of each man had been agreed on long ago in England. Nevertheless, as was usual in buccaneering ventures, the actual sight of such wealth gave rise to bitter disputes. In the division of the spoils, Pretty tells us, "many of the company fell into a mutiny against our General, especially those in the *Content,* who nevertheless were, after a sort, pacified for the time". But this was no place to linger, when at any moment an armed squadron might descend upon the interlopers. Having taken aboard two Japanese youths and a pilot knowledgeable about the East, Cavendish put to sea on 19 November, "joyously homeward towards England with a fayre wind", and leaving the *Content* astern, they "lost her company, and never saw her after".

So the ill-fated *Content* joined the tragic list of ships lost without trace, while her more fortunate consort followed Drake's route through the East Indies and round the Cape of Good Hope to England. Sails torn in Atlantic gales were replaced by new ones made up from the cargo. The *Desire* returned to Plymouth on 9 September 1588 to an England drunk with triumph over the defeat of the invincible Armada.

When, after refitting, they sailed up the Thames to a heroes' welcome, the gallant *Desire* had been decked out in true Elizabethan style. Her hull and upperworks were splendid in red, black, and gilt, her topmasts were wrapped in cloth of gold and her very sails were made of precious silks of brilliant hue. Nor were her horny-handed crew out of keeping. Everyone, down to the meanest cabin boy, was dressed in silks and satins that a prince would have envied. Thomas Cavendish, like Francis Drake before him, was knighted by Elizabeth.

To Englishmen it must have seemed that the way to the Pacific was now open. But Spain, though her expansive phase was over, was still a mighty power in defence of her possessions. When Richard Hawkins entered the Pacific with a squadron in 1594, eight years after Cavendish, his reception was very different. The entire fleet was defeated and captured by de Castro off the coast of Peru. English keels did not plough the Pacific again for almost a century.

The next period belonged to the Dutch. Within a scant quarter-century of the Netherlands' 1581 declaration of independence from Spain, the Dutch were already ousting the Spaniards from the East Indies and charting arid New Holland. The Dutch East India Company became a monopoly as powerful and jealous of rivals as the royal bureaucracies the Portuguese and the Spanish had established.

LE MAIRE AND SCHOUTEN OF CAPE HORN

The first Dutch attempts on the South Sea and the Moluccas were made via Magellan Strait before the end of the sixteenth century. Sebald de Weert's expedition ended in disaster; the irascible ex-innkeeper Oliver van Noort did succeed in circumnavigating the world, but added nothing to geographical knowledge. It was by way of the Cape of Good Hope that Dutch East Indian supremacy was established, and an all-embracing monopoly it became. The crew of the first Dutch ship to reach the Philippines had been garrotted by the Spaniards; the torture and execution of the English merchants at Amboina by the Dutch signalled their seventeenth-century mastery of the Eastern Seas. Nor was the company any more tolerant of encroachment upon its privileges by its own nationals. It issued a decree that no ship flying the Dutch flag other than a Dutch East Indiaman was allowed to sail to the East Indies either by way of the Cape of Good Hope or through the Strait of Magellan.

This prohibition was not to the liking of a crusty old merchant named Isaac Le Maire. He had not escaped from the Spaniards in his native Antwerp and settled in Amsterdam with his wife and twenty-two children to accept such a restriction in his adopted country. From his reading of an account of Drake's voyage he realized that there was a way of circumventing the monopoly while keeping within the letter of the law. Neither round the Cape of Good Hope nor through Magellan Strait, but below Tierra del Fuego, where "Atlantick and Pacific joined in a wide and free scope", his ships would go.

So in January 1616 the taut ship *Eendracht* ("unity") was boldly beating down the unexplored Atlantic coast of Tierra del Fuego below Magellan Strait. In command was the veteran Captain Willem Schouten, assisted by his brother John, also a sea captain, with Isaac Le Maire's twenty-nine-year-old son Jacob as supercargo, business manager, and overall expedition leader—a rather unlikely combination that worked remarkably well. They had sailed from the little town of Hoorn seven months before, the venture largely underwritten by the local merchants. Soon they were to immortalize the town's name.

But before we follow Schouten's fortunes into the realm of the cape pigeon and the wandering albatross, we must make a digression to avoid confusion. For at that very same time another *Eendracht*, under Captain Dirck Hartog of Amsterdam, was approaching the Cape of Good Hope on its way to the East Indies. Eleven years earlier, in 1605, only months before Torres had discovered his strait, the Dutch pinnace *Duyfken* had coasted Arnhem Land and the Gulf of Carpentaria. More recently the Dutch had learned to use the west winds to speed their passage across the Indian Ocean towards Java. Dirck Hartog took this new route and, holding on eastwards a little longer than usual, came upon the coast of Western Australia. The place where he anchored is still known as Dirck Hartog's Island, and the engraved pewter dish that he nailed to a post is preserved in the Rijksmuseum in Amsterdam.

While Hartog's *Eendracht* was doubling Africa, her namesake had come up with a mountainous land stretching away to the eastward, and separated from the Isla Grande de Tierra del Fuego by the fierce tide rips of a thirty-kilometre-wide passage. The land they named after the States General of the Netherlands, and Staten Island it remains; the new strait they called after Le Maire. Warmly clothed in wool and greased leather as the crew were, and free from scurvy by reason of a quantity of lemons obtained at the Cape Verdes, they were always hungry. Considerable inroads had been made into the five large cheeses that were aboard; dried fish and dried meat were holding out, but the more palatable items were beginning to run short. At the beginning of the voyage each man's daily ration had included a can of beer, rather more than half a pound of biscuit, and three ounces of butter and sweet lard. Now these allowances were much reduced.

Once through the dangerous Le Maire Strait, the *Eendracht* was "russeld mightily by a severe storm out of the West-south-west"—a restrained description of the labouring ship clawing to windward under close-reefed topsails, swept by icy seas that soaked everything below, and with every tortured timber shrieking its protest. After two days the gale eased and came round to north-east, a favourable slant; bleak rocky islands emerged from the murk to starboard. The fearsome cross seas were beyond the experience of even these hardy Hollanders, innured as they were to North Sea winter storms and black south-westers off the tip of Africa—towering hollow billows with fiercely tumbling crests. And, indeed, where could they have known them? For nowhere else do enormous rollers that have swept unhindered round the globe check and rear up towards the cloud wrack as they do in soundings off Cape Horn.

It was towards dusk on 29 January 1616, thirty-eight years after Drake had pointed the way, that the *Eendracht* brought the uttermost point in the Americas abeam and, leaving it astern, became the very first ship to round the continent into the Pacific. Schouten named the grim headland after his home town—Cape Hoorn.

A fortnight later the adventurers were past the Pacific entrance of the strait they had by-passed and well into the South Sea. Now they relaxed, "secure of their happy new discovery", and filled and refilled the wine bowl "which went three times round the company".

Now, while the Dutch were no more averse to plunder when any offered than were their contemporaries, their voyages were primarily trading and commercial ventures in somewhat of a modern sense; neither conquest for its own sake nor exploration was their main object. Young Jacob Le Maire was an exception. Like Mendaña, Quiros, and Torres before him, he was determined to look for the Unknown Southern Continent. He pursued, with greater consistency than Quiros, a southerly track across the Pacific and, in doing so, came upon two significant Polynesian archipelagos.

Before setting out on the long Pacific crossing the *Eendracht* stopped at uninhabited Juan Fernandez, now called Robinson Crusoe's Island, where water was obtained and an abundance of fish caught, but where the ship was unable to come to anchor. So, after two days' stay, they put to sea again "to the very great pain and sorrow of the sick", one of whom, the captain's brother, died shortly after.

A month later the expedition came upon their first South Sea islands, the Tuamotus, and passed through the archipelago more or less along Quiros's route. A repetition of the story of first contact between Westerners and Pacific Islanders occurred at the first inhabited atoll, where Tuamotuans armed with slings and spears tipped with swordfish spikes tried to molest a watering party and were shot down. The Dutchmen also seem to have been the first Europeans to record the extraordinary swarms of flies that so often plague coral atolls—in the absence of any obvious means of sustenance. For the flies of Rangiroa so infested the ship even days after its departure that Le Maire named it "Fly Island".

Leaving the Tuamotus on 18 April 1616, the ship continued westward without deviating to the north as Quiros had done. As these were uncharted waters, Schouten prudently reduced sail at night or hove-to altogether if the weather was thick. After three weeks leisurely progress, the *Eendracht* came up with a craft of a type never before seen by Europeans—a *tongiaki*, or classical Tongan double canoe. The people aboard were "red folk who smeared themselves with oil, and all the women had short hair like the men in Holland, whilst the men's hair was long". (This matter of Polynesian hair fashions was greatly to upset the missionaries, who seem to have regarded the men's long hair as the mark of the devil himself.) The *tongiaki* was probably bound from one of the main Tongan islands to Samoa, some four hundred kilometres further north.

For reasons known only to themselves, the Hollanders sent an armed party in a shallop after the double canoe, and raked it with musket fire, killing several of the natives. Two Tongans were taken aboard the ship, but were later released with gifts of beads and knives, which were surprisingly reciprocated by the ill-used

Tongan warriors in a tongiaki *attacked by a ship's boat from Schouten and Le Maire's expedition in 1616 off the northern Tongan islands.*

Tongans with mats and coconuts.

Continuing on their way, next day (10 May) a peak seven hundred metres high came over the horizon, and a few hours later a lower island one German league (seven kilometres) to the south also came into view. These were Tafahi and Niuatoputapu, two detached Tongan islands almost midway to Samoa from the main northern island of Vava'u. At least four more *tongiaki*, very swift under sail and steered by twin massive paddles, were encountered here. Their crews were entranced by the ship, which dwarfed their double canoes in height, beam, and capacity if not in length. They banged it with stones to test its strength and tried to extract every nail they saw. Not unexpectedly, these activities and other incidents resulted in bloodshed, in one instance by way of rusty nails and musket balls fired from cannon.

The Dutchmen were probably quite right in being wary of the powerfully built Tongan warriors with their hanging ear-lobes and waist-long hair, who were to become adept at obtaining their nails by burning ships after clubbing their crews. But then, as in later times, relations were not all stormy, and the Tongans traded pigs, poultry, coconuts, yams, and bananas with the sea-weary Europeans.

Cocos Eylandt

Verraders Eylant

A skirmish between the Eendracht *and Tongan double canoes,* tongiaki. *This and the engraving on page 125 were made by a member of Schouten and Le Maire's expedition.*

A day and thirty leagues (two hundred kilometres) beyond Tafahi-Niuatoputapu the *Eendracht* came to another rugged volcanic island, also inhabited by Tongans, which Schouten and Le Maire named Goede Hope. It was Niuafo'ou, the most isolated of all the Tongas. Its volcanic character was amply confirmed in the mid twentieth century when the population had to be evacuated for fifteen years following an eruption. In true Tongan style, the hereditary chief, Fusitu'a, returned first and lived alone for two years on the island to make sure it was safe before his people returned.

Niuafo'ou fell astern on 14 May, and now a disagreement developed. Le Maire wished to continue westward in hopes of coming across the Unknown Southern Continent, while the sea captain, Schouten, being fearful of not rounding New Guinea and being unaware of Torres's discovery, insisted they turn north-westward. The captain's council prevailed. Five days later the look-outs spotted two high islands separated by a narrow channel. These were Futuna and Alofi, whose Polynesian inhabitants are closely related to those of Samoa further east, though at the time of Cook, at any rate, they were part of the Tongan maritime empire. Le Maire named them the Hoornse

Eylanden, and Isles de Horne, part of French Polynesia, they remain. It was probably in Sigave Bay on the leeward side of Futuna, where a cataract spills down through the rioting tropical foliage, that the Dutch ship anchored. The expedition's stay of nearly two weeks, while not entirely peaceful, was one of the happiest of the voyage.

It is nothing less than a tragedy that only one-sided accounts of the first contacts between Europeans and South Sea Islanders have come down to us. From a later period, the early nineteenth century, there are the journals of Westerners who had been accepted into South Sea Island societies—like Will Mariner, who became a Tongan warrior, and Cannibal Jack Diaper; there is Marjorie Tuainekore Crocombe, a Cook Islander and my adopted sister, whose story of the eventful visit of the schooner *Goodenough* to Rarotonga, compiled from local tradition, is a masterpiece (these we will come to in later chapters). But from Le Maire and Schouten's time there is nothing. An even earlier incident that is illuminated by a knowledge of Polynesian custom, however, is Mendaña's reception in the Marquesas in 1595. White-bearded tribal elders had paddled their canoes round the Spanish ships waving palm fronds. This was rather naturally taken by the foreigners as a sign of peace, so they were understandably annoyed when the Marquesans later attacked them. Of course, far from performing a kind of Palm Sunday ritual, the priests of Tangaroa were making magic to remove the unwanted devil-beings; when the magic failed to work, it was the turn of the warriors.

We can only guess, therefore, at the reactions of the Tongans and Futunans to the things from another world—creatures whose incomprehensible equipment and patent ignorance of proper behaviour effectively removed them from any kinship category and put them outside *Maoritangi* (the right and correct way) altogether. For their part, the Western captains were responsible for the safety of their clumsy vessels on dangerous uncharted coasts; the requirements of safety from attack, fresh food, and fresh water were for them imperative.

This being so, the encounters at Futuna could easily have been more traumatic than they were. Friendly relations were established after an initial clash. Hostages were exchanged, but soon the sailors "got to be as free and easy as if we had been at home". They admired the physique of the Polynesians and were impressed by their accomplishments: the graceful dances of the young women before their chief to the rhythm of hollow log drums; the obvious religious zeal manifested by incessant praying "with much shouting and raving"; the agility of an under chief at climbing "cocker-nut" trees and husking the nuts on a sharpened stake. The workmanship of the four-metre-high circular palm-thatched houses was admired, as was the artistry of the "crowns of feathers" with which some of the officers were presented.

The hospitable Islanders feasted the sea-weary visitors on pigs, yams, and plantains cooked in an earth oven. Green drinking coconuts provided the usual beverage, but on ceremonial occasions the strangers were introduced to a far less familiar drink. A green herb was chewed into fragments, then stirred and kneaded with water in a large wooden trough. This, though the Dutchmen did not know it, was the sacred *kava;* their reluctance to partake of it must have offended their good-natured hosts. By way of return entertainment, the ship's trumpets were blown and drums were beaten. A discharge of cannon, however, was less successful, as it sent the terrified Fortunans racing into the bush.

Despite all this cordiality, the Islanders showed no reluctance to see the ship depart. Pigs were presented, which by then must have represented the last reserves of these tropical subsistence farmers. Under the circumstances, the return gifts of four knives, three small copper buckets, some beads, and twelve used nails were hardly overgenerous, though the two anchors that were foul in the coral and abandoned were doubtless salvaged subsequently by the near-amphibious Futunan divers.

Eighteen days passed and the expedition came upon a low atoll, where the Polynesian canoemen were heavily tattooed and armed with bows and arrows. This was the Polynesian outlier Nukumanu. Next day the land mass of New Ireland came up on the port bow (Schouten quite reasonably took it for New Guinea), and here began a succession of skirmishes with Melanesian warriors which continued along the coasts of New Hanover and the Admiralty Islands.

Most of the islands that the *Eendracht* was passing had never before been seen by Europeans. Often separate islands were taken to be one continuous coastline, and Schouten continued in his opinion that this was the north coast of New Guinea, whereas in reality they were skirting the arc of islands that extends some 250 kilometres off shore. At long last they came upon islands where Malay was spoken; they had reached the waters of the Dutch East Indies. On 28 October 1616, almost eighteen months after leaving Holland, the *Eendracht* ended her voyage at the Dutch East India Company's factory at Jacatra (now Jakarta) in Java.

It would be pleasing to record that the powerful state company took the perfectly constitutional breaking of their monopoly in good part. But it was not so. The *Eendracht* and all her cargo were confiscated; Schouten and Le Maire, with those of the crew who did not wish to take service with the company, were shipped home to Holland in the fleet of Joris van Speilbergen. Young Jacob Le Maire died en route—it was said from a broken heart. Indomitable old Isaac Le Maire, however, continued the fight to clear his son's name—and retrieve his own investment. After two years' litigation he was successful. The company was forced to return the ship and refund with interest the value of her cargo.

WILLIAM DAMPIER, BUCCANEER AND SCIENTIFIC EXPLORER

The terms *buccaneer, privateer,* and *pirate* are often confused. Buccaneers were English-speaking logwood cutters and hunters of wild cattle who maintained with musket and cutlass precarious settlements along the Central American coasts and off-shore islands from Belize and the Bay Islands off Honduras to the Mosquito Coast of Nicaragua. Their descendants are still there and remain the outstanding seamen of the Caribbean. Their English is quaint and archaic; I recall, when storm-driven to seek refuge in Roatan in the Bay Islands, that a dug-out canoe was termed *dory,* and *vessel* was pronounced "wessel". The original buccaneers, in addition to being sailors and doughty fighters, got their name through the sun dried beef—*bucan*—that they traded. (*Bucan* is of course identical with the Australian "jerky" and the Chilean *charque* and Brazilian *xerque*—both more or less pronounced "jerky".)

Now, in addition to defending themselves against the Spaniards, who claimed Central America, the buccaneers supplemented their incomes much as the old Norsemen had done—they went a-raiding. This was not a haphazard operation. The captain of a buccaneering ship in the seventeenth century made sure he held a commission—nominally from the King of France; generally purchased from the French governor of Petit Goâve in Haiti. The rub was that this was a personal commission and, as the mortality among buccaneer commanders was regrettably high, the quartermaster who assumed command upon his demise (oddly enough the quartermaster, not the mate, was second in command among the buccaneers) had no authority and was in risk of hanging as a pirate.

Some, like the heroic Captain Sawkins, cared little for such refinements. "We will bring our commissions on the muzzles of our guns," he told the governor of Panama, and shortly thereafter perished at the head of his twelve men in an attack on Pueblo Nuevo. Others, such as the brutal and treacherous Henry Morgan, betrayed and slaughtered his own comrades to be knighted and become governor of Jamaica.

Pirates, although the distinction was sometimes blurred, had not even token authority; they warred against everyone, including their own countrymen, and every man's hand was against them. They ended their careers, when caught, at Execution Dock or on the gibbet at Port Royal.

Privateers were a good deal more respectable than the sometimes dubious buccaneers. They functioned only when their country was at war. They engaged the national enemy as privately financed warships.

William Dampier played many parts in the course of a long career, which spanned the second half of the seventeenth century and the first quarter of the eighteenth: Jamaican planter, peaceful trading skipper (very briefly), Yucatan logwood cutter, buccaneer, even captain of a king's ship on an exploring voyage. Three times he adventured round the world. His character was full of contrasts. Too hot tempered and emotional to be any use as a commander, Dampier was one of the greatest navigators the world has ever seen, and as a scientific explorer he preceded Cook by more than a century. Indeed, Cook's respect for Dampier's writings was unbounded, and Nelson insisted that his officers study them.

All aspects of natural history and human behaviour were of interest to Dampier. Take, for instance, his treatise on trade winds; it can be read with profit to this day. Then recall the frequent assertion that Australian bush flies have only proliferated into a plague because of cattle dung. Not so, we find from Dampier. The Aborigines of New Holland, he observed, had their eyes so encrusted with flies that "they do never open their eyes as other People: And they cannot see far"—and there were no cattle then in the Kimberleys. Dampier was as observant of natural sea signs as any Pacific Islander. Approaching Guam from Mexico, he remarked on the "clouds which fly swift overhead, yet seem near the Limb of the Horizon to hang without much motion or alteration, where the land is near".

The conditions under which Dampier's scientific observations were recorded were hardly believable. A desperate band flees through the steaming Darien jungle with overwhelming forces at its heels; the exhausted buccaneers huddle for a brief respite round their campfires; all but Dampier, who is carefully inscribing his notes and sealing them in a hollow bamboo for protection against the tropic downpour and flooded rivers. Or take a Sumatran roadstead, with a battle raging in the port; Dampier is spending the night in an open boat tied up to a not very hospitable merchantman. His body is racked with the cramps and misery of dysentery, yet this incredibly heroic observer is engaged in writing a detailed description of an eclipse of the moon!

Originally the future explorer was not designed for the sea at all. But on the death of his parents he was removed from the Latin School "to learn Writing and Arithmetick", and was soon sent to sea in accordance with his own wishes. By 1673, when the twenty-two-year-old Dampier first sailed for the West Indies, he already had voyages to Newfoundland and Java and service in the Dutch wars to his credit.

Something of the calibre of Dampier's shipmates in cruises off Juan Fernandez, the Galapagos, Micronesia, and Indonesia is revealed in an anecdote he relates. An entire fleet of eighteen French ships of war and two buccaneering vessels drove onto the reefs round a desolate Cay. Here "many of those who got safe on the island, for want of being accustomed to such hardships, died like rotten Sheep. But the Privateers who had been used to such accidents lived merrily . . . and they told me, that if they had gone to Jamaica with 30*l* in their pockets, they could not have enjoyed themselves more." The hardy fellows made tents and carefully salvaged anything useful from the wrecks, so that they "were never without 2 or 3 Hogsheads of Wine and Brandy in their Tents, and Barrels of Beef and Pork; which they could live on without bread well enough, tho' the new-comers out of France could not".

This was a period when English buccaneers entered the Pacific either on foot across Panama, when they would rely on Indian dug-outs and captured Spanish vessels, or by way of Cape Horn. Dampier soon became a veteran of both routes. The island of Juan Fernandez, seven hundred kilometres off the coast of Chile, was a frequent rendezvous, but an insecure one since the shelter is dubious and the Spaniards were liable to descend in force without warning. Much more secure were the Galapagos Islands, which straddle the Equator a thousand kilometres out in the Pacific from Ecuador. This unique archipelago, part volcanic lava desert, part fertile uplands, was without permanent inhabitants in Dampier's day. It is a moot point whether or not the ancient *balsas* from Peru and Ecuador had used its anchorages. Certainly Ecuadorian pottery has been excavated, but so too, in close association, have been the clay pipes of English buccaneers. Ecuadorian pottery is not easy to date, and furthermore, no English buccaneering ship would willingly put to sea in the Pacific without Indian fishermen-hunters among the crew. The most favoured were Mosquito Indians from Nicaragua, and Dampier's story of Will, one of the most resourceful castaways ever and a member of this remarkable tribe, we will come to later.

Dampier seems to have come first to the Galapagos round the Horn in 1685 under Captain Cowley. The voyage had been remarkable for the welcome discovery that in the extreme cold of high latitudes "they could bear to drink three quarts of burnt brandy a man in twenty-four hours, without getting intoxicated". It was Cowley who gave names to all the islands in the group, names which the mostly Indian inhabitants were still using in 1968—although more recent and quite different designations appeared on the charts. Fifteen hundred bags of flour and sweetmeats were stored on the islands by Cowley's crew in case of future emergency when they sailed in a fruitless attempt on the Manila galleon. This seems to have been the first systematic use by the buccaneers of this isolated archipelago; it was to continue for over a century.

We will now move south again to the other Pacific buccaneering haven, Juan Fernandez, and relate the extraordinarily parallel stories of castaways Will, the Mosquito Man, and Alexander Selkirk, the real-life castaway who was the model for Daniel Defoe's Robinson Crusoe. Among the ships' companies of each of the four ships that in turn left or picked up the marooned men was William Dampier.

Will's story begins in 1681, when he was hunting goats ashore on Juan Fernandez and was unavoidably left behind after three Spanish ships hove in sight and the *Trinity*, in which Dampier was serving, had to leave hurriedly. The *Trinity's* company ultimately split; one party, of which Dampier was a member, returned to the east coast of Central America over the isthmus, the other, under the foolish and conceited Captain Sharp, sailed the ship back round the Horn. En route, Sharp took a Spanish vessel called the *San Rosario*, loaded with what he thought was lead. One ingot was retained for making musket balls and the prize set free. When the "lead" failed to melt, the buccaneers realized it was rough silver fresh from the mines of Peru. The *San Rosario's* cargo, which Sharp had so readily returned to its owners, had been worth a fortune.

The deserted Will, meanwhile, notched the blade of his machete and with it sawed up his gun barrel, "wherewith he made Harpoons, Lances, Hooks and a long knife; heating the pieces first in the fire, which he struck with his Gun-flint.... the hot pieces of iron he would hammer out and bend as he pleased with stones, and saw them with his jagged knife, or grind them to an edge with long labour, and harden them to a good temper." The resourceful Indian lived well on goats, fish, and seals and made his bed and bedding out of goat-skins. It was three years before a ship, which he recognized as English by the cut of her topsails, stood in towards Cumberland Bay. Having first killed and dressed with wild cabbage three goats, Will came down to the shore to congratulate the buccaneers on their safe arrival. It was a touching meeting, which affected even those tough, bearded cut-throats. The first man ashore was a Mosquito Indian named Robin who, "running to his brother Moskito Man, threw himself flat on his face at his feet". Dampier's account continues: "We stood with pleasure to behold the surprise, tenderness, and solemnity of this interview, which was exceedingly affectionate on both sides; and when their Ceremonies of Civility were over, we ... each of us embrac[ed] him we had found here, who was overjoyed to see so many of his old Friends."

One cannot help but feel that the obscure Will came out of his ordeal rather better than the well-known Alexander Selkirk, who was to follow him on the island. If Will was the inspiration for Man Friday in *Robinson Crusoe,* as some believe, then the relative stature of the White Man and the Black were reversed; it was the ingenious and self-possessed Indian who was the more resourceful.

Not that Selkirk fared too badly. This quarrelsome acting master of the *Cinque Ports* was marooned on Juan Fernandez in 1704 at his own request and remained alone for four years. To anyone who has anchored as I have in Cumberland Bay, above which Selkirk built his hut, his rejection of fish as part of his diet is inexplicable. For I know of no place where fish are so easily taken. "How many would you like for supper?" I would ask my wife and, putting a line over the side, proceed to catch the four or five she requested in as many minutes. Selkirk's complaint was not inability to catch fish but lack of salt, without which they gave him "a griping in the guts"—and this in a climate where you can readily dry out as much salt as you want from sea water in any rock hollow. Nor did he attempt to fashion the hunting gear that Will had; instead, when his powder was spent, he ran down goats for food—a tribute more to his fleetness of foot than to his ingenuity.

Selkirk's rescue we will leave to the next chapter. Dampier had already split up from Selkirk's enemy, Captain Stradling, before the marooning and headed north in the *St George* with sixty-four men towards the Galapagos in an attempt to intercept the Manila galleon. Times had changed since his last incursion into the Pacific. Queen Anne was now on the throne, and England was at war with France and Spain. Merchant-adventurers fitted out ships for service against the queen's enemies (and for profit), and the one-time buccaneers had achieved the more respectable status of privateers.

Not that this new semi-official status did Dampier any good. Coming up with the Manila galleon on 6 December 1704, his shilly-shallying and irresolution threw away a certain victory and allowed the Spaniards time to unleash their much superior armament and beat off the attackers. The disappointed crew split up once more, leaving Dampier to make his way in a rotten ship to the East Indies, where it was confiscated by the Dutch. He arrived in England penniless. It was some small compensation that the queen had him presented to her and allowed him to kiss her hand, but this left him still poor. His solution, a voyage as pilot to the very able commander Woodes Rogers, was a happy one.

$\mathcal{P}$rivateer and $\mathcal{N}$aval Squadron

A CRUISING VOYAGE Round the World", Woodes Rogers entitled his venture. To modern ears the phrase may conjure up pictures of graceful yachts in exotic waters, but in those days a "cruise" meant a cruise after prey—a privateering expedition. Such enterprises were privately financed; the shareholders' interests had to be considered no less than those of one's country and crew. Matters were made no easier when the chief shareholder himself accompanied the expedition, especially when he insisted on playing a leading role for which he was ill equipped. This happened on Woodes Rogers' voyage; the majority shareholder in question was a respected London physician named Thomas Dover.

Dover was a very good doctor. The pain-relieving potion he invented, out of opium among other ingredients, was unrivalled before the advent of aspirin and the like, and still appeared, when I was a young doctor, in the *British Pharmacopoeia* as "Dover's powder". But seamanship and commanding men in action were not Dover's *forte,* a fact which he somehow failed to grasp. Perhaps his resounding title of "Second captain, President of Council and Captain of Marines" went to his head. Not that the *Duke,* of 320 tons, and the *Duchess,* of 260, were particularly sound or well manned in any case. Since there were "not twenty sailors" on board the *Duke* when they left Bristol and few more on the *Duchess,* the flotilla put into Cork to refit and recruit more men.

The ships sailed again on 1 September, their complement still a motley one. "Above one Third were Foreigners from most Nations; several of Her Majesty's Subjects on board were Tinkers, Taylors, Hay-makers, Peddlers, Fiddlers, etc." Woodes Rogers' quiet confidence and sure competence comes out in his next remark: "With this mix'd gang we hop'd to be well mann'd, as soon as they had learnt the Use of Arms, and got their Sea-Legs, which we doubted not soon to teach 'em, and bring them to Discipline.''

The pilot Dampier's previous experience was drawn upon in rounding the Horn and heading north off Patagonia into kinder latitudes. On 31 January 1709 the ships made the island of Juan Fernandez in the afternoon and hove-to. Against Dampier's advice and Woodes Rogers' "inclination", the foolish doctor (now styled "captain") set out for the shore in one of the ship's boats, though the distance was no less than four leagues (twenty kilometres). Not surprisingly, darkness overtook the party, who were then alarmed at seeing a light ashore and pulled hastily back to their ship. French ships at anchor was the probable explanation of the light, and Woodes Rogers made ready to engage.

He stood in towards the south end of the island "in order to lay in with the southerly wind which Capt. Dampier told us generally blows there all day long". In the morning he "lay close aboard the land" but, being kept off by the erratic squalls that are characteristic of that place, he sent the pinnace to investigate. When it returned the origin of the mysterious light was apparent. The boat carried, in addition to "an abundance of Craw-fish" (for which the island is still famous) "a man cloth'd in Goat-Skins, who look'd wilder than the first Owners of them. He had been on the Island four years and four Months." He "had been Master of the *Cinque-Ports*, a ship that came here last with Capt. Dampier, who told me that he was the best Man in her; so I immediately agreed with him to be a Mate aboard our Ship"—a happy ending to Selkirk's solitary ordeal.

The fresh fruit and vegetables that Juan Fernandez afforded, together with goats caught for the men by "the late Governor", as Rogers termed Selkirk, soon recruited the health of the crew, which had suffered in the fearful hardships of the winter passage of Cape Horn. Ships were captured, but little plunder had been taken when the little flotilla resumed its way up the South American coast and the daring plan was conceived of capturing the major city of Guayaquil in Ecuador. And take it by storm they did, Dampier, Courtney (the captain of one of the prizes), Selkirk, and even Dover all distinguishing themselves in the action. The amount of ransom demanded was not forthcoming, so controlled plundering was resorted to to make up the sum.

The restraint exercised by the privateers is demonstrated by their council's decision "that money and women's ear-rings, with loose diamonds, pearls and precious stones", should not been taken. Not that the ladies of Guayaquil always played quite fair. Woodes Rogers relates the amusing anecdote of a house up the river where there were "above a Dozen handsome genteel young Women well dress'd". "Some of their Largest Gold Chains were conceal'd, and wound about their Middles, Legs, and Thighs, etc. but the Gentlewomen in these Hot Countries being very thin clad in Silk and fine Linnen, and their Hair dressed with Ribbons very neatly, our men by pressing felt the Chains, etc. with their hands on the Out-side of the Lady's Apparel, and by their Linguist modestly desired the Gentlewomen to take 'em off and surrender 'em." It is good to know that the ladies felt so little resentment at the privateers (who were under the command of Selkirk) that they "offered to dress 'em Victuals, and brought 'em a Cask of good Liquor".

The ships sailed from Guayaquil "very cheerfully", with "drums beating, trumpets sounding, and guns booming", and headed for Dampier's old stamping ground, the Galapagos. The veteran buccaneer, now in his fifty-seventh year, was unsuccessful in locating an adequate supply of fresh water. This was not surprising. Some of the Galapagos are without streams altogether, their lava slopes being covered with spiny shrubs, among which myriads of marine iguanas scuttle and giant tortoises lumber along. The more fertile islands are watered by mists and clouds that hang about at the thousand-metre level and feed lakes and streams, which, however, sink from sight into the porous volcanic rock before reaching the sea.

Here a bark commanded by Simon Hatley lost company, and all thought him lost. He did indeed experience great hardships after loosing the squadron, some said by reason of his having shot a black albatross. At any rate, Hatley ultimately got back to England where his misadventures formed the basis of Coleridge's poem *The Ancient Mariner*. It was now May, far too early in the season for the Manila galleon, so the fleet returned to Peruvian waters, where it cruised to little purpose. Disagreements about the distribution of these poor pickings brought about an incipient mutiny, which was quelled by firmness and compromise, the officers agreeing to give up a substantial part of their shares to the crew. Woodes Rogers wrote wryly that if any sea officer thought himself well endowed with patience, "then let him command a Privateer".

September found Woodes Rogers back at the Galapagos short of both plunder and provisions, stocking the ships with "land

and sea turtle", and afterwards repairing to the Three Marias Islands off Mexico to refit in preparation for the coming of the galleon. A measure of his thoroughness is the "sham fight" to exercise in the use of small arms the thirty-two Spanish Negro slaves who had agreed to join the expedition in return for their freedom. "To immitate business", redlead was sprinkled over them during the war games. Later, when one prize was unloaded she was found to be carrying boxes of bones "ticketed with the names of Romish saints", and eight thousand reams of papal bulls. The first were unceremoniously thrown overboard, but the latter were used to burn the pitch off the ships' bottoms.

The *Duke* and the *Duchess*, together with a prize that had been named the *Marquis*, took station off Cape St Lucas, the southern tip of Baja California, to await the Manila galleon, just as Cavendish had done with such profit 120 years earlier. And, like Cavendish, the raiders were kindly received by the poverty-stricken Californian Indians. But with all the good will in the world, the Indians could not supply the expedition with the food it now urgently needed, the privateers being forced to "prize decay'd Salt Pork and Beef" and wish they had more of it. By 20 December provisions were so low that they were on the verge of giving up their vigil and sailing for Guam, when "to their great and joyful surprise" the lookout on the *Duke* spied a sail.

The stranger was indeed a Manila galleon, one of the two that year, and she bore the resounding name of *Nuestra Señora de la Incarnacion Disenganio*. Light winds impeded the chase, and it was not until the next morning that the *Duke* came up with the Spaniard, the *Duchess* being still becalmed. For three hours broadside after broadside was exchanged until the superior English gunnery began to tell. A bullet "struck away a great part" of Woodes Rogers' upper jaw, and several teeth, "part of which dropt down upon the deck" where he fell. Unable to speak through pain and loss of blood, the gallant commander continued to direct the engagement by writing down his orders, until the galleon struck her colours.

The treasure galleon was a great prize indeed, but it was now learned that a consort was also on the way. A meeting was held to decide what was to be done, as had been the procedure throughout the cruise. The wounded Woodes Rogers, whose "Head and Throat so much swell'd" that he could hardly speak, was overruled by Courtney of the *Duchess* and Cooke of the *Marquis*. They had been prevented by lack of wind from playing a useful part in the recent fight and demanded that the *Duke* and her company remain at anchor off California while they redeemed their reputations (and their pockets). Woodes Rogers' recommendation had been to mount an attack with full force.

On 26 December the second galleon was sighted and the *Duchess* and *Marquis* engaged. The *Duke* made sail to join them but, since she was twenty kilometres to leeward, she had not much effect in the action that followed. The English were beaten off with a good many casualties and heavy damage to their rigging, and the gallant Spaniard continued on to Acapulco.

The galleon that had been taken, renamed the *Batchelor* after an alderman of Bristol who had helped to finance the expedition, was, against Rogers' wishes, placed under the nominal command of Doctor Dover. Nominal, because although he was appointed captain, captains Frye and Stretton were appointed to navigate, sail, and engage the vessel; Dover, who was most unpopular with the crew, was forbidden to "molest, hinder, or contradict them".

The expedition was now a brilliant success in terms of plunder, which was equivalent to several million dollars in present-day money. All that remained was to get home again. This presented a problem. All the ships had been damaged, and the galleon at the end of its long voyage from Manila had had no food left aboard worth taking. Latin America was much too hot to hold them. In the circumstances, the decision to cross the Pacific to Guam ten thousand kilometres away in hope of obtaining provisions was probably inevitable, though it was a bold one.

A number of the wounded died, their injuries compounded by "Scurvy and Dropsy"; the rest "began to be very much out of order", and were further weakened by having to pump continually. Nor can the "ancient custom of England" of "chusing Valentines", which was observed, have added much to their cheer. Woodes Rogers, in an unwonted departure from fairness, allowed six Negros the same ration as five Englishmen, "which should just keep those that are in health alive". Very welcome to all hands was the sight of Guam, which was sighted on 11 March 1710. "Flying proas", the unrivalled outrigger canoes of the Marianas, sped past but did not linger. It was not until the ships had anchored in the roadstead that the Spanish governor could be contacted. Guam was a weak garrison, and the Englishmen's promise to pay for all provisions and not molest the inhabitants (which they honoured) resulted in ample supplies of bullocks, limes, oranges, and coconuts.

The expedition went on to the Moluccas and to Batavia in Java, where the Dutch, who were currently allies, gave every assistance.

It was October before the "long and fatiguing" but highly successful cruise came to an end in the Thames. For the second time a Manila galleon had been taken. The feat was to be repeated once more; we will come to it under Anson's voyage. But first we owe it to William Dampier to add more about his remarkable career.

DAMPIER'S EARLIER VOYAGES

Dampier's voyage with Woodes Rogers was actually his last, and he only survived it by five years. But the buccaneer-scientist's adventures ranged so widely and covered such a long span that a full chronological account is well outside the scope òf a book of this length. But something must be said here about his experiences in the Pacific Islands and New Holland.

Dampier's South Sea Islands were the Marianas, especially Guam, and it is to him that we owe one of the best descriptions of the glorious "flying proas", which have vanished into history together with the aboriginal Chomoros, who once built and sailed them. The inhabitants of the Marianas (Guam, Saipan and their neighbours) were at this date, before Filipino and Mexican influences obliterated their original culture, closely akin to the people of the central Carolines seven hundred kilometres further south. Dampier noted that the Guam islanders ate no other food but breadfruit for the eight months it was in season; this is the case in Satawal and Puluwat in the Carolines today. The standard greeting, in fact, of a householder to a passing stranger is, "Goodday. Will you come in and eat breadfruit?" Similarly, the great "flying proas" of Guam that Dampier described so minutely were clearly very similar to the slender Carolinian *wa*, which still range far and wide across the open ocean.

"They are built sharp at both ends," wrote Dampier; "the bottom is of one piece, made like the bottom of a little Canoa, very neatly dug, and left of a good substance. This bottom part is instead of a keel. . . . From thence both sides of the boat are carried up to about 5 foot high with a narrow Plank, not above 4 or 5 inches broad, and each end of the Boat turns up round, very prettily. But what is very singular, one side of the Boat is made perpendicular, like a Wall, while the other side is rounding, made as other Vessels are, with a pretty full belly". This is the first European description of a common feature of Austronesian outriggers that change ends instead of tacking—the asymmetric hull. Its purpose is to balance the drag of the outrigger (which is always on the bulging side) and thus mitigate any tendency for the canoe to shoot up into the wind and be "taken aback" by the wind coming on the opposite side of the sail—a mishap likely to lead to a capsize.

Dampier goes on to describe the lateen sails and outriggers of the proas and the method of changing ends. The outrigger was always kept on the same side in relation to the wind, the weather side (a misprint here reads "lee"). The dextrous handling and extraordinary speed of these craft in the open ocean aroused Dampier's profound admiration. "By report, they will go from hence to another of the Ladrone Islands [Marianas] about 30 leagues off, and there do their Business, and return again in less than 12 hours." A round trip of sixty leagues is equal to three hundred kilometres—no mean speed. Dampier further reported (from hearsay) that one of these boats had gone express to Manila in four days. This would have meant averaging over four hundred kilometres a day, an impossible feat even for such fleet craft.

Fortunately, Dampier was too much a scientist to be content with second-hand reports. He tested with his ship's log the actual speed of a flying proa. The passage where he reports the results is a little ambiguous. She certainly logged twelve knots and, in his opinion, "would have run 24 Mile an hour". No wonder Dampier stated: "I do believe, they sail the best of any Boats in the World."

The voyage of H.M.S. *Roebuck* to New Holland is germaine to this book, for Australia is, after all, the largest land mass of the Pacific. On this one occasion William Dampier was a Royal Navy captain, even though his command mounted only twelve guns and carried a complement of fifty men and boys. The aim of the expedition was exploration for future settlement in the islands of the Pacific and the southern continent. The voyage was a disaster; from the start the objectives were compromised by Dampier's taking the Indian Ocean route rather than the Pacific route, thus following Portuguese and Dutch footsteps instead of breaking new ground. But as usual, it is Dampier the observant oceanographer rather than the Commander that compells our admiration. The determination of longitude was still a near insuperable problem, and estimates of the width of the major oceans still varied. Dampier's skill as a navigator brought him to the conclusion that the width of the Indian Ocean (and the Pacific) was commonly exaggerated. Thus, "Ships sailing from the Cape of Good Hope to New Holland . . . find themselves there, (and sometimes to their cost) running aground when they have thought themselves to be a great way off; and 'tis from this possibly, that the Dutch call that part of this Coast the Land of Indraught . . . but I rather think 'tis the nearness of the Land, than any Whirlpool, or the like, that surprises them.''

The *Roebuck* avoided this error and arrived safely at Shark's Bay in Western Australia. She coasted north, past what is now known as the Dampier Archipelago. Soon afterwards the expedition encountered Australian Aborigines (as well as swarms of flies, as we have seen), but no water. Attempts to capture one of the Aborigines, to find out from him the whereabouts of water, failed miserably; a sailor was speared through the cheek and an Aboriginal was shot and wounded by Dampier. Nor were the crew more successful at digging for water in the sand. It seems that Dampier, for all his contact with Amerindians, had no inkling of the scantiness of the resources relied on by hunter-gatherers— provided they roam in small bands as nomads. Because people were encountered, he reasoned that there must be wells or streams in the vicinity. Anyone with experience of the tiny soaks and rock-holes that often constitute Aboriginal "main waters" in Western Australia will realize that he was doomed to disappointment.

Nevertheless, Dampier patiently followed the coast, much closer in than had his Dutch predecessors. The *Roebuck* was repeatedly in soundings over uncharted shoals and plagued by alternating land and sea breezes. The birds and animals that were encountered, the sea snakes, sharks, and whales were all duly noted. But neither drinking water nor a good spot for careening could be found. Fifteen hundred kilometres of the Western Australian coastline had been covered in five weeks, when scurvy began to break out. Dampier abandoned the unrewarding exploration of New Holland and headed north towards Timor and New Guinea.

We will not follow Dampier further on this unsuccessful naval expedition. One misfortune followed another, and the ill-starred *Roebuck* did not even get home again. She sprang a leak and foundered at anchor off Ascension. All her crew got safely ashore and were returned to England aboard a ship of the East India Company.

Although our chronicle of Dampier closes with this unfortunate enterprise, it was of course not his last. Two years after the *Roebuck* sank in 1700, he was off to the South Seas again in command of a privateer (the voyage when Selkirk was left behind), and after that came, his fruitful association with Woodes Rogers in the cruising voyage round the world.

ANSON OF THE ROYAL NAVY

It would seem as if the plundering of Spanish colonial possessions was becoming steadily more respectable in England. The credentials of Cavendish had been dubious, Woodes Rogers was a privateer, but George Anson was a regular Royal Navy captain and his enterprise was an official act of war. At issue was the Spanish merchants' monopoly of trade with their own colonies; it was, said Prime Minister Sir Robert Walpole, a "war of the merchants". Thus the despoiling of Spain overseas was to be part of the role of Anson's squadron.

The fleet of six warships and two victuallers that sailed from England in 1740 was indeed a strong one. It is true there had been difficulties in recruiting soldiers, so that their numbers were made up with Chelsea Pensioners, rudely turned out of their retirement, and two hundred newly recruited marines who had not yet been taught how to fire a musket. Even so, it was nominally a strong expedition. The flagship *Centurion* mounted sixty guns and carried more than 400 men, the fleet as a whole 960. When the surviving ships came together at Juan Fernandez after spending three fearful months rounding Cape Horn in continual gales, 620 men had died. The *Centurion* alone had lost 200. The cause was scurvy. Incredibly, the prevention of scurvy with fresh green vegetables and fruits, practised successfully by the Spaniards a century and a half before, and by Drake even earlier, had been totally neglected by the Lords of the Admiralty.

Happily, by virtue of the fresh provisions obtainable on Juan Fernandez—greens and scurvy-grass, fish, seals, and goats—the sick began rapidly to recover. Selkirk, when marooned on the island thirty years earlier, had amused himself by running down goats and notching the ears of those he had no need of. "The first goat killed by our people at their landing," wrote Anson, "had its ears slit, whence we concluded that it had been formerly under the power of Selkirk. This was indeed an animal of most venerable aspect", bearing many marks of "extreme age".

One ship which was destined never again to rejoin the squadron was the twenty-eight-gun man-of-war *Wager*. Her story is so extraordinary, and even today subject to controversy, that it is worth outlining. The northern entrance to the labyrinth of southern Patagonian fjords is the desolate Golfo de Penas—Gulf of Rocks. Today, apart from a lonely lighthouse, there is no human habitation closer than three hundred kilometres. The latitude is 47° south, just south of New Zealand on the opposite side of the Pacific. Sailing that way in 1965, I was surprised to see by the chart that two prominent hills on a bleak, windswept island on the south side of the gulf did not bear the usual sonorous Spanish names. They were called instead "The Whale's Tits". It seemed probable that crude British sailors had been that way, and so it proved, for the island was Wager Island, and it was here, 224 years before, that the storm-damaged warship had struck on a sunken rock a musket shot from the shore.

Open mutiny broke out from the moment of the shipwreck. The crew armed themselves and proceeded to broach the ship's stores of liquor with such effect that some fell dead drunk into the flooded hold and drowned there. Some thirty lives were needlessly thrown away before the hundred survivors got safely ashore. A sharp divergence of opinion at once arose; the officers proposed to cruise in the boats up the Chilean coast, capture a Spanish bark and rejoin Anson at Juan Fernandez; the crew, to sail through Magellan Strait and undertake the formidable voyage in the ship's boats to Brazil (the Portuguese there were England's allies).

Anson's account of all this comes down firmly on the side of Captain Cheap and the officers of the Wager, as must have been virtually obligatory, but certain facts suggest that there may have been another side to the story. Captain Cheap fell down a ladder and dislocated his shoulder shortly before the stranding. He went below and ceased altogether to direct the desperate efforts that were being made to claw off the lee shore. Compare this throwing-up of the sponge with Woodes Rogers' continuing to direct an action with half his face shot away. Captain Cheap, it seems, was a poltroon, and the fears the crew expressed that he really intended to surrender to the Spaniards may have been well founded. Another important consideration in weighing the actions of the crew is that those of the mutineers who eventually reached home were pardoned, and mutineers in those days were not pardoned lightly.

Whatever the motives, the upshot was that something like eighty men set out in the longboat, lengthened and converted into a miniature schooner, on 13 October 1741, giving three cheers for the twenty officers and men who had elected to stay behind. Many of the longboat party died of hunger; some twenty remained ashore with the Indians at various points along the route; but the longboat itself, with thirty survivors, actually reached Rio

Grande in Brazil on 29 January 1742. Whatever the mutineers' sins had been, their courage and seamanship certainly merited the pardon they received.

Meanwhile, the weak and vacillating Cheap led his party from one disaster to another. Desertion of the barge with six men weakened the party, and only through the help of the Indians did the four remaining officers reach Chiloé and give themselves up. The Spaniards treated them with the utmost kindness and ultimately returned them to England. It is of interest that one of these four officers was Midshipman the Honourable John Byron (grandfather of the poet), who ultimately became an admiral known throughout the service as "Foul-weather Jack". His account of the shipwreck was used by Lord Byron in *Don Juan*.

Anson's ships, reassembled and refreshed at Juan Fernandez, began working their way up the coast of Chile and Peru, taking many rich prizes as they went. The large town of Paita was taken by storm, looted, and burnt. The Spaniards set their losses along the west coast of South America at five million dollars. But the greatest prize of all, the galleon from Manila, caught Anson napping by reaching Acapulco before he could intercept her. Moreover, the galleon's return voyage to Manila was cancelled for that year, since the Englishmen's presence had become known. It should be explained here that the Manila ships carried treasure in both directions. From Manila to Mexico they were laden with the silks and jewels of the Orient; from Acapulco back to the Philippines they carried Mexican silver to pay for these costly goods.

It seemed as if the treasure galleon, a major objective of Anson's, was for ever beyond his reach. His crews were so reduced by the ever-present scurvy that they were not capable of working all the ships, which in any case were mostly rotten. Three vessels had had to be burnt or broken up, leaving the *Centurion* alone, manned by some 350 men out of nearly 1,000 who had set out from England. But there were more places than Baja California for intercepting a galleon. Anson determined on a bold stroke; the attempt would take place off the Philippines. Without telling anyone of his real intentions, he laid course for China, to refit and there prepare for the enterprise.

The *Centurion* would not have reached China, let alone the Philippines, had not contrary winds driven her north of her intended course and brought her to Tinian in the Marianas. So weakened by scurvy were her crew that five hours were needed to furl the sails when they anchored. In the last two days at sea twenty-one men had died; in the two months that the ship remained at the island only ten more succumbed. For Tinian proved to be a veritable paradise, there being "an incredible number of cattle, hogs and poultry running wild on the Island. . . . the woods produced sweet and sower oranges, limes, lemons and coco-nuts in great plenty, besides a fruit peculiar to these Islands (called by Dampier, Bread-fruit)."

The *Centurion,* by displaying Spanish colours, had succeeded in capturing a flying proa with a Spanish sergeant and four "Indians" aboard. The prisoners gave the welcome intelligence that the island had no permanent inhabitants or garrison, but was simply used as a source of beef for the garrison at Guam, to procure which had been the task of the sergeant and his men. The sick were therefore disembarked, and they proceeded to recover with amazing rapidity. Meanwhile, from the "Indians" (they were Micronesians—Marianas Chomoros), and from his observations of the ruins of former habitation, Anson was able to piece together something of the story of the depopulation of Tinian and near-by Saipan, which lay in plain view. The islands had been thickly populated, Anson was told, Tinian itself having supported "thirty thousand souls". (This estimate was considered impossibly high by Anson, and so it was, probably by ten times.) Fifty-six years before, an epidemic had "destroyed multitudes of the people, the Spaniards to recruit their numbers at Guam, which were greatly diminished by this mortality, ordered all the inhabitants of Tinian thither; where, languishing for their former habitations, and their customary method of life, the greatest part of them in a few years died of grief".

The Chomoros were probably being cautious with the strange white man, for as their descendants were to point out bitterly forty years later, it was Spanish massacres that had depopulated the islands. The more fortunate of the survivors had fled south in their flying proas to settle among their kinsmen in the Carolines, where the origin of their little communities is still recognized. The rest were shipped as serfs to Guam, and Tinian and Saipan were left, as Anson found them, *sepi puun*—empty plates.

The English commodore may have had some inkling of the truth, for he added: "These poor Indians might reasonably have expected, at the great distance from Spain, to have escaped the violence and cruelty of that Haughty Nation", but the only advantage they received from their distance was "to perish an age or two later" than the Indians of America. The people who died on Guam pining for their native home had good reason, for "there were few countries more worthy to be regretted than this of Tinian". Leaving aside the relative morality of Spanish and English colonial rule, the Japanese and perhaps the world could hardly concur with the last sentence. Tinian *is* to be regretted, because it was from that island that the first atomic bomb was launched against Hiroshima in 1945. One cannot help but recall that it was on Saipan and Tinian around 1500 B.C. that the Austronesians established their first far Pacific settlements—a sad end to a splendid enterprise.

We have already remarked that colonies of Mariana exiles lived on among their close kin in the Carolines and that their flying proas, so ably described by Dampier, were very similar to the present seagoing outriggers of the central Carolines. Anson was as impressed with the proas as his predecessor had been and made detailed plans of the one he had captured. These drawings mouldered on library shelves until 1960, when the venerable Captain Ratsey, the famous English sailmaker, commissioned the Prout Brothers in England to build a proa to that design. I well remember her maiden voyage. It was March and very cold in England. The thirteen-metre craft's performance was impressive. Soon we felt we were experts and began to race along with the outrigger barely skimming the water, at times even airborne. But alas, we were no Chomoros. There was a sudden gust, the proa capsized, and the Prouts, my son Barry, and I were left floundering most uncomfortably in the Thames estuary. By the time we had been rescued we had developed a hearty respect for the seamanship of the men who had sailed such vessels across thousands of kilometres of the open Pacific.

After two months at Tinian the *Centurion's* people were fit to continue their journey to China, and on 9 November 1742 she reached Macao. By the time she put to sea again on 19 April 1743, her ship's complement had been augmented by twenty-three lascars and some Dutch seamen, and probably amounted to between three and four hundred men. Not until they were well out at sea did the commodore call the crew together and tell them his objective. The tidings were received "with great joy". Despite the formidable reputation of the Manila ships, everyone behaved as if the galleon was already taken, the ship's butcher even saving two sheep "for the entertainment of the General of the galleons".

Anson took station off Cape Espiritu Santo, the tip of the Philippine island of Samar, to await the silver-laden galleon from Acapulco. The topsails were kept lowered in case the *Centurion* should be sighted from ashore. And all day and every day the ship's company were trained in practical small arms shooting and the handling and loading of heavy ordnance. When, after two months almost to the day, the galleon *Covadonga* was sighted, it was a superb professional fighting crew that engaged the Spaniard.

The action was hard fought. Anson had taken the precaution of sending thirty picked marksmen into the tops before laying the *Centurion* along the galleon's lee bow. The sharpshooters aloft soon disposed of their opposite numbers and caused such havoc on the *Convadonga*'s deck that every officer but one was killed or wounded. Meanwhile, the English great guns swept the galleon's decks and put fifty shot through her hull, while the *Centurion*'s favourable position athwart the Spaniard's bow partly shielded her from the enemy's broadsides. Nevertheless, the galleon fought stubbornly, and it was not until sixty-seven men had been killed that she hauled down her colours. The *Centurion* lost only two men in the action, but it must be remembered that she was a warship, armed and crewed as such, while the much larger galleon was a merchant vessel.

In monetary terms the value of this prize was almost beyond belief, for she was carrying silver worth "near a million and a half of dollars" *in the currency of the time*—what it would be worth today is difficult to compute. Of greater moment, perhaps, to the exploration of the Pacific, was the secret Spanish chart of the northern Pacific Ocean between the Philippines and Mexico which was also taken.

Anson's was the last of the great freebooting voyages. In a very real sense it and its predecessors had succeeded in their main purpose—the breaking of Spain's monopoly of the New World and the Philippines. But even so, Anson's voyage was something of an anachronism. There was no hint of the enquiring attitude of mind so characteristic of the buccaneer Dampier. Even the methods of preventing scurvy, so well known to Dampier and Drake before him, had been forgotten. Another era was about to open in the Pacific—the age of the scientific explorers, which Dampier and Abel Tasman a generation earlier had already heralded.

9

The Scientific Explorers

Anthony van Diemen, governor-general at Batavia of the
Dutch East India Company from 1636 to 1645, was an
exception among his trade-obsessed compatriots. He sent
out ships to *explore,* to search for the unknown southern
continent which had so inflamed the imaginations of Mendaña,
Quiros, and Torres. As the widely regarded hydrographer Frans
Jacobszoon Visscher, who was to sail as Tasman's pilot,
expressed it: they should not only determine what lands lay east
and south of the East Indies, but also discover the rest of the
Southern Hemisphere, "whether it be land, sea or icebergs,
whatever God has ordained". Tasman and Visscher made two
voyages with these ends in view, and though the time was well
back in the freebooting era, their geographical discoveries were
only surpassed by Cook's.

Tasman Discovers Tasmania and New Zealand

It was in August 1642 that Tasman's two ships *Heemskerck* and
Zeehaen left Batavia in Java for Mauritius. Here they were
refitted, for Tasman reported the rigging to be "old, Weak and not
much to be trusted", so that he was obliged to add three extra
shrouds for security on each side of the main and foremast. This
seems an inauspicious start for a voyage into the Southern Ocean,
but these measures were the sign of a very fine seaman and a
prudent commander.

From Mauritius the expedition sailed south-east to 50° south,
whence they tended north again as they ran their easting down
before the gales of the Roaring Forties. Tasmania was discovered
on 24 November and named Van Dieman's Land. Along the east
coast only one landing was made, and although signs of
habitation were found, no Tasmanians were encountered.
Headwinds in Bass Strait precluded the unweatherly ships from

pushing westward or, indeed, of discovering the strait at all. Instead, they laid course eastward across what is now the Tasman Sea until the lofty snow-capped peaks of New Zealand's Southern Alps came into view on 13 December. Tasman turned north along the west coast of the South Island and, six days later, came to anchor in a bay on the southern side of Cook Strait.

"We have given this land the name of Staten Land ... since it could well be that this land is connected with the Staten Land [of Le Maire, near Cape Horn] but this is not certain. It seems a very beautiful country, and we trust this to be the coast of the unknown Southland," wrote Tasman in his journal. Here the New Zealand Maoris were met with, and an unfortunate encounter it proved to be.

The men, said Tasman, were "rough in voice and bones, their colour between brown and yellow, had Black hair right on top of the crown of the head fastened together in style and form like the Japanese at the back of the head but a bit longer and thicker of the hair; upon which stood a large thick white feather, their craft were two long Narrow canoes beside each other, over which some planks or other seating was laid" (punctuation was not Tasman's strong point). The sharp-pointed paddles were fully two metres long; the double canoe skimmed along swiftly, and the mat-clad paddlers, after inspecting the ships, sheered off in no very friendly manner.

ABEL TASMAN

The European ships were anchored a little way apart, and later, when the small boat of the *Zeehaen* was rowing between them, a double canoe containing thirteen paddlers suddenly charged it abeam and overran it. The foremost paddler "pushed the quartermaster Cornelius Ioppen in the neck several times with a long blunt pike so fiercely, that he had to fall overboard, whereupon the rest of them set to with short thick pieces of wood". (This was the first European taste of the *patu*—the short blunt stabbing club of the Maori, and of the mettle of a people renowned for their warlike qualities to this day.) Three sailors were killed and another mortally wounded. The quartermaster and the two remaining seamen swam towards the *Heemskerck* and were picked up.

The horrified explorers "shot hard with muskets and cannon", and, says Tasman, "we fired many shots with our forward upper and bow guns by and about their vessels, but struck none." The swamped boat "which these accursed men, luckily for us still let drift", was recovered and, without more ado, the ships up-anchored and hoisted sail. Eleven canoes swarming with warriors came after them; the *Heemskerck* opened fire as ineffectually as before, then the *Zeehaen* scored the one hit of this engagement, so remarkable for atrocious marksmanship, and the canoes "turned with speed for land, two of the Same Setting a type of Tingang Sails". (One would give much for a sketch of these sails, since only one New Zealand canoe sail has survived—a triangular one now in the British Museum.)

But the Dutch had lost all taste for anthropological investigation. They resolved, not unnaturally, "to hold this land's inhabitants as enemies", named the accursed spot "Murderer's Bay" (now Golden Bay), and set off northwards, tracing the whole west coast of the North Island. No further landings were attempted, the names Cape Maria Van Diemen and Three Kings Island at the northern tip of New Zealand mark Tasman's final point of departure on 6 January 1643.

The next landfall thirteen days later was a far happier one. Besides discovering Tasmania and New Zealand, Tasman was the first European to come on the main Tongan islands, of which Le Maire and Schouten had sighted the northern outliers twenty-seven years earlier. The inhabitants of Tongatapu and Nomuka were so friendly that the expedition spent a total of ten days at the two islands, obtaining ample supplies of yams, bananas, coconuts, pigs, chickens, fish, and fresh water. Articles of clothing, knives, and nails were the main objects of barter, a "double medium nail" being worth three to four coconuts.

What the Tongans thought of the strangers is not known. They certainly received them peacefully, for no weapons were seen; nor was anything stolen, apart from the *Heemskerck*'s skipper's pistol and slippers, which were afterwards given back. The Dutch specially commented on the "pants area" tattooing of the men and the grass skirts and short hair of the women. Tongan women are equally as beautiful as their Tahitian sisters, but these rather stolid explorers failed to note their charms; certainly there was no rhapsodizing such as the French visitors to Tahiti were to indulge in the following century.

After his departure from Nomuka, Tasman became the first Westerner to sight any of the Fijian islands (Vanua Levu, the second largest island in the group). The extensive Fijian reefs were avoided not without difficulty, and having added a little more knowledge of the islands north of New Guinea, the expedition reached its base at Batavia in Java on 15 June 1643. Out of the two ships' companies only fourteen lives had been lost.

Despite his great discoveries, Tasman aroused little enthusiasm. He was always the prudent seaman, kept well off shore and never pushed his luck. Certainly, the Dutch ships of the period were exceptionally beamy and extremely poor sailers to windward, though whether they were any worse in this respect than Spanish and English ships of the day is a moot question. The Dutch East India Company directors commented on his lack of perseverance in investigating those lands which he did discover, "leaving in the main everything open for a more curious successor". Again, after a second voyage, this time to the Gulf of Carpentaria, the directors in Holland were assured by the managers in Batavia that these new lands would in good time be explored "by more vigilant and more courageous persons than have been used so far. Exploration is not everyone's business."

Whatever Tasman's failure to exploit his chances, these comments by his superiors seem grossly unfair. Not even Cook, in infinitely more weatherly vessels, put more Pacific lands on the map than did Tasman. Poor gunnery apart, he respected the lives of the peoples he came across. He was solicitous of the well-being of his crews and brought his clumsy ships back intact from untravelled parts of the Southern Ocean and the reef-strewn tropical Pacific. Abel Janszoon Tasman deserves the honour due to a major explorer.

WALLIS DISCOVERS TAHITI

It is ironic that the archetype of all South Sea Islands, Tahiti, should not have been discovered by Europeans until 1767, and then by a rather undistinguished explorer named Samuel Wallis. The *Dolphin*, Wallis's ship, had already sailed round the world under the command of Commodore Byron, the redoubtable Foulweather Jack, who was midshipman on the ill-fated *Wager* of Anson's squadron. The *Dolphin* was a sixth-rate frigate, thirty-four metres long and eleven metres in beam. She was only the second vessel in the Royal Navy to be copper sheathed, an innovation that did not come into general use until much later (Cook's *Endeavour* was wood-sheathed, after the manner recommended by the Elizabethan Hawkins).

The purpose of the voyage was unequivocally to discover the elusive unknown southern continent. Wallis's orders stated that, as there was "reason to believe that Land or Islands of Great extent, hitherto unvisited by any European Power may be found in the Southern Hemisphere between Cape Horn and New Zealand ... an attempt should forthwith be made to discover and obtain a complete knowledge of the Land or Islands". In addition to the *Dolphin*, the incredibly slow and ill-found *Swallow*, under Lieutenant Philip Carteret, was placed under Wallis's command. We shall not follow the fortunes of the *Swallow*, which became separated from her consort off Magellan Strait, except to record that, against all odds, Carteret gallantly kept to grim southern latitudes, discovered Pitcairn Island of subsequent *Bounty* fame, and ultimately circumnavigated successfully.

A word about the *Dolphin*'s officers is appropriate. Wallis was a sound seaman with little of the intellectual curiosity proper to an explorer. To make matters worse he was ill for a good part of the voyage. But while Wallis was not an outstanding figure, his first mate, William Clarke, known on board as "Mr Knowall", was a disaster. He was of a nagging, spiteful disposition and a chronic prevaricator. Constant ill-health was hardly an excuse for his behaviour. It is perhaps significant that, after his return from the voyage, he was not again granted a commission.

Upon the two remaining officers devolved the running of the expedition. Tobias Furneaux, the second lieutenant, was virtually in command and acquitted himself with distinction. It is fitting that he was later to command the *Adventure* on Cook's second voyage. Furneaux's right-hand man was the thirty-six-year-old master of the *Dolphin*, George Robertson, who had joined the navy from the merchant service five years earlier, and had been immediately granted his warrant. A ship's master at this date was a transitional figure. The captain's duty was to fight the ship, and he was not necessarily much of a sailor; the master's role was to sail and navigate the vessel. It is noteworthy that both Cook and Bligh travelled this same road to become officers. On the return of the *Dolphin* to England, the Admiralty granted Robertson a commission antedated to two years before—a most signal mark of approbation. Of all the accounts of the voyage it is Robertson's journal that I have drawn on most in this chapter. One other non-commissioned officer must be mentioned: the master's mate, John Gore. Already a veteran of the *Dolphin*'s first circumnavigation, he proved completely reliable in every crisis. He was destined to be commissioned as third lieutenant in the *Endeavour* and to make his third circumnavigation under Cook's command.

"June 19th 1767 ... at 3 p.m. we saw the land bearing W.½S., it appeared to be a great high mountain covered with clouds." So was *Tahiti Nui, Tahiti Roa*, "Great and Far Tahiti", hub of the heartland of Polynesia, first glimpsed by Europeans. From the first, the proud young Tahitian warriors tested the mettle and temper of the uninvited strangers. The *Dolphin*'s people were desperately in need of fresh provisions, and the ship needed a safe anchorage, to find which much sounding from the boats was necessary. So hostile were the Islanders, who surrounded the barge with upwards of three hundred canoes, ramming it repeatedly and preparing to board, that Robertson, after futilely firing over the heads of the throng, had a marine shoot the foremost warrior. The first blood had been spilt in an inevitable clash of cultures and mutually incomprehensible attitudes. The *Dolphin* hauled off and, after some vicissitudes, including a stranding on the reef now known by her name, came to anchor in the beautiful and sheltered Matavai Bay, some miles east of where Papeete now stands. The troubles were just beginning.

Before we continue the story, however, an odd circumstance should be mentioned. The day Tahiti was sighted, the Dolphin's people were one and all convinced that they had seen high mountains to the south, from which Tahiti projected as a mere peninsula. This, they were sure, was the great southland. In view of this belief, engendered no doubt by anomalous and deceptive cloud towers, Wallis's failure to go south to confirm the new land's existence after leaving Tahiti is inexplicable except for reasons of ill-health. It was left to a subsequent explorer, Cook, to explode the centuries-old myth.

Relations with the Tahitians, while mutually wary, were at first cordial enough. An Islander, standing by the gangway, was butted unexpectedly by the ship's goat and, aghast at the appearance of the the awful creature, immediately jumped overboard, followed precipitately by his fellows. Good humour soon restored the situation, but meanwhile more and more canoes were gathering in the bay with unfriendly intent. It must have taken no little courage for Robertson to put off in the smallest boat to continue sounding. He carried his broadsword in his hand "without the scabert" and wore a pair of pistols. The five rowers, "the smallest lads in the ship", were unarmed, though two marines with muskets made up the party. As hundreds of canoes surrounded and harassed the little boat, the good Robertson cheered his "poor youngstres" with "a dram of good old Rum each", but was obliged to fire more than one shot and the ship to discharge her guns over the heads of the crowd before the anchorage had been thoroughly sounded.

Next day three hundred canoes surrounded the ship and began to trade "very fairly", exchanging hogs and fowls for nails and trinkets. There was a "fair young girl in each canoe", who distracted the crew with "a great many droll and wanton tricks", but not so completely that the sailors failed to observe the stones piled in every canoe. Now, from a great double canoe that lay off a kilometre away, her masts streaming with battle pennants, came a signal from her priestly commander, resplendent in scarlet and gold and high-plumed headdress. A rain of stones showered the *Dolphin*'s decks—"lyke hail amongst us," said Robertson, "which hurt a great many of our men". The ship's grapeshot made terrible reply, so that "the poor unhappy creatures that escaped immediately Jumpt overboard and hung by the remaining pieces of the canoe, until some of their friends took them up". The English mercifully held their fire while the outrigger flotilla, so rudely shattered in this unequal contest, withdrew to what they thought was a safe distance of two kilometres or so and rallied round the double canoe of the warrior-priest.

The gallant Tahitians were clearly re-forming to renew their attack, despite what they now knew of the odds, so the *Dolphin*'s ordnance opened up on the command canoe, blowing it in two. "But what surprised me most," wrote Robertson, "was the resolution of five or six small Canoes . . . who Constantly lay close by their King, and great men, when all the rest fled as fast as they could paddle off—this few poor fellows behaved so brave, that they not only carried off the Lame and Dead men, but they even towed off the shattered ends of the canoe to the end of a reeff."

The next day friendly trading was resumed, the Tahitians waving plantain leaves and green branches in token of peace. Two incidents here illustrate the integrity of the European explorers of this period in their dealings with the Islanders, but also the unconscious blind arrogance of Westerners towards the lands and governments of "primitive" peoples. A seaman, who had been wounded on the head by one of the stones the day before, defrauded an Islander of two fowls. For once the sick Wallis acted decisively. The culprit was immediately trussed to the grating and received "a Dozen of lashes" on his naked back. A stern warning was issued to any who might be tempted to behave likewise. The second happening was the annexation of the island in the name of George III. With all their good will towards the inhabitants, no one on the *Dolphin* seemed to realize that Tahiti had already its own land-owners, chiefs, and lawful government. So, amid good intent, ignorance, and blindness towards the rights of others did the unintentioned assault begin on the high culture of Polynesia.

A long pole was raised ashore to which was affixed a pennant in token of the annexation, a structure clearly taken by the priests of Oro to be an *atua* god figure. They laid offerings of pigs and fruits before it and eventually took it away altogether in return for two fat hogs—somewhat to the bemusement of the English.

They were enlightened the next day. Signal fires had illumined the night, and with dawn came a great flotilla of canoes by the shore, several thousand spearmen along the beach and a great body of warriors, with the pennant fluttering at their head, over the brown of Tahaara Hill ("Skirmish Hill" for Robertson). Once again artillery carried the day and seventy to eighty large canoes, capable of carrying eight hundred to a thousand men, were broken up. This was the last engagement. The Tahitians had absolutely no chance against the weapons of the strangers. They now made peace. As for the pennant, the high chieftainess, Purea, took it to her *marai*, or temple enclosure of Mahaiatea, where it was converted into a *Maro ura*, a sacred girdle, for her semi-devine son. When Cook saw it ten years later it was ornamented with red, yellow, and black feathers.

Trade now became the order of the day. The objects most coveted by the Tahitians were iron nails. The ship needed pigs, fowls, fish, vegetables, and fruit. The sailors wanted above all the proud, free, beautiful girls. Even today it is acceptable for a Polynesian girl, whose social status and freedom have always been higher by immemorial right than anything "liberated" Western women have yet attained, to choose the role of "Firebird"—"free woman"—in preference to that of monogamous wife. The girls were far from averse to accepting nails in return for their favours. Before long two-thirds of the men were obliged to lie on the deck for want of nails to sling their hammocks. The sailors even took to drawing nails from the ship's very timbers, so that eventually, to prevent her from being pulled to pieces, nobody was allowed ashore except for food and water.

One amusing encounter concerned a friend of Robertson's who became much enamoured of "a very handsome little woman", to whom he gave many presents, at first to no avail. She eventually consented to lead him to the seclusion of an outhouse, at which inopportune moment her burly husband arrived on the scene, so that nothing more romantic than fowls and fruit could be exchanged. Some days later, when the woman went aboard the *Dolphin*, her husband insisted on accompanying her aboard and followed her everywhere. Infuriated, the frustrated lady surreptitiously cast her husband's canoe adrift, and it was swept off rapidly downwind. When the innocent seamen went to launch a boat to retrieve the craft, she restrained them forcibly and pushed her husband overboard to swim for it. By the time the poor man had returned from his long swim the artful lady had achieved her desire.

On 11 July a personage of an entirely different order from those previously encountered visited the ship. This was Purea, the high chieftainess whom the English took to be queen of the island. She was "a strong well made Woman about five foot ten inches high, and very plainly drest," writes Robertson. "Her petecoat was White and Yellow and her Gown was Red", but, apart from pearls in her ears, she wore no jewellery. Red and yellow were the colours worn by chiefs throughout Polynesia. Purea's high rank was evidenced by the deference shown her, and also by another circumstance which puzzled the Westerners. When on board the *Dolphin* she smilingly refused all offers of refreshment, and when some of the ship's company dined with her ashore she was observed to touch no food with her own hands but to be fed by two beautiful young women who were seated on either side of her. This was *tapu* (taboo)—in this manifestation, the sacredness of the high chieftainess and the magic power she automatically conferred on anything she touched.

Next day, when Wallis and some of the officers dined with Purea at her pressing invitation, they were impressed with another feature of ceremonial meals in Polynesia—they were eaten in silence. This tradition is still alive; it was brought home to me in the feast that formed part of the sacred rights (*kapu*) for the crew of the double canoe *Hokule'a* when we were dedicated to the service of the ocean on the eve of our departure from Hawaii for Tahiti. Strict silence was imposed while we ate and while we drank the sacred *'ava* (*kava* or *yangona*), and we were forbidden the company of women until we should make landfall a month later. This was as recent as 1976. But the renaissance of Polynesian tradition is the subject of the last chapter.

Purea was not, in fact, the queen of Tahiti, nor was the lofty 107-metre-long building in which she received her guests her palace. It was the *Fare-hau*, or council house, of the district of Haapape, in which Purea herself was a guest. Nevertheless, Purea was a very great woman indeed. The Tahitians were divided into "clans", the chiefs of which ruled over various districts. Relations were controlled by a very precise system of custom and etiquette, whereby no one ruler was supreme. At the time of Wallis's voyage, we are told by Arii Taimai, a direct descendant of Purea, the Teva clan was in the ascendant. Its head was Amo, but he was eclipsed by his wife Purea, a far more dominant character. Their son, Teririrere, born in 1762, assumed from birth the title and sacredness of his father, in accordance with Polynesian custom. So sacred was such a royal heir considered to be that his parents must not walk on his shadow, and at least six human sacrifices would mark the successive stages of his passage to manhood. Purea became her son's guardian, the traditional high status of Polynesian women and her own strong character combining to exclude her husband from this role.

On Wallis's arrival at the great lady's guest-house, he and his companions were dressed in Tahitian robes and massaged by young girls, until the surgeon, warm after his walk and rather overcome by his reception, suddenly removed his wig—to the astonishment and terror of the fair masseuses. On the return journey, the sick Wallis refused the offer of a litter, and Purea herself lifted him over pools on the track as if he were a child.

Robertson, however, seems to have attracted Purea more than the ailing captain. Aboard the *Dolphin* she had one of her sub-chiefs examine his thighs for the traditional Polynesian tattooing, and was as surprised at its absence as at his hairy chest. Robertson would not allow himself to be lifted up as had the captain. But when the sub-chief indicated that he should pick up the lady he gallantly obliged. In his words, "which I did with one Arm and carryd her round the Cabin, this seemed to please her greatly and She Eyed me all round and began to be very merry and cheerful and if I am not mistaken by her Majesty's behaviour afterwards this is the way the Ladys here trys the men, before they Admit them to be their Lovers."

One is amused that the perceptive Robertson later was tactless enough to take so much notice of a "fine Young Lady" that he "almost forgot her Majesty", and when the queen spoke sharply to his young companion he felt impelled to take the girl in his arms to comfort her, whereupon the queen expressed her displeasure so forcibly that the offending one "soon after fainted". Robertson was then firmly seen off the island by the angry queen. Poor Purea! The charms of a beautiful young girl were also to stultify her infatuation with Sir Joseph Banks, on Cook's visit ten years later, when the future president of the Royal Society rejected her favours for those of one of her ladies in waiting. This was not the only cross Purea had to bear. The year after the *Dolphin*'s visit, when forty-six years old and arrogant with power, she so provoked the other Tahitian chiefs that they combined against her and her son, defeating them in a great battle at Parpara. When Cook anchored in Matavai Bay, supremacy had passed from the Teva clan and Purea had been reduced to the status of local chieftainess of Haapape.

By now relations between the English and the Tahitians were so friendly that several parties set out from the ship to tour the island. They found it very pleasant and populous, abounding in walled gardens and irrigated plantations. There were no real villages, the homesteads being scattered widely among their gardens. The inland valleys were heavily cultivated. This is no longer the case in Polynesia. Whether in the Marquesas, Rarotonga, Tahiti, or Hawaii, the picture is the same. Settlement now clusters round the coast, and once fertile valleys are destitute of inhabitants. Combined pressures of convenience for trade and easier control by colonial governments and missions have wrought the change. In Tahiti as in Rarotonga, once the coastal people were Christianized they denied the pagan inlanders their traditional access to the sea and destroyed their fish-traps and canoes, thus hastening the decline of a highly developed ecologically balanced civilization.

Despite its inauspicious beginning, the first European sojourn in Tahiti drew to its close amid expressions of mutual regret. Purea burst into tears at the news of the *Dolphin*'s imminent departure; despite an acute shortage of nails and the fact that inflation had halved their value in "girl units", the crew were no less sorry to quit the island. So it was a reluctant leave-taking, both ashore and afloat, when the *Dolphin* put to sea on 27 July after a five-week stay.

A digression is necessary here to explain an unwitting sequel to the visit, a sequel which was to give rise to much mutual recrimination between two European powers—the English, who made the first voyage to Tahiti, and the French, who made the second. The matter at issue was who introduced syphilis into Tahiti. Syphilis, like potatoes and tobacco, was a gift from the New World to the Old which, by the eighteenth century, was endemic throughout Europe. Although the then current treatment by mercury ointment was ineffective, the disease in its secondary and tertiary stages becomes latent. There is some excuse, therefore, for Wallis's honest assertion that the last case on board had been pronounced cured by the surgeon a full six months before reaching Tahiti. Bougainville's French expedition, which visited the island eight months after Wallis, were to suffer for the deficiencies in English medical knowledge.

The *Dolphin*, meanwhile, heading north-west from Tahiti, came upon but did not land at Uea, a Polynesian island in the group now known as Wallis Islands, west of Samoa. She proceeded thence to Tinian, where Wallis was disappointed at finding the country much less attractive than Anson's journal had led him to expect. Evidently the years of neglect had taken their toll, so that the once luxuriant if overgrown plantations had become obliterated in thorny jungle. Even the wild cattle had become scarce and were hard to hunt. The voyage to England was completed via Batavia and the Cape of Good Hope, and the gallant little *Dolphin* anchored in the Downs on 20 May 1768 after a circumnavigation that had been completed in a year and nine months.

BOUGAINVILLE AND THE NEW CYTHERA

Louis Antoine de Bougainville's circumnavigation from 1766 to 1769 in the frigates *Boudeuse* and *Etoile* must be seen against the background of the lately ended Seven Years War, in which England had effectively stripped France of her most important colonial possessions, and France's astonishing comeback as a world power fifteen years later in alliance with the North American colonies in their unthinkable defeat of Great Britain. Bougainville, who like Cook had fought in the Canadian campaign, played no little part in the rebuilding of French prestige and morale.

Bougainville was a remarkably versatile figure. He was a noted mathematician; part one of his treatise on the integral calculus was published when he was only twenty-two. Even the English enemy were constrained to elect him to membership of the Royal Society of London in 1756. Before ever he turned his hand to navigation and seaborne exploration, he had earned distinction as a diplomat and a soldier. There are strong nationalistic overtones to Bougainville's circumnavigation, which followed a frustrated attempt at colonizing the Falkland Islands, but the current climate of inquiry into every aspect of natural science provided equally strong motivation. The familiar quest for the unknown southern continent was a major object of the expedition.

Wallis had named Tahiti King George the Third Island after his rather dubious sovereign. Bougainville, who was at first unaware of the Englishman's prior visit, christened it New Cythera, after the Greek island (now Cerigo) where the goddess of love and beauty, Aphrodite, first rose from the waves. Allowing for the fact that Bougainville was a scholar of the neo-classicist Enlightenment, which theorized about the "noble savage", his title seems more apt than that of the unpoetic Englishman.

The peaks of Tahiti were sighted on 2 April 1768, and two days later a rather unsatisfactory anchorage was found inside the reef at Hitiaa, well to the east of the *Dolphin*'s Matavai Bay. From the first, relations with the Tahitians and their local chief Ereti were cordial and friendly, marred only by the Islanders' propensity to pilfer, with consummate skill that compelled the victims' grudging admiration. The expedition's stay was limited to ten days, so it is not surprising that much was misinterpreted, from navigation to social structure. However, the visitors' admiration for this friendly, gracious people did not altogether blind them to certain imperfections in this paradise.

"They choose the ugliest among them," wrote the anonymous author of the *Newsletter,* the first printed account of the voyage, "and dedicate him as a victim to the god of evil: they cover him with flowers, and a great throng of people accompanies him to the shore where he is cruelly killed by bleeding: the jugular vein is cut with a sort of knife of mother-of-pearl or a sharp stone. The sacrificed victim is layed out on a wicker mat, dressed in all the ornaments that were his during life; these are reddened with the victim's blood, and no islander would dare touch them or steal them for fear of exposing himself alone to the anger and vengeance of the god of evil."

But the good seemed to far outweigh the bad. "We consider this country as a friend, whom we must love with all his faults," wrote Bougainville. "Nature has placed the island in the most perfect climate in the world, had embellished it with every pleasing prospect.... Nature herself dictated the laws. The inhabitants follow them in peace and constitute perhaps the happiest society which the world knows. Lawmakers and philosophers, come here and look upon the establishment of what your imagination could not even conceive." Ironically, this was written upon the eve of a bloody Tahitian civil war.

Not unnaturally, it was the beauty and proud independence of the women that most impressed the Frenchmen, as indeed it had the English. A young girl standing beside the capstan "negligently let fall her robe and stood for all to see, as Venus stood forth before the Phrygian shepherd; and she had the celestial shape of Venus. The sailors and soldiers rushed to get at the hatchway, and never was a capstan turned with such eagerness." What a rude awakening it must have been when the illness of Venus, a result of the prior visit of the perfidious English (which at first the French were most reluctant to acknowledge), brought a painful return to reality.

This unhappy dénouement was yet to come when the ships departed, which they did with the loss of four anchors and bearing with them Ereti's brother, Ahutoru, amid expressions of friendship and grief at parting. The rest of the voyage, while less romantic and entailing hardship and hunger, was notable for geographical achievement. The Samoan group was re-discovered (the Dutchman Roggeveen had come upon Tutuila and Upolu forty-six years earlier) and named Navigator Islands, on account of the canoes that sailed round the ships as if they had been at anchor. Further westward the southern New Hebrides, south of the islands found by Quiros, were discovered. Bougainville now did what few of his predecessors had had the nerve to attempt; he pressed on directly towards the unknown eastern coast of New Holland.

For a week he followed the parallel of 15° south, carrying all sail by day, and at night creeping forward under reefed topsails with the lookouts at the alert—a bold enough venture in uncharted seas. On 4 June the first breakers appeared; by the evening of the 6th the ships were forced to turn north outside an endless line of reefs, upon which the sea broke with fury. This was the Great Barrier Reef, which Bougainville correctly judged by floating debris to stand sentinel before New Holland. Any attempt to penetrate the barrier with the trade winds blocking a return out to sea was not to be contemplated. The expedition had no alternative but to continue northward.

After crossing the Coral Sea and threading the maze of archipelagos east of New Guinea, Bougainville reached the Solomons, where his most important discovery was the great copper-rich island, now politically part of Papua New Guinea, which bears his name. The Solomon Islanders were far from friendly, the warriors of Choiseul assailing the ships' boats in ten superbly made shell-inlaid canoes; but the arrows of the Islanders were no match for the French muskets. In a captured canoe was found—in addition to clubs, spears, and wicker shields—the cooked jaw of a man.

The rest of the voyage to the Dutch East Indies was under constant threat of famine. The Dutch treated the Frenchmen well at Batavia, but so many were laid low by fevers that Ahutoru called it *enua mate*—land of sickness. They made haste to depart and reached France on 16 March 1769.

The results of Bougainville's voyage went beyond any discoveries he had made. In fact, Tahiti was not a discovery at all, but its impact on the intellectual salons of Paris, and hence on Western social thought, was immense. From the time of the Crusades, Europe had been influenced by Asia, but this was the first time that a non-European society, and a Stone Age one at that, was being held up as a model. Ahutoru aroused more interest than did Bougainville himself. The Tahitian was lionized by Parisian society. He was interviewed and admired by scientists, philosophers, and linguists. He helped inspire Diderot's *Supplement au Voyage de Bougainville,* a philosophical work which enjoyed wider currency and exercised more influence than the explorer's own book. In 1769 Ahutoru was formally presented to Louis XV. As to the "Tahitian prince's" own reactions, his passion for the Paris Opera soon became apparent and further endeared him to his hosts.

Thus began the legend of the romantic South Sea Islands, a conception not altogether devoid of validity. Subsequently, missionary zeal and traders' greed, with the armed support of the colonial powers, were to extinguish and alter much in Polynesian society. Yet through two centuries of overwhelming technological impact and denigration of island culture, something very enduring has remained. Today, as we shall see, the South Sea Island cultures are no longer disintegrating but are advancing.

James Cook

With Cook the Western exploration of the Pacific entered its ultimate stage—in charting, in the natural sciences, in anthropology. Cook left the map of the Pacific in all major respects complete. He delineated at last the mysterious east coast of New Holland and reduced the unknown southern continent to the boundaries of Antarctica. His secret orders instructed him to follow the parallel of 40° south, where "a continent, or land of great extent, may be found to the southward of the tract lately made by Captain Wallis in His Majesty's ship the *Dolphin*", but Cook went much further than this and, on his second voyage, circumnavigated nearer 60°.

James Cook

Viewed from the standpoint of the acquisition of geographical knowledge, the Western expeditions we have considered fell short of complete success. This was not necessarily the fault of the

COOK'S ENDEAVOUR

explorers themselves. Policies of national secrecy had much to answer for, as when Torres's discovery was pigeonholed for centuries. The early ships were unhandy in the extreme compared with later sailing vessels; nor were methods of navigation sufficiently accurate to locate newly discovered lands without ambiguity. Nevertheless, the sum of their contributions to geography was great. The major question Cook had to solve, apart from completing the map of Australia, was whether New Zealand joined the unknown southland, and whether the latter existed at all?

It was on Cook's first voyage, in the bark *Endeavour* from 1768 to 1771, that he mapped most of the New Zealand coastline and thoroughly examined the east coast of New Holland, which he named New South Wales, and Torres Strait. This was the voyage, too, when a long and productive stay was made at Tahiti to observe the transit of Venus and, more important, gather more factual data about Polynesian customs and voyaging technology than had ever been collected before.

The second expedition in 1772-75 was an extraordinary *tour de force* that took the two ships *Resolution* and *Adventure* far beyond the Antarctic Circle through the tabular icebergs to the margin of the pack ice; to Tahiti and New Zealand again; to Tonga, which Cook christened the Friendly Islands, unaware that Chief Finau and his colleagues would plan his murder but be unable to agree just where it should take place; to the discovery of New Caledonia; and, finally, to the charting of the fearsome southern coast of Tierra del Fuego—about the most stormy spot on earth.

It is generally agreed that Cook should never have allowed himself to be persuaded to undertake his last fatal expedition. He had been nearly forty years old on the eve of his first great voyage, and he now had behind him seven years of the unimaginable strain of command of ships in unknown waters—a strain that had broken the health and will of many another explorer. The *Resolution* was no longer the ship she had been when she set out again, in company with the *Discovery,* in 1776 to traverse Bering Strait in search of the North-West Passage. Nor was her commander the man he once had been. No longer was he tolerant of Polynesian pilfering. He was harsh with the Tongans, and on Huahine, near Tahiti, dealt with one "hardened scoundrel" by having his ears cropped. A number of houses and canoes were destroyed on his orders in an attempt to get back a stolen goat.

Whether this irritability and new-found readiness to resort to dictatorial methods precipitated the fatal outcome, we do not know. It could well have been that, coming upon the islands of Hawaii after the dangers and hardships of a passage between Alaska and Siberia into the Arctic Ocean, Cook was near the end of his tether and his judgement impaired. On 14 February 1779 the *Discovery* was at anchor in Kealakekua Bay on the island of Hawaii; a cutter had been stolen; Cook, with a party of marines, went ashore to seize the chief Kalei'opu'u as hostage for its return. He had abandoned the attempt and was retreating towards the boats when the news of a fatal skirmish on the other side of the bay reached the Hawaiians. Immediately they rushed the English party. Four marines were killed before Cook himself was struck down and stabbed to death.

So died the man who was probably the world's greatest

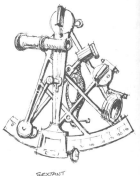

SEXTANT

explorer. For good or ill he had finally exposed the Pacific lands to the eyes of Europe. Their millennia of isolation from mainstream Western, Asiatic, and American worlds was now effectively ended. How did they fare? Part Three of this book is made up of episodes that give glimpses of a Pacific in transition. They range from the narratives of beachcombers, who were uniquely qualified to describe island societies from within, to the beginnings of the contemporary rediscovery and reassertion of ancient values.

THREE
Fa'a Pasifika

HOKULE'A

10

Clash of Cultures

$\mathcal{F}$ ROM TIME IMMEMORIAL the islands of Tonga were ruled by
the Tu'i Tonga, a sacred king who was the highest
representative of the gods on earth, the first of the line,
according to legend, being the son of Tangaloa, god of the ocean.
Around 1470 the twenty-fourth Tu'i Tonga changed the political
system by handing over temporal power to one of his brothers,
while reserving spiritual authority for himself. The temporal
king became known as the Tu'i Kanokupolu. The seat of the
kings was the major (and southernmost) Tongan island of
Tongatapu, the other main divisions of the archipelago being
Ha'apai, including the island of Nomuka, and Vava'u in the
north.

European contact with these main islands began with Abel
Tasman in 1643, followed by Cook in 1773, 1774, and 1777.
Various other explorers, including La Pérouse, Bligh, Edwards,
and d'Entrecasteaux visited them before 1797, when ten London
Missionary Society missionaries were landed from the *Duff*.
These last were singularly unsuccessful. One was soon "converted" by the native women and joined the entourage of a
Tongan chief, some were killed, and the remainder were taken off
by a passing vessel in 1800. The reason given by the Tongans for
killing three of the missionaries is interesting—and perhaps
contains a moral.

In 1796 a Welsh convict from Botany Bay named Morgan was
hidden aboard the American ship *Otter* by the master, Ebenezer
Dorr, and landed on Tongatapu, where "he lived on terms of
great friendship with the natives, and was much respected by
them". Morgan befriended the *Duff* missionaries when they
arrived, and, according to Chief Finau Ulakalala II, they shut
themselves up in a house where they sang and performed

ceremonies. After a time the missionaries quarrelled with Morgan over the possession of an iron pot, and with un-Christian spite told the Tongans that he was an outlaw in his own country whose life was forfeit. This betrayal was a virtual sentence of death on Morgan. "The people began to treat Morgan with every species of insult, so that his life was uncomfortable, and often in great danger." As it happened, there was an epidemic raging on the island at the time. The cause of this pestilence, explained the quick-witted convict, was the missionaries, who had been sent out by the king of England to perform witchcraft and make incantations to destroy the Tongans. "By and by you will all be cut off," he told the chiefs, "and the king of England will take posession of your islands." The chiefs took alarm and rushed upon the three resident missionaries and killed them.

These events coincided with the beginnings of a period of savage civil war and dynastic conflict in Tonga. Though this stormy era may have been precipitated indirectly by a realization on the part of ambitious chiefs of the potentialities of Western arms, the position was very different from that in Hawaii, New Zealand, Tahiti, and Fiji, where there had never been a single all-powerful monarch as in Tonga. Power was shared between district or island chiefs who were equals. This was an excellent and stable system until the islands were faced with predatory and powerful outsiders. Then the complex effects of alien incursion led in each case to furious civil wars that resulted, or aimed at, the setting up of a single national ruler—Kamehameha in Hawaii, Pomare in Tahiti, and Cakabau (Thakambau) in Fiji. Though the civil wars in Tonga were motivated by attempts to usurp the royal power rather than to establish a dynasty, they were bloody enough, and it was half a century before the ancient house (now Christian and in alliance with the missionaries) re-established its authority.

The fighting began in 1799 with the murder of the dictatorial Tu'i Kanokupolu by the unscrupulous Finau Ulakalala of Vava'u. The wives and favourite mistresses of the king, "the matchless beauties of Tonga, perfumed with the aroma of sandle wood, and their necks strung with wreaths of the freshest flowers", were slaughtered also, for Tongan custom dictated that the whole family of an enemy should be destroyed. Finau, before his death in 1809, established his rule over the northern islands of Vava'u and Ha'apai and intermittently over Tongatapu. Much of our knowledge of these events is due to the account of a well-educated English lad named Will Mariner, who lived four years in Tonga from 1806 as Finau's adopted son, and afterwards collaborated with a London doctor, John Martin, in writing his invaluable memoirs.

Will Mariner's Tongan adventure came about in this fashion. The 500-ton *Port au Prince* (formerly *Le General Dumourier*, taken off Port au Prince, Haiti, by an English ship of war and renamed) was commissioned to do duty as a privateer and also as a south whaler. She mounted thirty-two guns and carried ninety-six men when she weighed anchor at Gravesend on 12 February 1805. She was under the command of Captain Duck, and among her company was the fourteen year-old Will Mariner, the captain's clerk.

The ship's first enterprise, the attempted rescue of two English south whalers captured by the Spaniards and detained in the Chilean port of Concepción, was unsuccessful, but her subsequent exploits—plundering captured ships and towns, ransoming prisoners of war, and so on—were highly profitable. Headquarters were established on Chatham Island in the Galapagos (now San Cristobal) in the harbour still known as Wreck Bay. By August 1806, when the respected Captain Duck died, the privateer had accumulated much plunder plus the skins of 8,338 seals and the oil from fifteen whales. After Duck's sudden death nothing seemed to go right. The ship was leaking and in a poor state of repair, and the new captain, named Brown, inspired little trust in the men. Course was laid across the Pacific, with the aim of doing major repairs at Port Jackson or Botany Bay. But the leaks increased, and Brown put in at "Anahooroo" (Honolulu), where the chief refused him permission to enter harbour. Tahiti was the next objective, but being set too far to the westward, the *Port au Prince* made for the next group downwind—Tonga. She dropped anchor for the last time on 29 November 1806 at Ha'apai.

They were greeted effusively, presents of cooked yams and a large hog being brought on board, while Tongans, many of them armed, swarmed aboard. A Hawaiian resident ashore was at pains to reassure the English of the Islanders' good intentions, while some Hawaiians in the crew warned them of the opposite. Captain Brown unwisely believed the words of the first Hawaiian, to the extent of insisting that all arms be stacked below, despite the presence on board of more than three hundred Tongan warriors.

It is clear that the Pacific Islanders had learned their lesson about the power of naval gunnery and were not going to attack

head-on as the Tahitians had fought Wallis. The role of the
Hawaiian as a decoy was a strategy that had already been used
successfully in Tonga, when a shipwrecked survivor named
Doyle had in 1802 instigated the capture of the American ship
Duke of Portland at Tongatapu.

On the morning of 1 December, at a shout of command, the
Tongan warriors fell upon the crew with their clubs. When
Mariner, who was below, came on deck he found twenty-two
bodies with smashed-in skulls being stripped and thrown
overboard. The captain and several others were executed ashore,
but some twenty-five men, Will Mariner among them, were
spared. It seems that the Tongans, while having no objection at
all to killing, saw no reason for unnecessary bloodshed once the
ship was secured and, in any case, required experts to service and
man the ship's guns in the civil war that was raging. Mariner was
a special case, for he had already attracted the notice of the
formidable Finau Ulakalala, who took him under his protection
and later adopted him as his son.

From the beginning the young Englishman showed sensitivity
to Polynesian custom and language. He called out *"aroghah"*
(*aloha*) as a term of peace when he was first taken. When told to sit
down in a hut ashore he immediately grasped the vital point of
Tongan etiquette that requires one always to remain seated in the
presence of superiors. The survivors took longer to understand
another un-European way of acting. No one bothered to feed
them, until at last the hungry Will remonstrated with Finau. The
chief roared with laughter and explained that the custom in
Tonga was to enter any house where a meal was in progress, sit
down without invitation, and join in. He contrasted the Tongan
way with the "ill-nature and selfishness of the white people". The
custom of showing respect by seating oneself and of coming
uninvited to meals are both still strictly adhered to. I was once
very firmly reprimanded by a Tongan lady for my rudeness in
distinguishing between invited and uninvited guests.

The survivors of the crew were made to warp the *Port au Prince*
up to the beach, where she was run aground and anything that
appeared to be of value was removed, including the powder and
the carronades. (Two of these now decorate the lawn of the British
consulate in Nuku'alofa, gifts to their former enemy from the
chiefs of Ha'apai.) While the ship was being stripped before being
burnt, an incident occurred that demonstrated the dark side of the
oppressive Polynesian class system. An Islander, who was
removing the fid from the main-topgallant mast, was considered

by Finau too low class for such a responsibility, so the chief had him shot dead by one of the Hawaiians. When Mariner understood the language better, he asked Finau the reason for such cruelty, and was told that the man was only a cook, a low, vulgar fellow whose life or death was of no consequence to society.

At the time of the taking of the *Port au Prince* the Tongan civil war had been in progress for seven years. Finau was master of Ha'apai and Vava'u, but his eight assaults on Tongatapu had been unsuccessful. The inhabitants of this unhappy island no longer lived in scattered homesteads as they had in Captain Cook's time, but in fortified strongholds, each politically independent of the other. The one-time comparatively peaceful Tongans had not only been fighting among themselves but also taking part in wars in Fiji, where they learned more ruthless techniques. For instance, bows and arrows, formerly used only in hunting rats for sport, became more powerful and supplemented spears, clubs, and slings for the first time in warfare. The cannon from the captured privateer were to end the stalemate.

Four twelve-pound carronades were mounted on specially built carriages and were put aboard great double canoes in readiness for the annual assault on the fortress of Nuku'alofa (the present capital of the kingdom) on Tongatapu. Defended as it was by two four-metre ditches and a double wall of stakes and interlaced "wicker work" of "reeds" three metres high, and overhung by abutments for slingers and archers, the fort was a formidable defensive work. But it was utterly vulnerable against cannon. Indeed, when Nuku'alofa was finally stormed it was found that no fewer than 350 of the defenders had perished in the bombardment. Most of the rest, including the women and children, were slaughtered by the inrushing warriors.

THE 14-YEAR OLD WILL MARINER.

Mariner and his companions were congratulated by Finau for their conduct in the battle. For their part they urged him to follow up his victory by reducing the other forts on the island. But Finau preferred to return to Hapa'ai, and when he next came to Tongatapu it was to find massive cannon-proof earthworks barring his path. I will not try to write a history of the war, but will merely give instances from Mariner's account that throw most light on the manners and customs of this ancient Polynesian kingdom.

Brutal and savage as was Tongan warfare, with its insistence that an enemy's family merited destruction, there was a strong code of honour involved. Apart from the innumerable cases of suicidal bravery instanced by Mariner, there was the Tongan precept of obedience to the chiefs, right or wrong. This obligation was even felt towards one's hosts on a strange island, to the extent of fighting for them against one's own people should they attack the island where one was a guest. The Tongan sense of fair play was very far from that of an English public school, but it was very real for all that. For instance, in a later attack upon a fortified position Finau himself insisted that cannon should only be used against the defenders when they were sheltered behind their earthworks, for it was more honourable, he said, to fight man-to-man and the big guns gave him too great an advantage.

The high status and independence of women in Tonga (as in all Polynesia) made a strong impression on Will Mariner. When the capricious Finau had murdered his half-brother, the high chief of Vava'u, Finau's own aunt took the murdered man's place and roused and shamed the reluctant Vava'u chiefs into going to war against her nephew. In fact, though Mariner did not fully realize it, a sister in Tonga is automatically of higher rank than her brother. He did point out that only children whose *mothers* were chiefs could become chiefs in their turn.

Children, with one terrible exception, were well loved and cared for. Even if a person's own parents were living, he or she was at liberty to choose a foster mother—and still is. (This becomes apparent when one's Polynesian friends refer to more than one person as their mother.) Mafi Habe, one of Finau's wives, adopted Will Mariner and "had afterwards as much real esteem and parental affection" for him as she could possibly have had for her own son. The exception to kindness towards children, mentioned above, was the custom of strangling a little child, usually a chief's son by a commoner, to appease the gods at moments of national calamity. Mariner witnessed such sacrifices twice: once when a *tapu* had been violated by the killing of an enemy inside a sacred enclosure, and again during Finau's last illness.

It is perhaps only fair to inquire what the Tongans of this time thought of Europeans—*Papalangi*. Mariner had this opportunity when a chief and his wife who had been living for two years in Botany Bay visited their homeland again on board a *Papalangi* ship. At first, life had been so uncomfortable, they said, that they wished to die. They had been made to sweep and scrub, protesting to no avail that they were chiefs and unused to such menial tasks. If they saw anybody eating they were not invited to partake; indeed, when the chief lined up at a butcher's shop for what he took to be a food-sharing ceremony he was beaten. At last they understood that in New Holland it was money that made anyone a chief. Despite this bad start, the couple must have adapted to the town, because, having seen the social dislocation and even starvation occasioned by the civil war in Tonga, they elected to return to Australia.

The chief and his wife had travelled on a European sailing ship, but double canoe voyaging, guided by the systematic lore of the stars, sun, clouds, waves, and birds was still being actively practised at this period. Mariner witnessed the return to Vava'u of a chief named Kau Moala, who "for the sake of the excursion, and to mingle with the wars of those people" had sailed away to Fiji. Mariner does not mention it, but Kau Moala was the son of Akau'ola, the High Navigator of Tonga, and was himself one of those master navigators termed *kai vai*, or water-eaters. An analysis of the chief's wanderings is instructive, therefore, about Polynesian navigation. I have compiled one partly from Mariner's account and partly from Tongan tradition, told to me by the head of the Tuita navigator clan, rivals to Akau'ola and therefore unlikely to glorify Kau Moala.

The seagoing part of the saga opens when Kau Moala was returning home to Vava'u from Fiji in his *kalia* double canoe with his followers. This was a passage of 420 kilometres of open sea, and he had sighted his objective, when the "wind becoming unfavourable to land, and the sea running very high", he was obliged to change course for Samoa, which is 500 kilometres from Vava'u, "but the wind soon increasing to a heavy gale, drifted him to the island of Fotoona". Futuna is about 500 kilometres from Samoa and nearly 600 from Vava'u. The canoe, which was loaded with sandlewood, was broken up and a new one built for the chief according to normal Polynesian custom. About a year later he set out once more with thirty-nine companions, including four Futunans who had "begged to go with him that they might visit distant countries". They touched at the solitary island of Rotuma, 500 kilometres to the westward, and thence sailed 430 kilometres south to Fiji.

All the islands visited or aimed for by Kau Moala were well within the Tongan "empire". We know the *kalia* was big, since it could carry at least forty people in the open sea, and the navigator-chief's training certainly included the bearings of Samoa, Futuna, and Rotuma from different starting points, as well as the distances in days' sailing between them and the temperature of the various ocean currents to be encountered. The seamanship and navigational accuracy involved in these passages are nothing out of the ordinary for a trained Polynesian navigator; what was exceptional was Mariner's presence on the scene—and the record he made—when Kau Moala finally returned.

The feast given to Kau Moala by the Fijian chiefs on the eve of his departure reputedly included two hundred baskets of yams, two hundred fowls, two hundred hogs, and the bodies of two hundred slaughtered prisoners of war. On the subject of cannibalism Mariner is at pains to point out that the practice was largely of recent Fijian origin and was not fully accepted by all Tongans. For instance, after one of Finau's battles, sixty enemy slain were "given" to the gods; most were afterwards returned to their relatives for burial and only two or three were cooked and eaten. Furthermore, only about forty men of Finau's army took part in this business, and these, when they returned home, were avoided by the women because of it. Whether Mariner was right about the custom being a Fijian importation, cannibalism was certainly endemic in Melanesia and, New Zealand apart, rare in Polynesia.

Will Mariner was extraordinarily well adapted to Tongan life, and after Finau's death he continued to serve his son of the same name. But more and more he longed to return to his own country, and eventually he obtained the high chief's reluctant permission to do so when opportunity should offer. The captain of the first passing ship he hailed rudely refused to take him. He was left to paddle back miserably, inventing stories to prevent loss of face with the Tongans. A person's reputation is all important in Polynesia and Micronesia. It was considered in Tonga, as in the Gilberts, "better . . . to assassinate a man's person than to attack his reputation". Mariner therefore explained that the ship had been going to the wrong country and had come from a poor land where no knives or mirrors were available.

The castaway's luck changed, however, when the 130-ton brig *Favourite,* of Port Jackson, put into Vava'u, and the captain agreed to accept Mariner aboard. Finau the younger himself came to farewell his *Papalangi* retainer, bringing with him to the ship as gifts five large hogs and forty yams. The high chief dined with the captain, his perfect poise and good manners when handling such unfamiliar implements as a knife and fork quite captivating the ship's officers. So, after four years the nineteen-year-old Mariner began his journey back to London. Here he proved equally adaptable as he had in Tonga. After a voyage to the West Indies he collaborated with John Martin in writing his book, and in due course the former Tongan warrior carved out a successful career for himself in the London jungle—in the office of Mr Edward Hancock, stock-broker.

RAROTONGA, THE "BOUNTY", AND THE SCHOONER "CUMBERLAND"

Rarotonga, largest of the Cook Islands, lies some one thousand kilometres south-west of Tahiti, of which it is a small replica. It was one of the last major Polynesian islands to become known to Europeans, being discovered by Fletcher Christian in the *Bounty* in 1789, after the famous mutiny. The story of the *Bounty*'s wanderings "in search of a home" has been pieced together by the historian H.E. Maude, my one-time chief at the Australian National University. It is to him and to his Rarotongan collaborator, my adopted sister, Marjorie Tuainekore Crocombe, that I owe the main content of this section.

The *Bounty* mutiny took place on 28 April 1789 some fifty kilometres south of the Tongan island of Tofua. Captain William Bligh and his companions were set adrift, and the ship, under Christian with a crew of twenty-five, sailed into the blue. The island of Tubuai, five hundred kilometres south of Tahiti, was examined, and after a visit to Tahiti to procure pigs, goats, and chickens, the mutineers returned to Tubuai to found a settlement. Inevitably clashes over land and women developed between the newcomers and the Islanders. After three months the attempt was abandoned and the *Bounty* returned to Tahiti, where all but nine of the company elected to stay. A remarkable Tahitian traveller named Hitihiti, who had accompanied them to Tubuai, left them at this point. This was not his first voyage in a European ship, for he had accompanied Cook to Tonga, New Zealand, and the Antarctic; nor was it his last, as he afterwards sailed with Bligh in the *Providence*, when breadfruit was at last transplanted to the West Indies.

The *Bounty*, well stocked with growing taro, yam, and breadfruit for the next attempt at settlement, set out westward. She probably called at Mangaia (where an Islander seems to have been murdered). She sighted the previously unknown Rarotonga a few days later.

The account of this visit has been assembled from Rarotongan traditions collected by the first missionaries, and partly from the narrative of a Tahitian woman named Teehuteatuaonoa, or Jenny. She was first the wife of mutineer John Adams but left him for Isaac Martin, eventually returning to Tahiti from Pitcairn on the whaler *Sultan* in 1817.

"There came a very large ship," runs the Rarotongan tradition, "but the people did not land. Two canoes went off and bartered some goods with the white people. . . . As they left a man named Maia stole a large box from the ship, and in it was found the orange and the *motini* (pumpkin). . . . they had *taro* swamps and young banana trees, besides young break-fruit trees" on the ship. "It was from thence we obtained the first oranges."

The populous Rarotonga was obviously no place to settle, for Christian had learned his lesson on Tubuai and was now in search of an uninhabited land. Tongatapu and a Fijian island where the mutineers next called were no better suited, so Christian turned the ship's head eastward towards the uninhabited Pitcairn, which had been discovered by Carteret in 1767. Carteret's published account is known to have been among the books in Bligh's cabin. Here at last, after thirteen thousand kilometres of wandering since the mutiny, the *Bounty* found her last resting place and the mutineers a home.

Despite its discovery by Fletcher Christian, Rarotonga remained unknown to the outside world for the next two decades and more, until in 1813 Captain Walker of the brig *Endeavour* sighted "a new island" which, from the offing, appeared to abound in sandalwood. This was a magic word; the sandalwood groves in Fiji had been exhausted and those in the Marquesas were being kept secret by the Americans, as the scented wood fetched a high price on the Chinese market. Was there sandalwood in Rarotonga? The *Cumberland* (she is usually described as a schooner, but sometimes as a brig, so she was almost certainly a topsail schooner crossing square yards on both fore and main) was chartered in Sydney at twelve pounds a month and sailed from Port Jackson on 20 January 1814 under command of Philip Goodenough, with W.C. Wentworth (fresh from the expedition to find a way across the Blue Mountains) as second in command and charterers' representative. The company was a cosmopolitan one, including a Lascar, two Tahitians, two Maoris—Veretini and Tupe—in addition to nineteen European seamen. There were also two Tahitian women and one European one—the doomed Ann Butcher (known to the Rarotongans as Nati), the captain's consort. A call was made at New Zealand and the schooner arrived off Rarotonga in March.

Subsequent happenings were pieced together by Maude and Marjorie Crocombe from files of the *Sydney Gazette* on the one hand and the writings of Maretu (1871) and other Rarotongan traditionalists on the other. As Maude points out, the Australian sources tell what happened, but the Rarotongan ones explain *why* they happened—about which the white men were generally unaware. Both the social structure and the politics of Rarotonga were a closed book to the visitors.

Though the lush green island is only thirty-three kilometres round and eight in diameter, its precipitous peaks rise to fifteen hundred metres, giving the impression of far greater magnitude. Rarotonga was probably settled by East Polynesians around the seventh or eighth century A.D., but its chiefly lines date only from about the end of the twelfth century, when Tangiia arrived from the Tahiti group and Karika from Manu'a in Samoa (a recent excavation of a house site of about this date has uncovered two adzes, a Samoan and a Tahitian). In time the island came to be divided into three tribal districts or *vaka* (literally "canoe"): Takitimu, descended from Tangiia, with its shallow harbour at Ngatangiia (the people of Tangiia), where canoes are said to have staged *en route* to New Zealand; Aorangi in the west, also descended from Tangiia; Avarua, under *ariki* (high chief) Makea, a descendant of Karika. An uneasy balance of power existed between the three *ariki*, easily upset by frequent intrigues. It was into this unstable political situation, as Maude explains, that the *Cumberland* unwittingly sailed.

The white people were well received at Avarua by *ariki* Makea, and were soon persuaded to lend their support in a raid "to shoot Tinomana (of Aorangi) and his people". It appears that the marksmen on this occasion were one of the Tahitians and Veretini the Maori, and that four Aorangi people were killed. The anchorage at Avarua was not a safe one (that nothing has changed in this respect is evidenced by the bones of the brigantine *Yankee*, wrecked in the 1950s on the Avarua fringing reef), so the *Cumberland* was warped into the sheltered harbour at Ngatangiia in Takatimu country.

By now it was clear that there were no sandalwood groves on the island. Wentworth decided to load with the yellow dye-wood, *nono*, on the off chance that it would be marketable in Sydney. Sixty men of the Takatimu from Ngatangii were engaged to collect and load the dye-wood. The work-force was paid in tomahawks, mirrors, knives, and *toki* (axes; originally meaning stone axe in Rarotongan and Maori), but when it came to food and women, the arrogant Europeans simply mounted raids. Captain Goodenough was at this stage deserted by his lady friend,

Ann Butcher, who went to live with a Rarotongan chief. About the same time, Tupe, one of the Maoris, quarrelled with his shipmates and intrigued with the Rarotongans to kill the strangers. As if the situation were not already explosive enough, the whites began to make advances to the wives of chiefs and, even worse, to uproot *nono* trees from the sacred precincts of the *marae* (temple grounds).

Seeking to avoid a conflict with the Rarotongans, Wentworth and a sailor came ashore and shot Tupe as a troublemaker, but troublemaking was not at the root of the matter. The final straw was the desecration of Makea's *marae* at Avarua by the other Maori, Veretini, and two sailors, Strait and Travis. The Rarotongans could stand no more.

The warrior Rupe, half-brother to the Makea of Avarua, gave chase. While his men dispatched the two Europeans, Rupe himself went after the huge tattooed Maori. He came upon him, comatose from too much *kava*, being deloused by two women, and clubbed him to death. Wentworth himself had a narrow escape; his companion was killed.

The Europeans and the sanguinary Maoris probably deserved what they got. But an innocent and tragic victim of the general upheaval was Ann Butcher (Nati). Her new husband's people, openly boasting of their good fortune in having a European wife, enraged the Ngati Tamake'u, a lineage with whom they were already on bad terms. Taking advantage of the general chaos, the Ngati Tamake'u sent a raiding party, which killed the unfortunate Ann under a chestnut tree, known to this day as "The tree of Nati". Her body was cooked in an earth oven, thus qualifying her, says Maude, for the unenviable distinction of being the only European woman in all Polynesia to be eaten.

This was the end of active hostilities. Shortly afterwards, the *Cumberland* completed loading and sailed. She left behind her an unsettled people, overwhelmed by respect for the strangers' steel and muskets and the design of their ship. The strangers' god was clearly a most powerful one, and the Islanders' conviction of this must have been of considerable help to the missionaries John Williams and Papehia when they converted the island to Christiantiy nine years later.

As to the *Cumberland*'s crew, they played down much that had happened, for an order promulgated by Governor Macquarie the previous year expressly forbade the crews of vessels trading with the Pacific Islands from trespassing on native property and interfering in local "disputes, quarrels, and controversies". We

learn, without great sorrow, that the cargo of dye-wood proved to
be unsaleable and worthless.

CANNIBAL JACK DIAPER

William Diaper (or Diapea), who was to become known as
"Cannibal Jack" (on account of his residence in Melanesia, not
his eating habits) was born in Essex in 1820, the son of a yeoman
farmer. He was well educated, but in 1837, being "stimulated by
the desire of seeing foreign countries and strange manners", he
resolved to embrace a seafaring life and took ship for the South
Seas. Few men can have known the Pacific Islands so thoroughly
as Diaper did in the succeeding fifty-four years, during which he
lived for long periods in Fiji, Samoa, Tonga, and New Caledonia
and served on all manner of trading vessels and South Sea
whalers, as well as making some notable canoe voyages.

Around 1840 we find the wanderer settled at Natewa in Fiji,
living with three wives and trading in tortoise-shell. He became
the first white man to explore inland Vanua Levu. He also
acquired a very good-looking Rotuman (Polynesian) lady called
Henrietta as his fourth wife. Henrietta was the second wife of the
powerful chief Tu'i Macuata. Commodore Wilkes, of the United
States Exploring Expedition, remarked on her beauty and her
unhappiness and desire to escape the Tui. Diaper gives a highly
coloured account of how he rescued her from the strangulation
customary for widows in Fiji when her husband lay dying, but the
dates of the Tu'i's death and her advent at Natewa do not fit, and it
is likely that he acquired her in some less romantic way.

Diaper next took passage to Manila, where he sold his tortoise-
shell for over a thousand pounds. He returned to Natewa about a
year later, having made the last part of the passage, over three
hundred kilometres from Futuna, in a double canoe. It was not
wanderlust that prompted his next move but fear of the
formidable future king Cakabau, who in some way he had
offended, so that he was obliged to flee by double canoe to Tonga
(we will return to this voyage later, for it gives one of the best
surviving accounts of a passage in a *kalia*).

The versatile Diaper was a considerable linguist, speaking
Polynesian in several dialects, Fijian, and at least three New
Caledonian languages. Far more than most of his European
contemporaries he identified with the Islanders, and this got him
into more than a little trouble. He left New Zealand under a cloud,
being suspected of supplying arms to the Maoris during the

Taranaki War of 1860-61. A few years later "he was earnestly desired by the French on the north end of New Caledonia, for murder and for selling arms and amunition to revolting natives". He was also suspected by the French authorities of having acted as a decoy in the capture by the New Hebrideans of two whalers. Whatever the truth of the matter, he left New Caledonia by night in an open boat and landed in the New Hebrides, whence he worked his passage to Samoa in the missionary ship *John Williams*. In Apia Diaper obtained work in a French mission, but fled into the hills when he heard a French warship was expected.

Despite these lapses from the Westerners' cause, and notwithstanding his unconventional "marriages" and his salty language, William Diaper was well respected by nearly all the missionaries he encountered and by the Royal Navy officers for whom he acted as an interpreter. He was, in fact, employed by a mission in Samoa for several years before returning to Fiji, now on the eve of becoming a British colony, in a rather unconventional fashion. A Mr and Mrs Lawton, whom he met in an Apia tavern, wanted to go to Fiji. Diaper agreed to take them, pocketed the fare, and take them he did—all twelve hundred kilometres of the way in an open boat. Lawton thought at first that this was the dinghy conveying them to a schooner. He soon realized his mistake, but worse was to come. The voyage took five days, during much of which time the helpless Lawton was forced to steer while Cannibal Jack made love to his faithless wife.

Let us leave Diaper to his next less adventurous seventeen years in Fiji, and go back to his 1845 voyage from the Fijian Lau group towards Tonga in the double canoe of the Tongan chief Finau, a relative of the king who had befriended Will Mariner.

"There was a large new canoe just completed," wrote Diaper in his journal, "which had been built in Fiji by Tongan carpenters as was their wont in those times—Tonga not being equally famous like the 'lau' (weather islands) of Fiji for large timber. These canoes were regularly constructed of large planking, a matter of quite two inches thick when the canoe was of the largest size and intended to carry nearly and sometimes quite one hundred people." The planks were split from logs with axes, Diaper noted. They had strengthening ridges and panels through which innumerable holes were bored to allow the planks to be lashed together with sennit. Diaper gave it as his opinion that the seams were the strongest part of the structure, the salt water tending to swell as well as preserve the lashings, and he questioned whether this method was not superior to nail fastening.

These big canoes (called *ndrua* in Fiji and *kalia* in Tonga) were capable of very considerable passages. Diaper wrote of them making very long voyages "to the extent of 600, 800 or even 1,000 miles—being not infrequently absent a year or two from home, wandering and gadding about from island to island, going through all Samoa, Fiji, and all the 'Friendly Islands', not omitting even the more distant ones of Wallis' Island, Fortuna, Nieuafou, Nieuatobu tapu, as well as the three nearer groups of Tongatabu, Vavao and Hapai."

Finau's canoe had taken four or five years to build, during which time the chief had been obliged to make at least a dozen trips to Fiji to supply his Tongan carpenters with tools and "property" and to bring presents to the Fijian chiefs in return for their supplying the workmen with food and having their subjects haul the logs down out of the bush.

There were forty or fifty Tongans aboard the *ndrua*, women and children as well as men, when they sculled away from Vatoa Island in Fiji, hoisted the immense pandanus-mat sail and laid course by the heavens for Ha'apai. In command was Finau himself, "one of the most eccentric men perhaps in the world". The wind became contrary and strengthened, so that the sail had to be reefed. This was done by lowering away and re-hoisting only one corner. They beat to windward into the teeth of the strong trade wind, making much leeway in the process because, in Diaper's words, such craft "drawing so little water, and having no keels, of course they drift, having no hold whatever of the water".

Ultimately, the headwind and steepening sea became too much for them and, though nearer to Tonga than Fiji, they were forced to turn back towards Vatoa again. Food had been baked in "a flat sand and dirt bowl", the stones having been heated with difficulty "as everything was more or less wet from the seas, which every now and again broke over us". The cooked yams were shared out in an original manner. One man would lift out a couple of pieces of yam from the improvised earth oven. "Whose shall these be?" he would cry. Another man, seated back to back with him so that he could not see the portions would call out a name—an excellent and impartial system.

Meanwhile, the great double canoe, creaking and groaning in all its flexible fastenings, was scudding before the big seas, under reduced sail so that she could be controlled by the seven-metre steering paddle. All seagoing canoes (and wooden sailing ships)

leak under these conditions, and the *ndrua* was no exception.
There were two holds in each hull, and these required continuous
bailing. With enough people, and some to spare, for steering and
bailing too—provided they relieved one another in reasonable
spells—there was no need for anyone to grumble. But complain
"of the drudgery of the thing" they did.

Diaper had been warned not to expose himself by exhibiting
what he disarmingly described as his "own rather pronounced
eccentricities" in the presence of the "arch-demon" of temper—
Finau. The chief now showed his mettle. He flew into a furious
rage and ordered everyone out of the holds, threatening to kill
anyone who disobeyed. Then this incredible man kept the four
holds dry single-handed, "rushing from one to the other bailing
and drinking grog with superhuman energy for twenty-four
hours". Finau's self-inflicted ordeal was prolonged because it was
too rough to land at Vatoa and they had to go on to the next
island, Lakemba.

Diaper was safely back in Fiji, safe from the sea that is, but not,
as he put it, safe from Cakabau's clutches. Finau had for the time
being given up the idea of sailing home to Tonga, so the anxious
Cannibal Jack, fearing that a long delay in Fiji might land him
"in the oven", eagerly inquired for another Tonga-bound canoe.
He was fortunate, he thought, in finding a party of twenty-five
bound for Ha'apai and joined them. The voyage progressed "in
the usual way—eating, drinking, steering, sailing and bailing,
with the enlivening songs which we were all cheered by, as well as
by the beating of a large wooden drum", until they were no more
than thirty kilometres off Tofua in Tonga. The crew sank to their
knees to thank God for their safe passage (in less than forty years
Will Mariner's Tonga had become fervently Christian); grog was
prepared and drunk in celebration; then heavy black clouds rolled
up from the west and a sudden fierce gale raised seas that
repeatedly swept the canoe. Cooking earth-box, bundles of
tortoise-shell, Diaper's chests—all were swept overboard. As the
hours passed and the storm increased in violence, the canoe
became waterlogged; then it began to break up, all the while
drifting back towards Tonga.

It is a recognized technique in the Pacific Islands when caught
in a gale to swamp the craft, so that it lies just awash, offering no
obstruction to the waves. I have met Polynesian canoemen from
Taumako in the Santa Cruz Reef Islands who have had to do this,
and the famous Carolinian navigator, Piailug, whom we shall
meet in the next chapter, has been forced to resort to this desperate

measure three times. And desperate it is. Not for fear of exposure in tropical water—Pacific Islanders have enormous stamina—but because of sharks. Piailug had one of his crewmen taken from his side as they clung to the waterlogged hull. The same terrible fate befell Diaper's companions. Some may well have survived, but he was alone when, clinging to a piece of wreckage some days later, he was washed up on the shores of Komo island in the Lau group. He was back again in Fiji.

More dead than alive, the castaway was dragged from the water and nursed back to health by Litia, the chief's daughter. Not surprisingly, Diaper became deeply attached to this graceful girl, who herself was ailing, probably from tuberculosis. He seems to have become fatalistic now, or else his feeling for Litia overcame his fear of Cakabau, for he made no attempt to leave Komo and stayed with Litia until she died. Then he did bestir himself once more, and this, his third attempt to reach Tonga, was successful. The passage was in the *kalia* of Chief Joseph of Ha'apai; after two days at sea they landed safely in Ha'apai.

We have already passed lightly over the years that followed. Diaper even applied for a job as a civil servant in Fiji, but appears to have been turned down as a little too unconventional. Then, in the 1880s, the old wanderlust reasserted itself. Together with a younger man, Joseph Streeter, he built a cutter with materials advanced by a German firm. They sailed, laden with furniture and tools and carrying three children, without paying their debts, and arrived in the Loyalty Islands (off New Caledonia) with the unlikely story of having been blown away from Fiji by a storm. With a certain amount of poetic justice, they were in turn swindled out of their possessions and the cutter by a local trader. The colourful old beachcomber spent his last years peacefully on Mare in the Loyalty Islands and died there in 1891 at the age of seventy-one.

This chapter is called "Clash of Cultures". Unhappily, we have few early accounts by actual Pacific Islanders of this cultural clash between the West and Oceania. To try to bring their societies to life from the dawn of regular Western contact we have had to turn to the writings of outsiders. But Will Mariner, one of the first of the castaways, and William Diaper, one of the last beachcombers, became in a sense Islanders themselves. Far more than other Europeans, these men and their like had a genuine affection for and understanding of the people among whom they lived. They acted as "interpreters" of Western mores to the Islanders and so reduced the destructive impact of the Europeans—of missionaries burning the Island gods; of planters demanding labour; of government officials imposing their rule. Men like Mariner and Diaper were essentially human and tolerant. They wished to change no one.

But change there has inevitably been—enormous change, and it could hardly have been otherwise. Yet today the colonial era, which was foreshadowed from the days of Magellan onwards, itself is nearly ended. Few colonial possessions remain in the Pacific, and the process of their conversion into self-governing territories is proceeding apace. Are the independent Pacific Islanders of tomorrow wholly alien to their proud voyaging ancestors? I think not. The roots of South Seas culture have been extraordinarily resilient, and this is nowhere more evident than in the sea sagas that are still being lived today.

11

Voyages of Exploration into the Past

UCH HAS CHANGED in the South Sea Islands; the people are now part of a far wider world than ever before, but in the process of change the greater part of their seagoing culture, one of the greatest ever developed by mankind, has been lost for ever. One thing, however, has not changed. For the Polynesians and Micronesians the ocean is still a familiar, friendly place where they are at home; its vast expanse holds no terrors, for it is dotted with a multitude of islands. In the words of a living star-path navigator of Tikopia: "It is my island. It is where I follow the stars where to go. I shall find." He has put his confidence to the test and proved it well founded. The following two stories of the Cook Islands illustrate this spirit of *tangata o moana,* men of the ocean.

THE RESOURCEFUL LOVERS

In the little library-museum at Avarua in Rarotonga, half-way between the church of the missionary John Williams and the overgrown *marae* of Makea Nui Ariki, I came upon a manuscript written on pages out of a school notebook. It was not old; it dated from the early 1920s; and it was written by a Cook Islander named James Masters. In 1920, when he was a deckhand on the trading schooner *Tiare Taporo,* he fell in love with a girl, Tepou Masters, who lived on his home atoll, Palmerston. They were cousins, though distant ones, being both descended from one of the three wives that the patriarch John Masters had brought with him to the atoll the previous century, but the relationship was still too close in Palmerston eyes for them to be allowed to marry.

Tepou accompanied James on the schooner to Tongareva, where they hoped their relatives might be more accommodating. Not unexpectedly, since Tongareva had been the home island of the original Masters' three wives, the lovers met with the same disappointing response. The best thing for them to do, they decided, was to steal a boat and make for uninhabited Suwarrow. Here they would stay a year or two, and when nature had taken its course, as James put it, they would return and no one could prevent their marriage.

They secretly provisioned an eight-metre ship's lifeboat that was lying at anchor in the lagoon, putting on board a five-gallon kerosene tin of water, 250 coconuts, a sharpened wooden stake for husking them, a piece of iron with which to break them open, and half a pearl shell with which to scrape out the meat. They also had a mat, two pillows, and their clothes, and the boat was equipped with oars, mast, and sail. There was no chart or compass. When James was asked later if he thought they were adequately equipped for a six-hundred-kilometre voyage between tiny atolls visible from no more than seventeen kilometres, he made no mention of chart or compass; he answered simply that they should have taken a bush knife.

In the dead of night the couple rowed across the big Tongareva lagoon to the reef pass on the western side, where they hoisted the lug sail and squared away before the south-east trades, running Tongareva out of sight by dawn. The course for Suwarrow, James judged correctly, was somewhat to the left of the position where the sun set at that time of the year—roughly south-west. Manihiki and Rakahanga, which lay just north of their course about half-way, might be sighted *en route*. For five days they held this bearing, with the steady trades on the port quarter, but no sign of land did they see. "Even the great sea birds that give notice of land seemed to have deserted us," James wrote. At this point a shark nipped the steering oar, seemingly trying to push it round. James took this as a sign and altered course due west. This was a pity, because their old south-west course had been accurate, only they had not sailed nearly far enough in that direction.

Pukapuka, Swains Island, and the Tokelaus must lie to the west, the young Cook Islander reckoned, and he was quite right. In fact, they must have missed one or more of these islands very narrowly before they again changed course. This time to the north. James retained his orientation throughout; he knew which way they were sailing, had some idea of how far they had gone on each leg, and retained in his head a fairly accurate picture of where the islands around them lay. But week followed week and still no land appeared.

The rather meagre ration of fresh water was supplemented by

rain water caught in the sail. At night flying fish came aboard, and the hungry couple were glad enough to eat these raw. They were in good health though, and James says they had not lost any weight. But eventually the supply of coconuts, their mainstay for both food and drink, became nearly exhausted. For the first time they began to be afraid. Then on the twenty-eighth day the feathery palms of an atoll came up over the horizon ahead. It was Hull Island in the Phoenix group.

As the salt-stained open boat neared the fringing reef, the American manager of the copra plantation and a Gilbertese labourer came off to them in a canoe. One would have thought the two pathetic ocean waifs would be only too anxious to land, but no. "I did not like the look of the American because he was carrying a rifle," James recorded. "So I said, 'Fill us up with coconuts and we will be on our way.'"—a modest enough request in the circumstances. But the American was not so fierce as he appeared. In fact, he was a kindly man who soon persuaded the wanderers to come ashore. They must have been fit enough, in spite of what would have been an ordeal to anyone but South Sea Islanders, because James began work on the plantation the very next day.

Tepou and James took passage on the next copra schooner, leaving the ship's lifeboat behind on Hull. For nearly a year they worked on different islands before ending up on Rarotonga. The manuscript ends on a poignant note: "Here," James wrote, "we quarrelled and Tepou married a man from Manihiki."

The Castaways from Manihiki

While in Rarotonga in 1965 I had the privilege of meeting Teehu Makimare, a shy, thirty-year-old Cook Islander from Manihiki. The previous year, he and six companions had been sailing to near-by Rakahanga (Quiros's "Island of Beautiful People") in a 4½-metre open cutter, when a sudden easterly gale drove them far out of sight of land. The little boat had no keel and could never hope to beat back against the strong trade winds, far less the gale, so Teehu decided to run before the wind in the general direction of Pukapuka or, beyond it, Samoa.

Despite the absence of a chart or compass, the young captain nearly made it. After 450 kilometres of empty sea the castaways spied one night the petrol flares of canoes netting flying fish off Pukapuka. Alas, the flares were far up to windward, as inaccessible as if they had been on the moon. There was no alternative but to continue westward before the wind. With heavy hearts, the lonely little party watched the lights dim, then disappear altogether.

Now the ordeal began in earnest. Surfing before heavy seas, the tiny vessel capsized and what little food remained to them—a few yams and taro—was lost. Three weeks later in the night there was a second capsize. The two youngest men, both in their twenties, were too weak to cling to the waterlogged boat through the long hours before it could be righted and bailed out. When morning came they had disappeared. All the water, mostly what had been collected in rain showers, was gone, together with their only containers. Stubbornly the survivors kept going, becoming weaker day by day but never losing hope that an island must soon come up above the horizon. The only water they had was wrung from their shirts after rain, supplemented with a little sea water; their only food was a rare flying fish.

Where were the islands that they knew dotted the Pacific? By the worst of ill fortune they were sailing down a corridor, with Samoa, then Uvea, then Fiji to the south of them, and Tokelau, Tuvalu, and Rotuma to the north. Week succeeded week, but still the five men refused to lose heart; above all, it was Teehu's confidence that kept them going. The party had been two months at sea when high islands appeared in the distance. Now the wind, which had handled them so roughly, became light and fickle, so that their progress was slowed to a snail's pace. The oldest man on board—he was well into his forties—died that day. Another man died as they crawled up the beach at Eromanga in the New Hebrides four days later. The tenacious castaways had been at sea sixty-four days and had come 3,700 kilometres.

The three survivors were not yet safe. The coast appeared deserted, an overgrown plantation being the only sign of former habitation. None of them could walk. Painfully, they crawled up the beach to the foot of a papaw tree. They could not stand or lift up a stick to knock down the fruit; the flame of life was flickering very low. Still they would not be beaten. Lying beside the tree, the three men proceeded to chew through the soft pulpy wood. After hours, it seemed—Teehu had lost all sense of time—the tree fell and they feasted on the fruit. A new lease of life. They slept.

Salvation came with the morning in the shape of a gigantic New Hebridean surrounded by a yelping pack of dogs. Now, there are no dogs on Manihiki, and neither of Teehu's companions had ever been off the island before. Horrified, they burst into tears. These were tigers, they thought, come to devour them. But their ordeal was really over at last. The three living skeletons were carried on litters to the nearest village and tenderly nursed back to health. Telegrams to families in Manihiki were dispatched from Vila. An intensive air and sea search that had been mounted when the cutter first went missing had been long since abandoned; the party had been given up for dead for nearly two months.

Teehu's courageous leadership was in due course acknowledged. Shortly after I left Rarotonga, he was flown to London to receive from the Duke of Edinburgh the Stanhope Gold Medal, the Royal Humane Society's highest award.

Tevake, the Tropic Bird

Tevake, a wrinkled old Polynesian from the Reef Islands of Santa Cruz, was the first Polynesian navigator I ever sailed with. He was also one of the greatest. He had taught his nephew Bongi some of his art, but otherwise he stood alone, the last of a navigator line that stretched back in time to the Austronesians and beyond.

TEVAKE
THE NAVIGATOR

Tevake was no mere traditionalist in theory; he was a restless voyager. He had personally ranged in his thirteen-metre *te puke* canoe with its clew-shaped sail all through the Santa Cruz islands, and further to solitary Tikopia and the northern New Hebrides. His big sailing canoe had been wrecked a few years before, but he took me voyaging in my own ketch stripped of chart, compass, and all navigational aids. I became his pupil; he became my friend.

Our first non-instrumental voyage was to Taumako, where the knowledgeable chief Tumai had told Quiros about seventy islands so long ago, and where Quiros had seen twenty-metre canoes, much larger than any built this century. Nor was Tevake's geographical range anything like as extensive as Tumai's had been. Nevertheless, Tevake's performance bordered on the uncanny. On our return from Taumako he guided the helmsman for eleven hours solely by the ocean swells, for the sun was obscured throughout by low cloud and heavy rain. Yet the experienced old man made his desired landfall precisely half-way between two adjacent islands.

I made other passages under Tevake's tutelage, notably to Vanikoro, when he showed me the luminescent underwater "lightning", called *te lapa,* which flashes towards land afar off; as well he expounded much star, wave, and current lore. Tevake was a great navigator and a man dedicated to the sea.

The Tikopia, within the same voyaging sphere as the Santa

Cruz Reef Islanders, speak of being lost at sea as "sweet burial". When Tevake felt himself too old and sick to voyage any more, he gave himself to the element that had been home to him all his life. Some time after I had returned to Australia Tevake wrote asking if I was setting down all he had taught me. He was feeling very weak now, he said. I replied, explaining how his teachings and his picture (which I had already sent him) were going into the book I was writing.* Several months later the district officer wrote me that Tevake, feeling death coming upon him, had said a formal farewell to his relations and friends before paddling out to sea in a tiny canoe on a voyage of no return. So ended an era.

Tevake's death severed one more major link with the past, but even so, the chain was not entirely broken. Bongi, the old man's nephew, has himself navigated a *te puke* to Taumako, Vanikoro, and all the other Santa Cruz Islands, though Tikopia and the New Hebrides are outside his range. This is a losing battle; each succeeding generation of South Seas navigators knows a little less than the preceeding one. However, while this is the position throughout most of the Pacific, there are signs in certain areas that something more significant is taking place—an actual revival of far voyaging.

The Carolines Captains

We saw in the second chapter how the navigator Hipour from the Carolinian island of Puluwat retraced the old sea road to Saipan, using methods that were probably ancient before the first of his Micronesian ancestors set sail out into the Pacific. This voyage served as a catalyst; it stimulated others to emulate and surpass it, and they in turn set up a chain reaction. Nowhere was this more than in the Carolines themselves where a remarkable series of long-distance passages were initiated.

Foremost in this renaissance were the chiefs and navigators of Satawal, a little atoll of four hundred souls, 216 kilometres west of Hipour's Puluwat. These proud men felt shamed at Hipour's exploit and were determined to go one better; they would make the return voyage to Saipan *by canoe*.

Repunglug and Repunglap are two of the most respected navigators on Satawal. They had been taught the star course to

---

* *We, the Navigators* (Canberra: Australian National University Press; Honolulu: University Press of Hawaii, 1972).

Saipan by their father thirty years earlier, though he himself had never made the passage. The Repung half-brothers would be in command, the chiefs decided, supported by three crewmen. The nine-metre canoe, or *wa*, finally chosen belonged to their own clan and was of traditional construction—strakes, keel, and end pieces all adzed out of breadfruit logs.

As provisions for the voyage, the men took approximately twenty-seven kilograms of pounded taro and eighteen kilograms of cooked breadfruit, as well as drinking and "meat" coconuts. As on any long passage, there was a basket of cured coconut fibre for making rope and extra poles to splice any booms, spars, or outrigger supports that might be broken during the passage. The party set sail on 26 April 1970, leaving in the morning so as to make the ten-hour trip to uninhabited Pigailoe, ninety kilometres from Satawal, before dark. This little island (corresponding to Pic on the Puluwat–Saipan route) was their only staging place. The Repungs waited there for a favourable wind, filling in time by catching turtles and gathering coconuts.

The wind veered to south-east and early in the morning of 30 April they began the 720-kilometre open sea passage, heading towards the setting position of the Little Bear (about 355°) at 4½ knots. This was practically the geographical direction of Saipan (353°) but, watching the receding island carefully, the navigators detected a west-flowing current and altered course to *Feusamakut*—the pole-star—due north. This direction was maintained until the last evening at sea, when the "geographical" Little Bear course was resumed.

On the second day out the wind died down, so the sail was lowered and Repunglug slept for the first time since leaving Pigailoe, while his brother stayed awake to watch the weather and swell patterns. The calm was of short duration, however, the wind coming in again from the same favourable southerly quarter. Twice on the third day strong gusts forced the party to lower sail and lie ahull. In neither instance did the canoe drift far enough off course to alter its position materially. The navigators' confidence was well founded, for early in the morning of the fourth day, Saipan was sighted dead ahead.

During their stay on Saipan, the Carolinians met with the High Commissioner and put forward certain demands that had been entrusted to them by the chiefs of Satawal. These included the cessation of building on a small reef island which was the burial place of their great chief Agrup, and a grant of land. Stormy weather was encountered during the return trip; heaving-to and battling against head winds and seas prolonged the passage, so that Pigailoe was not reached for a full week.

Puluwat, stung in its turn, was not going to be left out of the running. The master navigator Ikeeliman, despite atrocious weather, made a successful voyage to Guam in 1972. From Pic, the staging island in passages from Puluwat to the Marianas, calms, gales, and headwinds plagued them successively. The canoes (there were two) were driven downwind of their objective. This displacement from course was deduced by Ikeeliman according to his *etak* system of dead-reckoning, so after four days without sight of land, he began tacking to windward in the direction in which he calculated Guam lay. Two days later the big island duly appeared in the expected direction.

Two more Satawal canoes made the Saipan return voyage in 1973, navigated by Repunglug. Among the crew were four recent graduates of the Outer Islands High School, who were brought along by their elders to further their traditional education. Another feature of this voyage was that the return passage was made direct to Satawal—a distance of nearly eight hundred kilometres. The following year, 1974, the voyage was accomplished again, this time under the command of Piailug, the third great navigator from Satawal.

These voyages by Hipour, Ikeeliman, the Repungs, and Piailug have been far too consistently successful over distances of the order of seven hundred kilometres of unbroken open ocean to have owed anything to chance. Neither did they depend on Western navigational instruments or charts. The navigational aspects of all these voyages—the steering stars used and the like—are known, and some have been recorded in writing. So clearly, this is no flash in the pan. But how many navigators of such competence remain in the Carolines. Are they dying out?

A former Peace Corps volunteer named Mike McCoy, who has settled on Satawal, estimates that there are at least seventeen trained navigators of the highest calibre, all young and active enough to stand the rigours of canoe voyaging, in the central Carolines today. In addition, there are six or seven young apprentice navigators on Satawal alone, including Repunglug's son, Olakiman, who is a freshman at the University of Guam, and Epoumai, the island's schoolteacher.

Repunglap surpassed himself in 1975 by moving right outside his traditional voyaging range altogether. First, he and his crew sailed to Saipan, then up the Marianas chain. So far the navigation had been traditional. From this point on the canoe was accompanied by a Japanese yacht which gave them the courses to steer, Repunglap translating them into star compass terms. The rest of the journey was a test of endurance both for the scantily clothed Islanders and for the canoe in icy seas, for they crossed no less than fifteen hundred kilometres of stormy ocean to Okinawa, Japan.

"OUR GREAT BAURUA"

A huge outrigger voyaging canoe—known as a *baurua*—twenty-five metres long was built in the Gilbertese island of Tarawa in 1976. The people of the whole Gilberts took it to their hearts. It was spoken of with pride as "our *baurua*". I had the good fortune to sail on this superb vessel on her first inter-island passage.

The idea of building the *baurua,* the first of her kind to be constructed in the Gilberts for about thirty-five years, was the inspiration of a New Zealander named Jim Siers. She was built in little more than three months by fifteen men of the Tarawa village of Taratai. Metal tools and imported timber apart, her design and construction were in every way traditional. The planks were held together edge to edge by coconut fibre lashings at six-inch intervals; the frames were subsequently inserted and similarly lashed in place. Altogether some ten kilometres of sennit lashings went into the construction and the rigging. Twenty-five coconut palm trunks, sawn lengthwise, were used for the outrigger booms and supports. The sails were of pandanus matting, though the ones used on the trials that I attended were of cloth.

Sailing canoes are still very much a living tradition in the Gilberts; a hundred of them fish out at sea from Tarawa alone. But only old men remembered the last big *baurua,* and no one living had helped build one. Thus the present one was made rather too slender compared with the published dimensions of its predecessors, and this made it very wet in a seaway. As to navigation, there were still some three living *tia borau* (trained navigators) but all these were elderly and too infirm to embark on an ocean voyage. So the *baurua* was navigated by Western methods when, at the end of May, she set off for Fiji, 2,500 kilometres to the south.

The crew were selected from the builders and commanded by Tananoa from the same village. There were several New Zealanders and an English navigator. Storm damage necessitated a lengthy stop at Rotuma, but the *baurua* reached Fiji safely at the

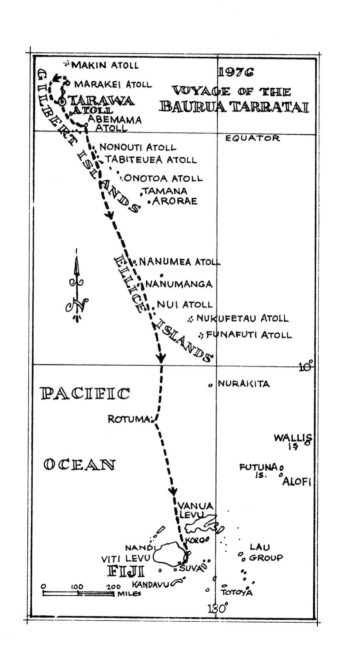

1976
VOYAGE OF THE
BAURUA TARRATAI

MAKIN ATOLL
MARAKEI ATOLL
GILBERT ISLANDS
TARAWA ATOLL
ABEMAMA ATOLL
EQUATOR
NONOUTI ATOLL
TABITEUEA ATOLL
ONOTOA ATOLL
TAMANA
ARORAE

NANUMEA ATOLL
NANUMANGA
NUI ATOLL
ELLICE ISLANDS
NUKUFETAU ATOLL
FUNAFUTI ATOLL
N
10°

PACIFIC
NURAKITA

ROTUMA
WALLIS IS

OCEAN
FUTUNA IS.
ALOFI

VANUA LEVU
NANDI
KORO
LAU GROUP
VITI LEVU
FIJI
SUVA
KANDAVU
0 100 200 MILES
TOTOYA
180°

beginning of July, to the great pride and satisfaction of the Gilbert Islanders. It is a sad commentary on the present age that the *baurua*'s crew had to appear in court in Fiji for not having visas, though perhaps the treatment of strange voyagers would have been a good deal worse in an earlier age.

The Gilbertese crew returned home, and the *baurua* was shipped to a museum. Encouraged by the success of the venture, the enthusiastic Jim Siers persuaded a Fijian village to follow the example of Taratai. At the time of writing they were building a huge *ndrua*, similar to the Tongan *kalia* used by Chief Finau and Cannibal Jack on their ill-fated voyage.

The tradition of building great canoes is a little further removed in Fiji than in the Gilberts. None the less, one was actually constructed on the island of Ongea in 1943 to carry copra. She was sixteen metres long and her deck platform carried fifty or more people. The sail was pandanus and the rigging made from plaited wild hibiscus bark. With a full load she made good eight knots downwind.

Hawaii to Tahiti—the Double Canoe Hokule'a

The urge to revive the ancient voyaging technology is stirring in places far and away more Westernized than the Carolines, Gilberts, or Fiji. The double canoe *Hokule'a* ("Star of Gladness"—Arcturus) was a product of Hawaii, where the Hawaiians are a depressed minority in their own land and are hardly even Polynesians any more. Yet out of such unpromising material arose one of the most significant Polynesian cultural revival projects of recent times. And like the Tarawans with their great *baurua*, the people of Hawaii, the Tuamotus, and Tahiti took *Hokule'a* to their hearts.

Since regular contact with Tahiti lapsed, perhaps five hundred years ago, the mariners of Hawaii have been coastal sailors, venturing no further than between their own high islands and rarely out of sight of land. Canoes, as in New Zealand, ceased to be fit for far voyaging and became increasingly adapted for paddling, with auxiliary sail having a steadily decreasing role. The Hawaiian craft in particular had to be efficient surf-boats. Not only did design alter over the centuries, so did construction. An abundance of large trees favoured dug-out over traditional Polynesian planked construction. Moreover, dug-out canoes were more robust when it came to surfing in to exposed beaches and being dragged ashore.

Many were the problems, then, that faced those concerned with the *Hokule'a* project (I was privileged to be one of them). No tradition whatever remained of the design of the ancient voyaging canoes, though their voyages had become the stuff of many myths and legends. Nor were many present-day Hawaiians accustomed to the use of sail. We had to turn to other parts of the Pacific for inspiration. By a happy chance, Captain Cook left drawings of two classical Polynesian voyaging canoes—the *tongiaki* of Tonga and the *pahi* of Tahiti—and it was found that the underwater lines (which determine performance) of these craft from very distant areas were identical.

The object of the *Hokule'a* experiment, which became the official bi-centennial project for the State of Hawaii, was to evaluate open sea performance of a reconstructed voyaging canoe along the five-thousand-kilometre contact route to Tahiti, to judge the efficacy of traditional star-path navigation for the voyage (no instruments were carried), to transport the Polynesian-introduced plants and animals, and to try out foods preserved in the traditional manner. All except the last were successfully accomplished.

Hokule'a was designed to be a "performance equivalent" replica. The underwater lines, together with her Polynesian claw-shaped sails, ensured that she was. Community feeling dictated that she should be "Hawaiian" in appearance rather than Tongan or Tahitian; financial considerations that she should be constructed of modern materials. This last point caused a lot of confusion, though it should have been apparent that performance and carrying capacity, unlike the strength of coconut fibre lashings (which we had no intention of testing), were quite independent of the building material.

On 1 May 1976 the twenty-metre double canoe put out from the island of Maui, heavy laden with dried fish, taro, bananas, fresh root vegetables, sugar-cane, and coconuts. Showers of spray swept the slatted deck platform as we threshed to windward in the teeth of the strong north-east trade. Behind lumbered the big motor-sailer that was to act as chase boat—for safety and for the convenience of movie and still photographers. Unlike the Tawara *baurua*, we were to be shepherded all the way. There was a strict understanding that no navigational information whatsoever would be passed over to *Hokule'a* from the guard vessel.

The seventeen men aboard were a little subdued after the solemn *'ava* drinking ceremony that had preceded our departure. By dint of the sacred drink and the sacred meal we had been purified and dedicated to the ocean. We were under *kapu,* and until it was lifted by our arrival at a new land, drink and the company of women were forbidden us. Our non-human passengers were subdued too, but for a different reason—they were seasick. The little golden-haired *poi* dog, Hoku, was huddled up miserably in her tiny sleeping bag; Maxwell the pig was, for the first and last time, off his food; the cock and the hen in their wickerwork cage over the stern seemed mere bundles of feathers.

I was delighted to see how well our tall claw-shaped sails were drawing. They had been reconstructed, not without difficulty, from the drawings of Cook's artists and from Hawaiian rock carvings. The classical sails of Hawaii were of the basic Polynesian claw type, which are found far to the west on Tevake's *te puke* and certain double canoes of an Austronesian New Guinea people. A modified form, the half-claw, was used in Tahiti. It is of interest that in the course of our search we came upon three Hawaiian petroglyphs depicting typical Tahitian sails of five hundred years ago.

The first few days were occupied in tacking round the big island of Hawaii, a distance of nearly six hundred kilometres. Mostly we were out of sight of land, but on the third day the snow-capped peak of Mauna Kea ("White Mountain"), 4,600 metres high, broke through the overcast and gave us our point of departure. By this time everyone, including the animals, was feeling better. Cooking was done on a metal plate, with coconut husks for fuel. According to tradition, a wooden framework filled with coral gravel was used.

Piailug of Satawal, he who had made a return voyage to Saipan, was navigator and sailing master. He had been informed what currents to expect (they were very similar to those in his familiar seaways) and where the islands lay. For the rest, he relied entirely on his well-tried art. The height of the pole-star, measured in *ey-ass,* or hand spans, told him our latitude north of the Equator. Once into the Southern Hemisphere, I made the latitude determinations by reference to zenith stars. Up to the Equator our course was towards *Tumur,* the point on the horizon where Antares rises, or south-east. After crossing the Line we altered to *Majemehas,* the Southern Cross half risen, or south-south-east. These courses were designed to counteract the generally west-flowing current (deduced from the direction of the prevailing wind) and bring us up-wind and up-current of Tahiti to an initial landfall in the Tuamotu archipelago.

In practice, navigational necessity dictated that we sail on a close reach on the port tack, that is, as near the wind as a canoe is ever sailed, and a wet and uncomfortable business it was. *Hokule'a* made good a steady average of 200 to 220 kilometres a day until, at the end of the second week, we entered the doldrums, the belt of equatorial calms. Piailug estimated that we were then in 6° north and well on our track to windward (subsequent comparison with the chase boat's position showed we were actually sixty kilometres further south than this). Now followed a frustrating week of fickle breezes and calms that tried everyone's patience to the utmost. Apart from Piailug himself, the Hawaiian mate, a magnificent Hawaiian crew member named Sam Kolelau, Rodo Williams, a Tahitian, and me, none of the crew had had deep-sea experience. They were expert paddlers and surfers but in other respects were an urbanized American minority group. Already they had persuaded the good-natured but indulgent captain to obtain food from the chase boat, so spoiling the food part of the experiment. For the record, it must be mentioned that certain crew members had, against strict orders, smuggled a radio receiver aboard. Neither Piailug nor Rodo nor I knew of this until we landed. Fortunately the culprits were too ignorant of the radio's navigational potential to use it in a way that would have compromised Piailug's navigation.

The crossing of the Equator, roughly the half-way mark, was made at the beginning of the fourth week. Piailug put us in 0° 40′ north, thanks to a clearly visible pole-star that was almost kissing the horizon. This, it turned out, was only ten kilometres north of our real latitude. Longitude, which has to be guessed at by dead reckoning alone in default of instruments, was not so accurate. We were 110 kilometres west of where we thought we were. (I should explain here that Piailug expressed our position in terms of distance and bearing; I translated these into latitude and longitude for ease of subsequent comparison.)

The animals were very fit now, the cock crowing each morning, Maxwell eating dried fish and coconut so greedily that he required a new cage, and Hoku the pet of the ship, perfectly at ease and apt to bark defiance at any dolphin or booby bird that threatened to encroach upon her territory. The living plants that were stowed in the hulls, carefully wrapped in damp moss, *tapa* cloth, and matting, were doing well too. There were some twenty species aboard, all ones that the Polynesian ancestors had introduced into the empty islands they discovered (of course the migration route had been *from* Tahiti *to* Hawaii, not the other way round as we were sailing). Among the plants were breadfruit seedlings, sprouting coconuts, sugar-cane roots, sweet potato and yam tubers, paper mulberry seeds, and many more. All subsequently took root and flourished in Tahiti, despite the salt water they encountered on the voyage.

On the night of 29 May, when we had been four weeks at sea, we estimated that we were due to pass close east of the uninhabited Caroline Atoll, which had been sighted by Quiros. I was not a little concerned that we might come upon its low shores unexpectedly in the darkness. We were still a little east of Tahiti, and Hawaii was now 3,500 kilometres astern according to Piailug. The island lay in 10° south; the zenith star I was using was Spica, which culminated a little before midnight in 11° south. Patiently I peered up along the mast while the star ever so slowly mounted towards its zenith. At last it stood above the trajectory traced by the masthead—Spica was a shade south of the elipse the masthead was tracing—not much, certainly under a degree, half a degree perhaps. This would put us in about 10°30′ south. At any rate, we were comfortably past the atoll and could relax. The zenith star confirmed Piailug's dead reckoning that Tahiti was only 750 kilometres to the south.

The ship's company were all in good physical condition. Apart from the provisions obtained unnecessarily from the chase boat, the dried foods were keeping well, and were supplemented by fresh dorado, bonito, and tuna. Fish were caught almost every day—sometimes three or four. Nor were we short of water. We had been able to fill all our containers in the doldrums by spreading out sails in the tropical downpours (admittedly, our containers were plastic cans instead of the gourds and hollow bamboos of long ago, but this was of little moment).

My main concern at this time was the unseasonable headwinds that persistently pushed us off course to the west—downwind. We were in some danger of missing the Tuamotus and, if the wind direction persisted, of dropping to leeward of Tahiti itself. I mentioned my fears to Piailug. He was not a bit concerned.

"Today Sunday," he said. "If no island by Thursday, we know we well south of Tahiti and the Tuamotus. We tack then, and head north-east on starboard tack. Tahiti islands and Tuamotus lie east and west for hundreds of miles. If we cut through them at an angle like this"—he illustrated the oblique approach with a gesture—"we see their screens of birds and waves and clouds, we find an island all right—in maybe a week from when we pass downwind of Tahiti."

This exposition of Piailug's outlining the method of making an oblique approach to one's target, which is "expanded" by birds and other land signs, illustrates one of the main principles of Polynesian navigation. I had seen it applied previously by both Tevake and Hipour. It was a practical way of getting round the difficult question of longitude.

We were spared from having to follow this strategy, however. On the evening of 31 May, unmistakable signs of the nearness of land became evident. The great swell from the south-east was abruptly cut off. Clearly we had come into the lee of a mass of islands. These could only be the Tuamotus. About the same time Rodo Williams spotted two *ititae*. These, he explained, were a species of tern that never flew further than fifty kilometres from land.

As night closed in everyone was watchful. The Tuamotus are known as "The Dangerous Archipelago" with good reason. The razor-sharp coral can tear a hole in a vessel before ever the dim silhouette of a low atoll is visible through the darkness. Our care was rewarded. In the early hours of the morning a dark line became visible across the horizon on the port bow. We promptly hove to to await daylight. There were only two atolls in our latitude, Mataiva in the Tuamotus and Tupai north of Bora Bora far to the west. Rodo favoured Mataiva. And so indeed it proved to be when it lay fully revealed in the daylight. The navigational part of the voyage was now virtually over. Tahiti lay only 285 kilometres away and was such a large target that, if we sailed in anything like the right direction, it could not be missed.

The welcome of the Tuamotuans and the Tahitians was already beginning. Every island in French Polynesia had composed songs in honour of *Hokule'a*; there were some even from the far-away Cooks. We were entertained royally on the little atoll of Mataiva, where we spent a day and a night. Then on to Tahiti, where the governor declared a public holiday. As we approached the land off Matavai Bay, we were met by nearly a hundred yachts and launches; aircraft swooped overhead, and flotillas of outrigger canoes erupted out of Papeete reef pass. The foreshore was black with people, so that it seemed that every living soul on the island who was not afloat was gathered there. None of us could ever forget that welcome. It was clear that the voyage of *Hokule'a* had tapped deep well-springs of Polynesian identity.

The effects of *Hokule'a*'s achievement have spread through the islands like ripples from a stone tossed into a pond. Soon after,

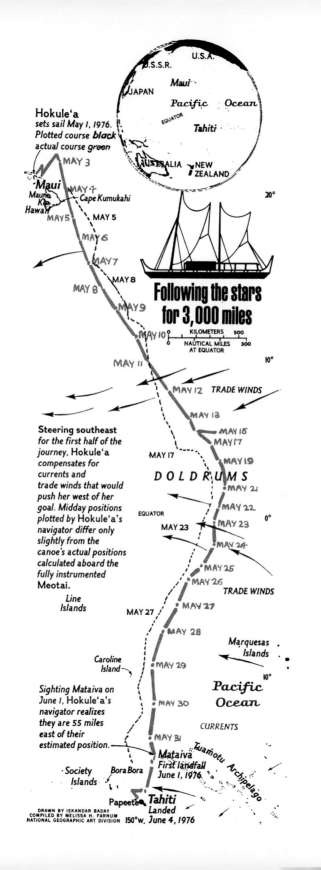

U.S.A.

U.S.S.R.

Maui

JAPAN

Pacific   Ocean

EQUATOR

Tahiti

AUSTRALIA   NEW
ZEALAND

20°

Hokule'a
sets sail May 1, 1976.
Plotted course **black**
actual course **green**

MAY 3

Maui
Mauna
Kea
Hawaii   Cape Kumukahi
MAY 4

MAY 5   MAY 5

MAY 6

MAY 7

MAY 8
MAY 8

MAY 9

Following the stars
for 3,000 miles

MAY 10

KILOMETERS   500

NAUTICAL MILES
AT EQUATOR

MAY 11   10°

MAY 12   TRADE WINDS

MAY 13

Steering southeast
for the first half of the
journey, Hokule'a
compensates for
currents and
trade winds that would
push her west of her
goal. Midday positions
plotted by Hokule'a's
navigator differ only
slightly from the
canoe's actual positions
calculated aboard the
fully instrumented
Meotai.

MAY 15
MAY 17
MAY 17

MAY 19

D O L D R U M S

MAY 21

MAY 22

EQUATOR   MAY 23

MAY 23

MAY 24

Line
Islands

MAY 25

MAY 26

TRADE WINDS

MAY 27   MAY 27

MAY 28

Marquesas
Islands

Caroline
Island   MAY 29

**Sighting Mataiva on
June 1, Hokule'a's
navigator realizes
they are 55 miles
east of their
estimated position.**

MAY 30

*Pacific
Ocean*

10°

CURRENTS

MAY 31

Mataiva
**First landfall
June 1, 1976**

Tuamotu Archipelago

Society
Islands   Bora Bora

Papeete   **Tahiti
Landed
June 4, 1976**

DRAWN BY ISKANDAR BADAY
COMPILED BY MELISSA H. FARNUM
NATIONAL GEOGRAPHIC ART DIVISION   150°W.

new voyaging canoes came under construction in Tahiti and Hawaii; the Islanders are beginning to rediscover the dignity of their voyaging heritage.

Fa'a Pasifika

The phrase *Fa'a Pasifika*—"The Pacific Way"—can be heard nowadays throughout the Pacific. It is an indication of the cultural renaissance of the South Sea Islands. The revived traditions of far voyaging are playing a notable part in this, but the concept embraces many other aspects of the life-style and attitudes of the Pacific peoples as well as their maritime past.

What are some of the manifestations of the "Pacific Way"? They are cultural facets which are ancient and traditional or else modified European introductions. They have spread far and wide from their islands of origin. They include the use of kava, songs and dances from Hawaii, Tahiti, and Rarotonga (hula and *tamure*), gift exchange symbols in the form of flower or shell *leis*, the use of greetings like *aloha*. Then there are the meanings of words like "mother" or "brother", which in the West refer to blood relationships only, but in the South Seas denote *social* relationships as well. Everyone belongs; all one's peer group may count as brothers; one may adopt or be adopted by a "mother". The traditional ceremonial foods are staging a comeback for even the most formal occasions—earth-oven-cooked pork and root vegetables (now joined by the ubiquitous corned beef wrapped in taro leaves). Eating with the fingers is again in vogue.

Some aspects of the *Fa'a Pasifika* are examples not only of common sense but also of the Islanders' growing self-confidence. The discarding of shoes, especially indoors, is one example; the substitution of the *lava lava* or *sulu*, the loincloth, for uncomfortable trousers is another. Not that the *sulu* is endemic. Through most of the South Seas men wore scanty breech-clouts and women grass or bark skirts. In some places they still do, but the *sulu* seems likely to become almost universal. Though missionary introduced, it has more in common with traditional wear than trousers have.

Fa'a Pasifika is becoming increasingly important in the field of religion. Pacific Island cultures were all intensely religious, but when the islands were converted to Christianity the old pagan religions were suppressed with a firm hand; they might well have been extinguished—but they are not. In many parts of the Pacific the old faiths have made not inconsiderable modifications to the local brand of Christiantiy. In 1974 the Pacific Conference of Churches produced a book called *Worship the Pacific Way*. We hear of a Chimbu priest saying mass in traditional regalia, a Fijian whale's tooth being presented to a bishop at his consecration, and a New Caledonian minister administering communion with coconut water instead of wine. And these are but random examples.

More indicative still of the Islanders' growing self-confidence, because awe at the white man's power was coupled with respect for his god, is that the pre-Christian religions are growing increasingly respectable. *Hokule'a* was blessed both by Christian priests and *kahuna* of the old religion. On arrival in Tahiti the two sacred *tiki* that had watched over us on the passage were unlashed from the sternposts and, wreathed in sacred *ti* leaves, solemnly presented to the high altar of Taputapu Atea on Raiatea—the most holy place of worship in all ancient Polynesia. One may of course be cynical and say that all this is good for the tourist industry. True enough, but there is something deeper.

I do not wish to exaggerate the significance of *Fa'a Pasifika*. There are powerful contrary trends tending to absorb everything that is individual and unique into one amorphous television culture. At the most there are about five million Pacific Islanders (including Papuans); they are spread across a third of the earth, and they once spoke between them some twelve hundred languages. No easy unity here. Some have scorned the Pacific Way as merely "film Tahitian", but it is far more than that. It is a synthesis of old and new by peoples with a very tenacious culture indeed. And as for the ancient arts of the star-path navigators, whose methods enabled men to settle the Pacific in the first place—men like Piailug are still carrying on. It may be fanciful, but I can picture old Tevake, now with Tangaroa, god of the ocean, looking on and feeling very proud.

Bibliography

Bibliography

Many published works have been drawn upon in the preparation of this book. The most important are listed below, divided into books and periodicals. Those which seem likely to be most useful to readers desiring fuller information are marked with an asterisk, and their relevance to particular parts or chapters is indicated.

BOOKS

Anon. *Periplus of the Erythraean Sea, by a Merchant of the First Century.* London: Longmans, 1912. Refers to part 1.

Anson, G. *Voyage Round the World.* London: Knapton, 1749.* Refers to part 2.

Bass, G. *A History of Seafaring from Underwater Archaeology.* London: Hudson, 1972. Refers to parts 1 and 2.

Beaglehole, J. C. *The Exploration of the Pacific.* London: Black, 1966.* Refers to part 2.

Crocombe, R. *The Pacific Way.* Suva: Lotu Pasifika, 1976.* Refers to part 3.

Dampier, W. *Voyages.* Edited by John Masefield. 2 vols., London: Richards, 1906.* Refers to part 2.

Darby, H. C., ed. *Pacific Islands.* 4 vols., *Naval Intelligence Handbook.* London: H.M.S.O., 1945. Refers to parts 1 and 2.

Davis, L., ed. *News from New Cythera.* Minneapolis: University of Minnesota Press, 1970. Refers to part 2.

Diapea, W. *Cannibal Jack.* London: Faber and Dwyer, 1928.* Refers to part 3.

Diderot, D. *Supplement au Voyage de Bougainville.* Paris: Nouvelle Revue Français, 1921. Refers to part 2.

Doran, E. "The Sailing Raft as a Great Tradition". In *Man Across the Sea,* edited by Riley. Austin and London: University of Texas Press, 1971. Refers to part 1.

Edwards, C. *Aboriginal Watercraft on the Pacific Coast of South America.* Berkley and Los Angeles: University of California Press, 1965. Refers to part 1.

————— . "New World Perspectives on Pre-European Voyaging in the Pacific Basin". In *Early Chinese Art and Its Possible Influence in the Pacific Basin,* edited by Noel Barnard. New York: Intercultural Arts Press, 1972. Refers to part 1.

Friis, H. R., ed. *The Pacific Basin.* New York: American Geographical Society, 1967. Chapter 4, "The Geographical Knowledge of the Pacific Peoples", by G. Lewthwaite; chapter 5, "Geographical Exploration by the Chinese", by Chiao-min Hsieh; chapters 7, "Geographical Exploration by the Spaniards", and 8, "Geographical Exploration by the Portuguese", by D. D. Brand; and chapter 9, "Geographical Exploration by the Dutch", by Jan O.M. Broek. Refers to parts 1 and 2.

Finney, B. ed. *Pacific Navigation and Voyaging.* Wellington, N.Z.: Polynesian Society, 1976. See D. H. Lewis, "A Return Voyage between Puluwat and Saipan"; M. McCoy, "A Renaissance in Carolines-Marianas Voyaging". Refers to part 3.

Gunson, N. ed. *The Changing Pacific.* Melbourne: Oxford University Press, forthcoming. See D. H. Lewis, "The Pacific Navigators' Debt to the Ancient Seafarers of Asia". Refers to part 1.

Haddon, A. C. and Hornell, J. *Canoes of Oceania.* Reprint of 3 vols. in 1. Honolulu: Bishop Museum Press, 1975.* Refers to part 1.

Hakluyt, R. *The Principal Navigators, Voyages, Traffiques and Discoveries of the English Nation,* vol. 40. Glasgow; Maclehose, 1904. Refers to part 2.

Henry, T. *Ancient Tahiti.* Honolulu: Bishop Museum, 1928. Refers to part 2.

Hornell, J. *Water Transport.* Cambridge: Cambridge University Press, 1946.* Refers to part 1.

Innes, H. *The Conquistadores.* London: Collins, 1969. Refers to part 1.

Levison, M.; Ward, R. G.; and Webb, J. W. *The Settlement of Polynesia. A Computer Simulation.* Canberra: A.N.U. Press, 1973.* Refers to part 1.

Lewis, D. H. *We, the Navigators.* Canberra: A.N.U. Press; Honolulu: University Press of Hawaii, 1972.* Refers to part 1.

Markham, C., ed. *The Voyages of Pedro Fernandez de Quiros.* 2 vols. London: Hakluyt Society, 1904.* Refers to part 2.

Martin, J. *An Account of the Natives of the Tonga Islands. Compiled ... from the Extensive Communication of Mr. William Mariner.* 2 vols. Edinburgh: Constable, 1827.* Refers to part 3.

Mason, A. E. W. *The Life of Francis Drake.* London: Hodder and Stoughton, 1941. Refers to part 2.

Maude, H. E. *Of Islands and Men.* Melbourne: Oxford University Press, 1968.* Refers to parts 2 and 3.

Megaw, J., ed. *Employ'd as a Discoverer.* Sydney: Reed, 1971. Refers to part 2.

Needham, J. *Science and Civilisation in China.* vol. 4, part 3, *Civil Engineering and Nautics.* Cambridge: Cambridge University Press, 1971.* Refers to part 1.

Parr, M.C. *So Noble a Captain.* London: Hale, 1955. Refers to part 2.

Pigafetta, A. *The First Voyage Round the World by Magellan.* Edited by Stanley of Alderley. London: Hakluyt Society, vol. 52, 1875.* Refers to part 2.

Riesenberg, F. *Cape Horn.* London: Hale, 1950.* Refers to part 2.

Robertson, G. *The Discovery of Tahiti.* London: Hakluyt Society, 1928.* Refers to part 2.

Rogers, Woodes. *A Cruising Voyage Round the World.* 1712. London: Cassell, Seafarers' Library Edition, 1928.* Refers to part 2.

Sharp, A. *The Voyages of Abel Janszoon Tasman.* London: Oxford University Press, 1968. Refers to part 2.

————. *The Discovery of the Pacific Islands.* London: Oxford University Press, 1969.* Refers to part 2.

Taylor, E. G. R. *The Haven-Finding Art.* London and Sydney: Hollis and Carter, 1971.* Refers to parts 1 and 2.

Temple, R. C., ed. *The World Encompassed by Sir Francis Drake.* London: Argonaut, 1926.* Refers to part 2.

Tilman, W. *Mischief in Patagonia.* Cambridge: Cambridge University Press, 1957. Refers to part 2.

Wycherley, G. *Buccaneers of the Pacific.* London: Long, n.d.* Refers to part 2.

JOURNALS AND MAGAZINES

Allen, J., and Green, R.C. "Mendaña 1595 and the Fate of the Lost Admiralta". *Journal of Pacific History* 7 (1972): 73-91. Refers to part 2.

Ambrose, W., and Green, R.C. "First Millennium B.C. Transport of Obsidian from New Britain to the Solomon Islands". Vol. 237, May: 31. Refers to part 1.

Bellwood, P. "The Prehistory of Oceania". *Current Anthropology* 16 (1975), no. 1.* Refers to part 1.

Fry, H. T. "Alexander Dalrymple and New Guinea". *Journal of Pacific History* 4 (1969). Refers to parts 1 and 2.

Golson, J. "The Remarkable History of Indo-Pacific Man". *Journal of Pacific History* 7 (1972).* Refers to part 1.

Hilder, B. "The Discovery of Torres Strait in 1606". *Navigation* 4 (1973), no. 2. Refers to part 2.

————. "Drake's Passage". *Navigation* 5 (1976), no. 1. Refers to part 2.

Husain, Sidi 'Alt Re' is ibn. *Muhit* (The Ocean), extracts trans. von Hammer-Purgstall. *Journal of the Asiatic Society of Bengal*, nos. 35, 56, and 70 years 1834, 1836, 1837, 1838. Refers to part 1.

Legg, C. "William Diaper". *Journal of Pacific History* 1 (1966). Refers to part 3.

Lewis, D. H. "Hokule'a Follows the Stars to Tahiti". *National Geographic* 150 (1976), no. 4. Refers to part 3.

Ling Shun-sheng. "The Formosan Seagoing Raft and Its Origin in Ancient China". *Bulletin of the Institute of Ethnology, Academia Sinica* (Taipei), no. 1. Refers to part 1.

McIntyre, K. G. "Portuguese Discoverers on the Australian Coast". Address to the Royal Historical Society of Victoria, 23 April 1974, printed in the *Victorian Historical Magazine*. Refers to part 2.

McKnight, C. "The Nature of Early Maritime Trade ... Indonesian Archipelago". *World Archaeology* 5 (1973), no. 2. Refers to part 1.

Pawley, A., and Green, K. "Lexical Evidence for the Proto-Polynesian Homeland". *Te Reo* 14 (1971). Refers to part 1.

Prinsep, J. "Note on the Nautical Instruments of the Arabs". *Journal of the Asiatic Society of Bengal*, December 1836. Refers to part 1.

————. "Notes on the Muhit". *Journal of the Asiatic Society of Bengal*, September 1838. Refers to part 1.

Smith, H. "The Introduction of Venereal Disease into Tahiti." *Journal of Pacific History* 10 (1975). Refers to part 2.

ABOUT THE AUTHOR

David Lewis has had a lifetime of adventure. At the age of seventeen he made a solo 725-kilometre canoe trip from Wanganui to Auckland, New Zealand. While at medical school in Otago he took part in nineteen first ascents and traverses in the Southern Alps of New Zealand and was New Zealand University downhill ski champion in 1938. In 1960 and 1964 he sailed in the first and second single-handed transatlantic races, coming third to Francis Chichester's first in 1960. In 1964-67, together with his wife and two young daughters, he made the first circumnavigation of the world in a multi-hull (the catamaran *Rehu Moana*), by way of the Strait of Magellan, sailing the Tahiti-New Zealand leg by Polynesian methods, without instruments. In 1968-69 he sailed the ketch *Isbjorn* from England to Australia.

Perhaps the best known of David Lewis's exploits is the remarkable voyage made in 1972-74 in the steel sloop *Ice Bird*, the first single-handed voyage to the Antarctic continent. Since then he has travelled thousands of kilometres in the desert country of Central Australia studying the route-finding techniques of Australian Aborigines; and he was one of the navigators on a twenty-metre double canoe which made the voyage from Hawaii to Tahiti in 1976.

David Lewis was born in New Zealand in 1917. He qualified as a medical practitioner in Leeds in 1942 and served as a medical officer in the Second World War. He has practised in the West Indies and in London, and now lives on Dangar Island in the Hawkesbury River, near Sydney.

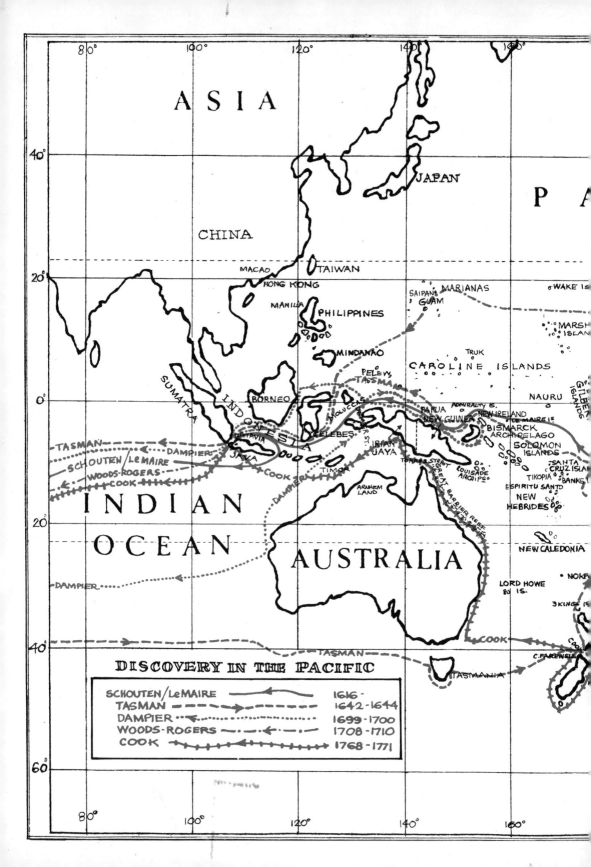

DISCOVERY IN THE PACIFIC